come back
alive

Doubleday

New York   London   Toronto   Sydney   Auckland

come back alive

alive

The Ultimate Guide to Surviving Disasters, Kidnapping, Animal Attacks, and Other Nasty Perils of Modern Travel

robert young pelton

A MAIN STREET BOOK
PUBLISHED BY DOUBLEDAY
a division of Random House, Inc.
1540 Broadway, New York, New York 10036

MAIN STREET BOOKS, DOUBLEDAY, and the portrayal of a building with a
tree are trademarks of Doubleday, a division of Random House, Inc.

Although every effort has been made to ensure the correctness of the
information in this book, the publisher and authors do not assume, and
hereby disclaim, any liability to any party for any loss or damage caused
by errors, omissions, misleading information, or any potential problem
caused by information in this guide, even if such errors or omission are a
result of negligence, accident, or any other cause.

For updates, links, and resources, visit us at *www.comebackalive.com*

Book design by Claire Naylon Vaccaro
Illustrations by Robert Myers

Library of Congress Cataloging-in-Publication Data
Pelton, Robert Young.
Come back alive: the ultimate guide to surviving disasters,
kidnapping, animal attacks, and other nasty perils of modern travel /
Robert Young Pelton.
p.   cm.
1. Survival skills. I. Title.
GF86.P45   1999
613.6'9—dc21   99-17325
CIP

ISBN 0-385-49566-8

Printed in the United States of America

July 1999

First Edition

1   3   5   7   9   10   8   6   4   2

To Linda, Lisa, and Claire,

who taught me that

there is adventure in love

as well as danger

acknowledgments

I would like to thank Bill Thomas and Eric Simonoff, who conspired to convince me that I should and could write an entertaining survival guide. I also want to thank Wink Dulles, Marcus Wynne, and Rob Krott for actually agreeing with them and encouraging me throughout the painful process.

disclaimer

Many of the situations and activities described in this book are inherently hazardous. If you can avoid them, you should. If you can't, experience, common sense, and caution are your best protection and should be exercised at all times. In any event, the information in this book is to be used only as a last resort, in extreme emergency, and should never be used as a basis to seek out or invite any of the dangerous or potentially dangerous situations described in this book. No book can provide guidance on how to behave in all of the specific situations with which the reader might be confronted, and the reader must tailor the information he or she derives from this book to each situation that arises. The reader should supplement information from this book with information from other sources, including information about the particular place or conditions in which the reader is likely to find him or herself. All risks of injury are assumed by individual readers, who are responsible for taking appropriate safety precautions and using appropriate equipment at all times. Neither Author nor Publisher assume any liability for accidents or injuries suffered by readers who use this book. Furthermore, individuals are responsible for confirming and complying with any local regulations that may apply to the activities in which they engage.

contents

come back
alive

introduction

The Art of Survival

When people head for parts unknown, there seems to be no shortage of survival guides. Today, many well-prepared adventurers get succor and life-sustaining courage from carrying around a small paperback book that carefully explains how to get out of any deleterious or baneful situation. In my opinion, this is the literary equivalent of wearing a helmet when skydiving. You'll look good going down, but if things get ugly, your beanie won't help you when you get to where you're going.

I am not a big fan of survival guides. I don't care how good beaver tail tastes and I don't know why I need to see daylight through the anus of my freshly cleaned and gutted deer. Do I *really* need to master semaphore? Will I ever need to start a fire by rubbing two sticks together or should I just use my BIC? Do I need a three-week or a four-week supply of food in case of a nuclear attack? Should I jump up and break my assailant's neck with a flying kick, or should I just assume the Angry Crane with Hemorrhoids position to scare him off? The truth is, I really don't know. And after a lifetime of scrotum-shrinking adventures and close calls, I still don't know.

If you need to be taught very simple things or if you think that you can master a lifetime of military, navigational, and bush skills in one good toilet read, then you are probably better off left in the woods with a survival guide to die, blissfully but erroneously confident in your ultimate survival. Such is the esoteric and delusional world of survival guides.

The majority of survival books—brought to you by barrel-chested, strong-limbed, granite-jawed experts who live in a world of remote forests, blistering deserts, and frozen wastelands—are great sources of vicarious entertainment and stern warnings but frighteningly disconnected from real-world scenarios. They instill pure terror by harping on esoteric conditions that perhaps affect 40 percent of the population, only 5 percent of the time. In other words, they all blithely ignore real life.

True survival means knowing the risks, weighing the benefits, and then taking responsibility for your actions. It's the stuff they forget to put in tourist brochures and nature shows. Survival also demands being versed and comfortable with the basic principles of navigation, emergency procedures, and wilderness skills.

Most people enter into adventure with the same confidence as a drunk who steps into an open elevator shaft. There isn't a whole lot there to warn you before you get into trouble. Too many of today's travelers have been raised in a Naderesque, consumer-cocooned society where the dangers are all printed on the label, slippery spots are roped off, and an attendant is always on duty in case the amusement park ride breaks. When we screw up, there's 911 to call, and when someone else screws up, we can sue them or get a free year's supply of whatever they make. In other words, it's always someone's fault and problem if things go wrong.

How to, Not What to, Survive

What the world needs now is a manual that disseminates the psychology of survival rather than another tome that misleads folks into thinking that there is a simple survival tip for every nasty situation. I actually have a survival guide (thankfully long out of print) that offers survival tips in the event you're paid a visit by extraterrestrials. Their advice? "Remain calm, make no threatening moves." ("Remaining calm," of course, is the single most repeated tip in every survival situation.) Even the well-credentialed "Lofty" Wiseman has penned an urban survival guide that explains (on page 250) how to read and understand warning signs, including how to read a sign that prohibits your dog from defecating. Hey, what about a book that tells you how to survive survival guides?

Why This Book Is Different

You're not going to see a lot of drawings of some fifties-era guy in a baseball cap trying to trap rabbits or right a flipped navy life raft. There won't be any paranoid pontifications about New World Order and I won't explain how to make a bazooka out of your neighbor's drainpipe. There will be no instructions for tying knots or wilderness recipes for cooking grubs. This book won't tell you how to build a seaworthy vessel out of Popsicle sticks or give you lyrics to campfire songs. We are going to dig into odd and esoteric things most survival guides tiptoe around, and we're going to learn how to survive with style.

Inside, you'll encounter survival philosophies and models for the third world, adventure travel, urban jungles, remote regions, war zones, terrorism, crime spots—even your own house (the place you're most likely to get into trouble). You'll learn how to make the relative and appropriate transition required from the gray drudgery of day-to-day living to white-knuckle terror—imagined, real, sought-after, or completely unexpected.

We'll look at the obstacles you can overcome and those you may as well straighten your clothes and leave a good-looking corpse. You'll understand why the choices on a restaurant menu are statistically more dangerous than climbing a mountain.

We'll talk about adventure, fear, bravery, and just how fast you can die (or survive) when you least expect it.

We'll spend some time learning how to keep from getting lost. You'll find out why maps, compasses, altimeters, and even satellites can get you into serious trouble.

You'll find out where to sit (and sleep) on an airplane and when you should eat with your fingers. We'll talk about the world's deadliest animal, what to do when a grenade rolls under your bed, and even how to piss off a crocodile. You'll learn how to survive five-hundred-pound bombs, gangsters, punks, and the cops.

You'll learn a few tricks to impress your friends: navigation and distance using birds, telling the time with your fingers, using bees to find water, why there are sixty seconds in a minute, finding remote islands with your testicles—all the neat tools your long-lost ancestors used before they became civilized.

Then we'll visit some dangerous places, like your home and office, before calling on some safer spots like war zones and xenophobic dictatorships.

When you finish this book, you will begin to understand why some people survive and some don't.

You'll get it.

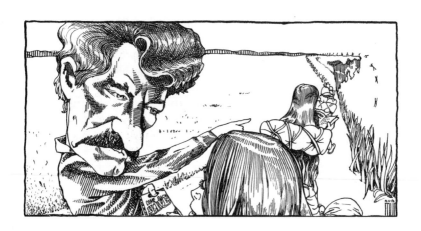

· 1 ·

the adventure quiz

Are You a Survivor? Time's Up! You're Dead

What is survival? Who is a survivor? Take this quick quiz to see just how bulletproof and survival savvy you are in this big nasty world:

1. **Most people die of:** _____
   (Heart disease)

2. **Most young people die due to:** _____
   (Car accidents)

3. **The most likely cause of accidental death for hikers in the United States is:**
   _____
   (Dying in a car accident)

4. **The most dangerous job in America is:**
   _____
   (Truck driver)

5. The most dangerous creature in the world is the: _____
    (Mosquito)

6. The most dangerous wild animal in America is: _____
    (Common deer)

7. The most dangerous place in the world is: _____
    (Your home)

8. Most animal attacks in National Parks are caused by: _____
    (Family pets)

9. When attacked, your most powerful self-defense move is: _____
    (Running away)

10. The most dangerous activity in America is: _____
    (Driving)

11. Nasty bugs in water are always killed by: _____
    (Boiling)

12. The best way to signal for help is to: _____
    (Use a SatPhone to call the local sheriff's office)

13. The best things to eat in the bush are: _____
    (The food you brought with you)

If you took the test and got all the answers right, you don't need this book. It seems you are blessed with an overabundance of common sense. If you are like most normal people, you should have flunked miserably, proving that, like most of us, you were raised on nature shows and cheap thrillers.

What Is an Adventurer?

Many of the dangers in the quiz are things you navigate every day. So it may strike you as odd that adventurers have to do weird and exotic things just to show you how, well, adventurous they are.

In well-defined societal structures these people were originally called extroverts, attention seekers, nonconformists, and, of course, nuts.

The term "extroverts" covered this group until the conformity of the fifties spurred on researchers to more neatly categorize these malcontents. When they realized that needing attention vs. being adventurous were two different things, the term shifted to "Type A" personalities. "Type B" personalities were considered normal quiet folks who colored inside the lines. Type A folks were fast-moving, all-consuming overachievers who were destined to keel over at an early age from a massive stroke. When researchers then learned that adventurous people didn't inaccessibly die of heart attacks any faster than dull people, they came up with "T-Type." T-Types came in four flavors: "T-Mental" (for intellectual risk takers), "T-Physical" (for more corporeal risk taking), T-Negative (for destructive traits), and T-Positive (for positive traits).

Other labels like "HSS," or "High Sensation Seekers," were used to focus in on the root causes of addiction, juvenile delinquency, and poor societal integration. There is even the spill over in the "ADD," or "Attention Deficit Disorder" that links short attention spans, a need for stimulation, and poor learning with the need for adventure.

Finally there is the vogue for adventure, thrill seeking, and disaster watching that seems to appear in cyclical waves in entertainment media, thrill rides, sports, and news coverage.

The incontrovertible point that all these studies and theories come to is that a need for adventure, a skill for survival and success are present in people who are considered adventurous . . . if your skills are identified and channeled in a positive manner. If your devils drive you to the dark side, you may find yourself being equally successful at robbing banks, being a mercenary, running drugs, or just being caught in your own *Clockwork Orange* hell of vicarious overstimulation. Adventurous people can be both good and evil.

Better Surviving Through Chemicals

The real test of whether you are a survivor or not lies in understanding some basic chemistry. Neurochemistry to be exact. To test whether someone is a high or low sensation seeker, medical researchers will look at the effects of sensations of the EKG scans. Your brain's volume knobs are regulated by neurotransmitters. Two of them (norepinephrine and dopamine) directly control stimuli and pleasure and serotonin dampens arousal and excitement about as fast as sitting naked on a steel autopsy table.

Low sensation seekers (known by their nontechnical name: "wimps") will actually have high levels of norepinephrine and dopamine and augment incoming stimuli reaching the cortex. It doesn't take much to make these people jittery. This higher sensitivity leads to faster overloading and possibly a longer life span. It also leads to panic, which can dramatically reduce life span when quick thinking is called for.

These people have a high level of monoamine oxidase (MAO), the enzyme used to regulate arousal, your inhibitions, and your pleasure stimuli.

Adventurous people have a low level of this enzyme and require greater levels of stimulation (i.e., naked fear) to get nervous or excited. When they do get wired, their amps go to eleven as *Spinal Tap* would say.

Dopamine is a stimulator designed to increase awareness, physical strength, and processing speed, but it can also create an addictive sense of arousal and pleasure much the same as cocaine can. The faster dopamine rushes to the brain, the bigger the "rush." This rush is usually triggered by fear.

I am being charitable when I use the term "adventurous" because this assumes that you are channeling this craving for excitement into healthy sports and activities. Unfortunately, this chemical imbalance is found in quite a few juvenile delinquents, gang bangers, and criminals.

The upshot of understanding this chemical structure is that if two people are exposed to the same stimuli, one can be terrified and panicked, while the other is snoring soundly. In some people this rush of dopamine causes "fight or flight" syndrome and can induce panic. In adventurous types dopamine creates pleasure and interest. Identifying this effect can set you on the right path to harnessing your talents. People who work in rescue, paramedics, climbers, explorers, and special forces thrive on constant challenge. I find myself being completely relaxed and focused on the front lines, racing my bike, off-roading, or exploring jungles. That makes me quite odd unless, of course, I make my money being an adventurer. It is a source of great amusement to my adventurous friends when they find out that I actually worked in an office for most of my life.

Adventurers Are Made, Not Tweaked

I interchange the word "adventurer" with "survivor" simply because an adventurer is someone who continually put themselves in situations that have no certain outcome. The daily dealing with problems and choices, or "surviving," can provide our satisfaction. It's when you can gain enjoyment from this barrage of uncertainty that surviving becomes adventuring.

These days it's quite popular to confuse thrill seeking or even antisocial behavior with adventuring. Base jumping, snowboarding, skateboarding, surfing, street racing, drug use, and juvenile sports are considered "bad" sports that require tattoos, piercings, sticking your tongue out a lot, and waving your fingers around like you're drying a booger. Little is said about dealing with the stress of day-to-day living and keeping a sense of wonder and humor.

Remember that this generation who grew up in car seats, Jolly Jumpers, day care, and bungee jumping. Their "dull" grandparents lived through world wars, mass genocide, nuclear bombs, and global depression. So it's not surprising that the simple act of riding a skateboard or surfboard with your tongue sticking out is considered extreme. Other generations had D-Day, Vietnam. This generation has *The Simpsons*. Today's untested generation doesn't have a whole lot of heroes or much sense of direction. Ergo, the current demand for adventure.

Who Is an Adventurer?

Just what can this generation do to express their need for adventure? Admittedly, only about 20 percent of the population (and they are predominately young males) is considered as "risk seeking."

In an era where you can't take your first head, go off to fight a war, sail to the New World, or even swing through jungles to drag off girls, what's an adventurous fella to do?

The more civilized a society is, the more outrageous their adventures. The Victorian era in England spawned some of the most colorful adventurers in history. Even today icons like Richard Branson are perfect examples of high-risk lifestyles being used to thumb their noses at the status quo. Today's outlet seems to be "high-risk" sports. I put the quotes there because many of the cinematically friendly extreme sports are neither dangerous or high-risk. They just look good on film. In the UK they haven't reported a skydiving or hangliding fatality in years. Skiers who attempt high vertical descents spend days planning; climbers and rafters who film those spectacular adventure docos are chosen for their predictability in returning with the goods, not filming their demise.

Risk seekers will end up in one of three camps:

The reprobates: People who skip the social skills side of things and straight for the cheap thrills afforded by pornography, promiscuous sex, drugs, and cheap thrills. Statistically, there are enough of these people to fill the jails and clinics. An interesting footnote is that minor junior offenders were offered a hitch in the Marines as alternative to jailtime. The judges thought this would put a little discipline in them, would teach them to channel their needs in more productive ways. This is where you don't want to go. If you feel that you're banging your head a little too hard at concerts or packing in a little too much synthetic fun, you need a hobby.

The dilettantes: Often we never tap in to the things that drive us and the real world sweeps us into its current. Locked in to a good job and monthly payments, we get to escape on the weekends and holidays where we feel strangely at home in remote and foreign locales. These folks sit at the Y junction of life, not quite knowing whether to take the "adventure" path or the "security" path to their final destination. I would suggest that mastering the adventure will always make the security path seem like a detour. There is nothing wrong with achieving a balance of security and certainty and indulge your passions for adventure. I have met a number of solid citizens who decide to invest in emerging markets, climb mountains, do aid work on their vacations, or work as sheriffs on their weekends. There is a middle ground in this adventure and survival thing.

The adventurers: Those who have the good fortune to hook up with a positive role model and have the tenacity will probably migrate into a career that combines their love of challenge with the security of knowing they are very good at it. You can work as a mountain guide, a commodities trader, a professional athlete, film producer, field worker for the UN, in medical ER, or even as a journalist. Any occupation or hobby that offers an ever-changing multitasking approach to work and play is going to provide satisfaction and enough hits to keep you interested and happy.

So let's come to terms with who we are and not try to build our life on a keel of hard sobriety or wild-eyed adventure. Don't be sucked in by the thinking that says you are either black or white, dull or crazy. Realistically, everyone has a wild side and dull side.

Whither Adventure?

We've learned that people who are tuned for survival are considered adventurous. We also know that there is no one profile, gender, shape, age, size, or color for adventurous people. There are statistical clusters, medical indications, environmental influences, and physical limitations, but it's up to you to create yourself in your image. Finding an occupation, hobby, or outlet for your interest is made much easier by the glut of clubs, schools, camps, tours, and even indoor adventure centers that let you get adventurous with training wheels. These days it's possible to fly a MiG fighter, hang-glide, skydive, raft, or rock-climb with somebody right next to you guiding you through it. If you hit the panic button, don't worry, you're roped in, tied down, cushioned, and protected. If you dig it, then sign you up for the course and get serious.

Do You Fear or Enjoy This Book?

A question worth asking yourself is whether fear, excitement, or ignorance drives you forward or pulls you back. Is your interest in survival prompted by a desire to actively learn skills and increase your confidence, or is it inspired by a vicarious desire to feel better by being entertained by other people's misfortunes? There's no judgment here, since many a filmmaker, writer, and even myself benefit from the phenomenon of people fascinated by others' adventures.

If you enjoy this book, it is probably because you are seeking the opportunity to employ some of these tricks and tips and realize you couldn't come up with them yourselves. If you fear this book, it's probably because you have been victimized by an event and realize that there is little one can do once the hand of nature and luck take hold.

You need a respect and an understanding of both points of view to use this book properly.

Survival will be dictated by a healthy fear of danger as well as the resourcefulness to dig into a grab bag of tricks to defeat it. It is worth remembering that Danger is a friend you don't want to meet too often, but it's good to keep in touch.

Enjoy Life and Die Happy; Fear Life and Die Scared

It's odd that even lawnmowers have owners' manuals, but humans come stripped and without packaging, warranty, or instructions. It's not my goal to provide a manual on life, but maybe a set of parameters that allow you to color between the lines with a more flourish.

Most people are handicapped but do not know what their limitations are. A number of survival schools have been set up to show us that many of our limitations are self-imposed. Every time we think we can't go any farther, come up with a solution, or are ready to ring the bell, a bit of instruction and motivation can show us how to carry on. This education can be applied to everything you do in your life, not just your weekends.

There is also an odd intersection in our lives where young teens feel they can do anything but can't and older folks ease back and choose to do less but could do more. The military takes full advantage of youthful optimism and caution of experience. This can be your philosophy too. When young, seek out as many experiences as possible, try as many jobs as you can, read as many books as your head will hold, and never underestimate the benefit of training from seasoned pros. It's one thing to teach yourself how to be a road racer; it's another to live long enough to learn from your self-induced mistakes.

Lessons to Live By

Be creative. Create your own mission, goal, or style and make it count. Come up with something you've always wanted to do and avoid emulating things you see on TV or read about.

Never stop learning. "Been there, done that" is a phrase that prevents knowledge. There is education in every new conversation, every magazine article, book, TV show, Web site, new destination, and lecture. My best advice is to continually expand specific areas of knowledge before moving on to the next area. Write down what you are learning and doing to aid in retention and actively do something related to your area of interest.

Reach out. Many of us feel that we must self-generate knowledge and activity. Being somewhat shy, I find it difficult to write people letters or call them on the phone. Yes, there is plenty of diffidence and rejection, but the people you connect with can dramatically expand your life. In fact, this is one of the hallmarks of successful people who make connections to expand their circle of friends. On the back side is giving your knowledge to other people through mentoring, volunteer work, or charitable activities. This starts the cycle anew.

Set goals and achieve them. If you want to climb Mount Everest, then do it. If you want to explore remote jungles, stick a pin in a map and start planning. There are plenty of obstacles in your way and money is not the toughest one. Many people start off small. I had a map of Africa on my wall for years before I ever got there.

Seize the moment. There is no master plan for your life unless you make one. You may never achieve any of your goals or you may rewrite them every day. If you have a direction, then you can make a constructive decision when you come to a fork in the road. Every day we make dozens of minor decisions and if we don't apply them to a greater goal, we end up just going around in circles. Most major goals are achieved by a series of smaller forward-moving decisions.

You will soon find that the real pleasure in life is not setting one goal and then achieving it but in your mastery of overcoming obstacles in getting to those goals. This is not an empty motivational guide but a manual on how to work the odds and avoid the open manhole covers.

Early on, I strove for a balance in my life and I worked hard in all aspects of my life. When I reached my forties, all aspects of my life magically and effortlessly blended together when I found myself making a lot of money at doing what I used to do for my vacation. You can too.

Some tips for those who want more out of the short time we are on this planet:

- Try a number of activities to find something that turns you on.
- Learn as much as you can about your passions.
- Learn from others and from doing.
- Integrate all aspects of your life toward being the best at what you do.
- Once you feel comfortable in your expertise, share your knowledge and skills with others. You might find you'll learn even more.
- Focus on what makes this world work and work to alleviate some of the problems.

Mastering survival and adventure gives you the feeling that you can master your environment and make you more likely to seek out challenges. Ignorance of survival thinking and shunning adventure forces you to accept the status quo, view change as bad, and can ultimately affect your view of your position in life as being predetermined and unchangeable.

· 2 ·

survival

Holy Sh*t, There I Was! The Myth of Survival

In this chapter we are going to explore the survival myth. This is a separate phenomenon from survivalists, people who pursue self-sufficiency in their lonely wait for the next apocalypse. I would also toss out the folks who have great survival skills but consider it everyday living: natives, aboriginals, trappers, boaters, guides, commandos, and other professionals who don't dress up to survive.

What I'm talking about when I write the Myth of Survival is the mindset that gets people *into* trouble, not out of it. We've all read the stories. Every time I flip through the channels or visit the bookstore, I am beguiled by tales of heroic survival. Whether they are real stories like Audie Murphy holding off Germans from the back of a burning tank or half-frozen climbers staggering down from a disastrous attempt on Everest, the Myth of Survival is propagated over and over and it goes something like this: Person sets out to do something adventurous, stuff happens, forcing him to overcome great odds and distinguish himself meritoriously. He returns quiet and calm with a strong message to pass on to other, weaker mortals. It helps if the hero is good looking and if at least half a dozen people were disposably less heroic but sufficiently noble in their expiration. These people can fully present their heroics in a flattering light—minus self-doubt, shaking knees, bugged-out eyes, and skid-marked shorts. Hell, these folks, by virtue of their survival, have become *experts*.

Frankly, I think that this is baloney. Too often we think that doing something dangerous has some romantic sense of glory in its execution. If you need to use your survival skills, you've probably already screwed up.

Survival is a journey through statistics and whatever is graciously acceded to self-preservation.

People who plan, get it right, and avoid problems just can't seem to get the same book or film deals, but they are the ones to write books about.

Today, class, please find the glory or heroism in the following examples.

- One frigid winter night a man visits his daughter's home, finds her not there, and decides to sneak in through the bathroom window. He gets stuck and the next day the postman sees his legs sticking out the half-open window but finds the man dead, frozen as stiff as an ironing board.
- A young man and his girlfriend decide to satisfy their passion while driving down the highway at over 70 mph. His girl enthusiastically rides the pink pony, unintentionally blocking his view. At the moment of blinding passion he veers into an oncoming Audi, killing everyone.
- Yellowstone has at least two gorings a year from tourists who pose their families next to wild bison or elk. Large signs warn visitors of the deadly effects of 212°F thermal pools, but still curious tourists scream in pain as they dip their hands in to see just how hot it really is.
- Elderly Korean bus tourists climb over fences, walk past graphic warning signs, and then steam themselves in Hawaii's volcanic geysers in some health kick or bizarre death ritual.
- A tourist from France decides to get back to nature in our oldest national park. He finds a pool just above the spectacular waterfall, and, while splashing around, he slips on the rocks, gets sucked into the thundering current, goes over the six-hundred-foot waterfall and is smashed to his death. His last souvenir? A photo in which he is seen posing next to a park service sign that states below, "If You Swim Here You Will Die." There is even an illustration for foreign tourists of a man falling down the waterfall to his death.
- Four prisoners in Wisconsin decide to escape for the Milwaukee city jailhouse. After getting down to the basement they take off the

grille of a ventilation duct and one of the prisoners gets stuck. His cohorts become so angry at him, they sodomize him and return to their cells, leaving him for the guards to arrest.

Fun, huh? So let's just say that reading this book or any other will not prevent or provide advice to prevent the aforementioned scenarios.

I mention that real survival is found in the parched scrub of Southern Sudan, where knob-kneed, potbellied kids eat grains of rice that fall off empty aid trucks, or under freeway underpasses, where grubby homeless people make dinner out of taco wrappers. Real survival isn't pretty or heroic, so let's agree that the first step in survival is common sense tempered with the respect that most of us will never truly have to use what we learn.

Re$cue, Dollars from Distress?

So why am I so down on part-time survival? Because these days survival as a hobby seems to be the biggest reason people get into trouble. Hunters, hikers, climbers, rafters, and adventurers who want to push themselves within well-defined limits quickly become blundering accountants, welders, clerks, and waitresses when the stuff hits the fan. And stupidity is expensive.

When millionaire balloonist Steve Fossett ditched 480 nautical miles off Australia's northeast coast in his attempt to circumnavigate the globe, he and the world automatically assumed that someone would come and rescue him.

The task fell to the French (from their territory of New Caledonia) and the Australian taxpayers. The Australians were also called upon to rescue a French yachtswoman, which drained another $3.5 million from the exchequer. And when wedding photographer and yacht racer Tony Bullimor was trapped in his sailboat, it cost the Aussies $5.9 million to get him on dry land. His four-day ordeal sparked offers for film, news, and spokesman deals, casting the whole idea of people attempting adventurous things in a truly preposterous light. Tony's comment on it all? "There is something a little absurd about the tremendous cost of rescuing people who do foolhardy things." Amen, brother.

If adventurers and explorers were left to die as they were a hundred years ago before the age of global positioning systems, turbocharged helicopters, and massive, mobile sea-air-ground rescue teams, folks might have a bit more reticence about doing silly things, like piloting a balloon around the globe or jet-skiing across the South Atlantic.

In Alaska there are about fifteen hundred rescues each year at a cost of over $9 million. It's one thing to pull a fisherman off a sinking boat, it's another to pluck dead people off mountains who went up for a week of fun. The Park Service at Mount McKinley spent over $220,000 to rescue a British climbing team, some of them dead. In Aspen, seven weekend warriors skied out into a blizzard and high avalanche conditions. Twelve snowmobiles, two Arctic Cats, a couple of helicopters, and a small army of ski-borne searchers brought them out at a cost of $16,000. The local newspapers charitably described them as "having the brain capacity of Arctic Lichen."

In general, the cost for a single land-based rescue can run around $3,000 to $7,500, depending on how easy you make it to be found. Usually, this money comes out of small budgets of rural counties with small tax bases. Often the military, Coast Guard, and local volunteers chip in. To avoid adventurers from being rescued and then beaten to death by pissed-off rescuers for their stupidity, states are now beginning to charge for what they consider "high-risk, personal pursuits." The folks at Mount McKinley originally thought they would collect a cash deposit of $1,500 for U.S. climbers and $7,500 from foreigners and keep 10 percent . . . if they were alive to get their deposit back. They finally settled on a $150 fee and sixty-day advance registration—a long way from Mount Everest's six-figure climbing fee, but the start of a new trend. The Grand Canyon now charges for a helicopter evacuation out of the canyon, and tickets are being issued by most parks to people who are rescued for doing dumb things. In this way fatalities have been cut in half and rescues by just under half.

So if you are pulled out of the wilderness, don't be surprised if you are handed a warm drink and a large bill. The good news is that they'll be happy to work out time payments.

If you're not budgeted for being extracted by a Wyoming SWAT team, your best bet is to get lost at sea, preferably near the U.S. coastline. The U.S. Coast Guard does not charge for yanking folks out of shark-infested oceans, as balloonists Steve Fossett, Richard Branson, and Per Linstrand happily discovered over umbrella drinks after ditching their balloon off the coast of Hawaii in December 1998. So if you spin the wheel of fortune for fun, be prepared to lose.

Survival vs. Looking Good in Khaki

There are a number of survival schools where the real journey is an inner journey. Despite their locations in scenic and remote places, their goal is to get you to reach a little deeper into your resources for self-confidence, creativity, and intelligence. It doesn't really matter if you make it to the top of a mountain, the end of a trail, or the mouth of a river, it's how much you enjoyed getting there. This is self-sufficiency rather than survival.

So the next time you overhear someone in a bar saying, "Holy shit, there I was," ask why he wasn't smart enough to stay out of trouble in the first place.

· 3 ·

fear

When Your Brain Checks Out and Your Body Is Left with the Bill

With fear, the important thing to recognize is the difference between fear generated by a realistic threat, and fear caused by anxiety, lack of preparation, supplies, training, or knowledge. Why? Because the downside of fear is panic or stress, both of which take an enormous toll on our mental and physical conditioning.

When things are going swimmingly, and life is good, you are in what they call the homeostasis zone. Homeostasis is the normal stress-free condition of the human body at rest. This is where most people should be.

Stress is the enemy of homeostasis. Stress is an animal feeling that something is wrong; it's also something that makes your brain pay attention and kicks the body into action. Stress can be induced physically, such as a blow to the head or extremes in temperature. Stress can also be mental: Worrying about losing your job can be as stressful as a man holding a gun to your head. In fact, long-term mental stress can actually be physically damaging, causing health problems that can range from chronic headaches to ulcers.

When stress is introduced (whether real or perceived) the following occurs:

1. **Anxiety:** With the onset of low stress a person becomes visibly irritable and edgy. Concentration is lost, and there may be diarrhea, loss of appetite, lack of interest, and emotional outbursts.

2. **Alarm:** Often called "fight or flight." This is a high state of stress triggered by being startled or perhaps by a loud noise or a physical confrontation. The endocrine glands begin pumping adrenaline, increasing muscle strength and heart and breathing rates. Sensory awareness is also heightened as chemical signals are sent through the body. The adrenal glands (on top of the kidneys), which secrete epinephrine, provide extra strength.

3. **Resistance:** If the person chooses to take action, the muscles tense, an aggressive posture and attitude develops, and the person readies for a fight or flight. At this point, people may choose to do irrational or heroic things, since logic and common sense have been abandoned. Body strength is high, sense sharp, and the heart is pounding.

4. **Exhaustion:** This is the final, short-term stage where the body has burned an extraordinary amount of blood sugar and weakens. Your knees may begin to shake and you may feel dizzy or weak. This stage usually occurs after a threat has passed.

Fight It or Ride It

To channel the natural physical and mental symptoms of fear, the military spends a lot of time training soldiers how to react. A human's natural instinct when shot at is to duck, take cover, or run away, but a soldier is supposed to attack when shot at, even when this course goes against his better judgment. Training is the way the military ensures that. In self-defense you also learn to harness fear and how to use the assailant's force against him.

There is no such training in adventuring. You can read books and learn survival skills, but nothing really prepares you for the first time you stumble into a bear or over a waterfall. At that point, there are so many conditions, options, and choices that the mind is at a loss to choose the right way to react.

The solution is to get as much experience as you can in a wide variety of terrains, conditions, and scenarios. Associate with people who deal with emergencies, take courses, and deliberately think through and practice what you would do in dangerous conditions. In this way, when something happens, you may not know exactly how you will react but you will probably be calm enough to think it through.

The secret to surviving fear is to learn to use it. Welcoming the clarity of thought, extra strength, and heightened sense to accomplish what must be done. Make fear your friend and he will come to your aid when you need him the most.

leadership

Who's in Charge? Me? I Thought You Were!

Learning to lead may save not only your life but the lives of the people around you. In the event of disaster and fear, it is natural for humans to panic. The last thing most people are concerned with in a panic situation is assuming personal responsibility for their actions. That's why you'll see normally responsible adults stampeding over babies in a dash to get to the lifeboats or to the nearest fire exit. It's a matter of personal survival. It's a damn strong instinct.

You can see this unrehearsed reaction on video surveillance cameras shot during earthquakes: Normally placid folks start waving their hands and screaming like they were at a revival meeting full of crazed joggers. It's morbidly funny to watch people scattering and stampeding without a single lucid thought in their heads. Unless of course they are blocking the only exit in a burning building. Then you get angry. Panic is a natural outgrowth of fear and group dynamics. One or two people can start a whole football stadium panicking.

But we've learned to harness fear. How do we harness the fear of others? If you read adventure disaster stories, it doesn't take long to see how bad or no leadership plunges people into disaster. It is also important to pay attention when leadership can save you. Airline pilots, medical crews, sea captains, soldiers, priests, and teachers are trained to take a leadership role in times of crisis. But what about burger flippers, truck drivers, typists, plumbers, or, worse yet, news crews who will not only stand around but ask you to move your bloodied head a little to the left so they can catch a better shot for the six o'clock news? In an era of legal liability, dispassionate citizens, and apathetic bystanders, just who is going to save you?

In emergency situations with groups of people, leadership makes the difference between disaster and survival. Firm, direct intervention can turn panic into progress.

The first leadership lesson is to stay calm and appraise the situation. Remember, they've got to burn off all that adrenaline in the veins. But don't worry. They'll burn out in a couple of minutes. Although it sounds selfish, your first impulse should be to save yourself so that you'll be around to help other people. Then, when it is appropriate, gather people around you, form a consensus, and delegate tasks based on individuals' skills or attributes. Your major gift should be to bring calm and clarity to a situation. By not burning up your blood sugar by running around, you will be calm and collected, not exhausted and desperate.

Everybody Wants to Rule the World

The other extreme is people who take charge in emergencies only to dish out bad advice and deadly succor. Leadership is learned, not figured out on the spot, but that doesn't stop some people from telling you what to do in an emergency. These people are the "rub butter on it if it's burned" or "hey, help me drag this guy out of his car" school of ad hoc rescuers. Heroes who learn their stuff from *Kojak* reruns are deadly.

If you are in an emergency situation, the smartest thing you can do is to ask if anyone is an EMT or has first-aid or other medical training. If someone does start barking orders, ask him what training he has so you can be sure it's appropriate for the situation.

Before You Follow the Leader, Check Credentials—and Your Instincts

Too often in the big bad world of adventure, expedition, and the military, the egomaniacal, mentally unstable, or just plain pig-stupid and brutal rise to the top. I have been on a number of expeditions led by these "colorful" characters—a hollow core wrapped up in egomaniacal drive ignited by emotional instability. For instance, I once had a knife pulled on me by an expedition leader—in front of the ruler of an African nation and in full view of the world's press—because the rugged gentleman in question did not want to get his kilt wet by being thrown in a pool.

What Is Leadership?

Is leadership that quality that makes you so tough that your crew mutinies, sticks you in a lifeboat, and makes you travel halfway around the world like Captain Bligh?

Or is leadership making your team love you so much that they "win one for the Gipper"?

Leadership is neither hard brutality nor sappy patronizing. It is a management skill that can be learned by anyone. As in most endeavors it does help to have some assistance from your brain and personality, but it is not a prerequisite.

To weed out the 2 million or so candidates for the Camel Trophy, the world's toughest off-road event, the organizers ask people to fill out questionnaires. They then pull the forms that show a good grasp of reality, enthusiasm, and a commitment to teamwork. Proficiency is important but not the main criterion. A well-rounded person with an easygoing personality is the ideal candidate. Not very glamorous specs, but . . . one that is required when the going gets tough.

The handful who make it to the training period are sent to a remote, cold place for a weekend of hell. One of the main tasks is called leadership, in which the contestants are faced with a scaled-down version of the British Military Officer candidate test. The idea is to present candidates with a number of complex and/or seemingly insurmountable tasks and judge them on how well they accomplish them.

There is a spiderweb of rope and a request for all ten candidates to pass through the gaps without touching the ropes. There is a teetering log on which the applicants must switch positions from left to right without a single person falling off. Every challenge gets tougher and each appears impossible. The only ray of hope is that this has been done before.

The final, cold candidates are always eager to please, and one usually begins to bark out orders and "take charge." This person always fails, as do those who sit back and simply try various permutations. On the other hand, the person who suggests an idea but needs help is the person who does well.

Overall, what these candidates discover is that the problems presented require the total mental or physical resources as well as the cooperation of the entire group. It is the persons who can facilitate and focus the entire group who become the natural leaders.

Remember then that leaders don't always take charge; they enable others to get the job done.

Saving the Day

The most important responsibility of leadership is to focus and harness whatever skills and resources are at hand. But what is the other thing fearless leaders are supposed to do? In a situation where people are thrown together for a long time or in expeditions, there are some things every leader should know.

Establish Structure

If you choose to take charge, it is important to gather people around and discuss what you feel needs to be done. Create a regular forum by saying, "Let's all put our heads together and come up with a plan." If people do not want to comply, ask them to join in and give their opinion. If there is someone you feel is more capable than you are, suggest that he take charge of the specific task. After a while, a natural hierarchy will emerge.

If it is an accident scene, the key needs will be first aid, securing help, and directing traffic. If it is a fire, it may be evacuation. More complex examples might be a lost hiking group, the aftermath of a natural disaster, and an expedition gone awry. The important point is, whatever needs to be done should be done in concert.

For example, the key tasks for an outdoor group include:

- **Food:** gathering of fuel and food, preparing, serving, and cleaning
- **Sanitation:** latrines, washing clothes, cleaning camps, supervising hygiene

- **Accommodations/camp:** choosing and building camps
- **Security/safety:** preventing theft, incursion from animals, hostile elements
- **Health:** prevention of disease, inspection, treatment, and education
- **Maintenance/repair:** repair and upkeep of clothing, cooking supplies, equipment
- **Navigation/communications:** setting courses, maintaining contact

Your job is to smooth out any squabbles and move things along. If you think you might be together for the long haul, a more formal survival process needs to be instituted:

- Apply names and titles to each person or group.
- Construct a plan and how the group will achieve it.
- Hold a daily briefing of any modifications to the plan.
- Point out accomplishments by group members and give them group praise.

Establish Mission

If you are faced with a good or even desperate mission, you can drum up support by involving everyone in the planning stage. Often there will be much disagreement on whether to stay put or leave, or which route is best. If there are duplicate resources and a need to travel light, it is possible to break into subgroups. As a rule, however, you should stay together because you could end up with one found group and more lost groups.

First, establish a forum where you discuss who, what, and when. You may notice the "why" is missing. The why part should be voted on, and if the mission is stated clearly, there should not be an in-depth discussion of different methods. If there is heated discussion or argument about various methods, it is wise to isolate the detractor and suggest that he/she stay out of the discussion until the group comes to a consensus. Inevitably, your detractors will deal with stress by arguing. They may even cross their arms and pout their lips. Resist the urge to suggest eating them and try to talk with them away from the group. Worst case, hold a vote to abandon or ostracize the malcontent.

Another method, less confrontational but ultimately more damaging, is to democratically determine the group's path and force the detractor to defend his position in public. Group dynamics are damaged by these naysayers, however, and they usually continue to sabotage your efforts. Consequently, I have found it is usually best to remove naysayers and rabble-rousers to maintain group focus and productivity.

Maintain Momentum

It is important to tap into the natural ebb and flow of human endeavor and work quickly to solve your predicament. Pushing too hard will create resentment and fatigue. Waiting too long to embark on a course of action only leads to more waiting. Soon energy, resources, and willpower are depleted, leaving you with no option but to stay. To that end:

- Tap into a common goal (be rescued, get off mountain, attract rescue, gather food, hike out) and be motivational about the end result.
- Identify and specify specific, immediate goals (gather ten fish, build three huts, build two rafts, get off the mountain).
- Give each person a specific part in the task and praise his/her contribution.
- Review, manage, and assist where needed (give encouragement, pitch in, solve problems, build morale).
- Review progress and modify tasks or goals if needed.

Being the Boss

Maintaining your leadership position is important for group dynamics. Having established yourself, and won their confidence, members of the group will expect you to look after their interests and ward off potential problems. They will also emulate your style and attitude to help keep up their spirits and hope. In order to fulfill their expectations, you will need to:

- Support and raise the morale of the group through humor, entertainment, encouragement, and praise.
- Rise earlier, work harder, and go to sleep later.
- Discuss the situation with others to keep track of the group's mood.
- Dive into unpleasant situations and solve them before they get out of hand.
- Deal with the dirty work of punishment or admonishment fairly but unequivocally by a system determined by the group.
- Provide a role model by your personal conduct and eagerness to help.
- Never show doubt, anger, depression, or confusion.
- Ensure the safety and well-being of the group.

- Provide feedback for ideas and complaints.
- Make time for recognition, relaxation, and encourage productive celebrations.

Essentially, your job is to maintain an easygoing democratic process in a tough autocratic environment. This also includes giving impromptu or formal recognition of individuals for accomplishments, real or imagined, creating entertainment to let off steam, drawing out quieter members of the group to balance the extroverts, and generally maintaining the group as a working whole.

I Am the Boss, Aren't I?

Often there will be a pre-identified leader (as in the case of an expedition, camp, ship, aircraft, or the military) who may or may not be qualified for the post. (In fact, he or she is probably the person that got you into the jam in the first place.) If the person in charge is a true leader, he will listen to your opinions or ideas if they have merit. If he is a Stalinesque twerp, you are in trouble. Big trouble.

The only solution you have at that point is to assert what rights you have for independence. Be sure to do this in the calmest, most nonconfrontational manner possible, as the appearance of a mutiny can cause more problems. (For example, captains, soldiers, and police have the right to arrest or even jail you if they think you will be a danger to a group. You may be proved right later but it will be a little too late.) Best advice is to go with the flow, suggest, suggest, suggest, and then split if things are too insane.

Are You the Boss?

Still unsure whether you're the leadership type? Perhaps the following quiz will help you to ascertain whether you are ready, willing, and able.

Finally, the joys and penalties of leadership come to us all as a parent, big sister, team manager, driver, or even a friend. All you can hope is that you are better at it than others.

So far, you should have harnessed fear, harnessed the skills and enthusiasm of the people around you, and now all you need is some specific survival tips, which we'll cover in the rest of the book.

are you a leader? a quiz

1) Leaders are born, not made.   True ___ False ___

False: Leaders lead by example or social mandate. In survival situations people will follow those who set an example by action.

2) People are smart enough to figure things out on their own. This leadership thing is overrated.   True ___ False ___

False: When resources (food, water, fire) are limited, someone has to make the decisions on how the group will use them. Also, people will not equally apply their skills to the many mundane chores required in groups (gathering, fire, cleaning, cooking, signal making).

3) Leaders are busy leading, so they should have special privileges.   True ___ False ___

False: Leaders have the job of leading but there is no special reward.

4) People need to be told exactly what to do each day or hour if necessary. If they don't, they should be punished.   True ___ False ___

False: The leader's job is to identify the goal, not to lay out the methodology. People also need some leeway to come up with better or faster ways to get the job done.

5) Leaders don't have time for whining and petty squabbles.   True ___ False ___

False: Sorry, that's exactly what leaders are for: resolving minor problems before they become major problems.

6) **Men are better leaders.** True __ False __

False: Although this is not true, it is statistically more likely that men will have more experience, training, or skills in a wilderness environment. Women are better leaders under stress due to their less dictatorial approach.

7) **Leaders lay down the law and don't take crap from whiners.** True __ False __

False: A double whammy here because leaders must use their authority to shift group dynamics toward positive steps. How you deal with dissenters will determine how easy or difficult this becomes.

8) **Leaders need to kick ass and take names.** True __ False __

False: Directly confronting group members is a destructive policy that leads to griping and backstabbing. There are always one or two people who won't go with the flow. Usually, they need to be singled out and made to prove their point or opposition. In other words, dissenters need to be harnessed.

9) **Young people and women can't lead as well as older men.** True __ False __

False: We've already broached the gender part of this but all things being equal, experience, social position, and style will determine who will lead the group.

10) **These days there is no upside to being the boss, only misery and criticism.**   True ___ False ___

True: There will be no reward for leading a crew of lost souls to safety or organizing a rescue during a flood. It will be something that springs naturally from yourself and will be aided by a sense of confidence.

But even if you know nothing, the test of a good leader is the ability to encourage people to take themselves to where they never thought they could go alone.

· 5 ·

home

Why Horror Movies Take Place at Home

Let's assume that you've got the right mental attitude. Now let's try it out in the world's most dangerous place. The most dangerous place in the world? Well, it's not some gulag in Siberia or the central African jungle. It's your home.

Why? Because you spend a lot of time there. In between shaving your armpits, drunken parties, Saturday BBQs, raging domestic fights, stupid pet tricks, and washing dishes, stuff happens. More than one-third of all injuries resulting in emergency department visits occur at home. Sure, the highways do more damage, but they can't compare with the cornucopia of horrors that hide in your home.

What Makes a Home So Dangerous?

Look around your house. How many objects, situations, or events do you view with an eye to safety? Is there a nice glass-framed picture above your bed waiting to fall on your head in an earthquake? Do you keep meaning to tighten that banister? Are those empty paint cans going to get tossed . . . as soon as you get around to it? Then think of where you work, where you shop, where you travel to, and even the car you drive. Life is regulated to the point of ridiculousness. Hell, you even have to take the elevator twelve stories down and freeze your butt off outside to smoke a cigarette.

But your house is a disaster waiting to happen.

When you bought that marvelous glass coffee table with nice shiny bezeled corners, did you get a safety lecture from the salesclerk? Does your five-year-old do a semiannual inspection of poisonous materials, loaded handguns, top-heavy TVs, and scabby extension cords? No, of course not, but you do, right? Oh, you don't? Well then, I guess you should know that slippery bathtubs, fires, nonignited gas stoves, power tools, ungrounded receptacles, and slippery carpets kill about sixty people every day.

Let's go over the drill.

Falls: Falls are the most likely cause of death around the home if you are an adult. Half of all home deaths are from falls. Victims over sixty don't bounce too well, and the usual culprit is having a second story in your home. You need two banisters, a runner, and a carpet at the end of the stairs to absorb some of the shock. If you are getting doddery, you might want to trade in that Georgetown home for a ranch house in Irvine.

Poison: This category makes up a third of home deaths. Even more surprising is that most of these deaths are from drug overdoses or complications from ingesting drugs. Maybe you'll want to put on your reading glasses next time you get up in the middle of the night for some sleeping pills.

Fires: The last major killer is death by fire or as a result of burns. Most fires take place between 4:00 and 8:00 P.M., but most deaths from fire take place between midnight and 4:00 A.M. Cooking is the prime culprit of fires, followed by electrical devices. Fires by tobacco smoking cause the most deaths. Smoke detectors, emergency lighting, and a rehearsed nighttime evacuation plan seem to fill the bill here. Understand just how flammable your house is and move lamps, replace drapes, install fire extinguishers, and have a plan for putting out a cooking fire.

Children: After the elderly, children are the likeliest accident victims around the home. Most deaths under the age of four occur when children go exploring and end up choking, drowning, suffocating, being shot, burning and harming themselves because an adult left something out or did not supervise them. The answer is simple. Childproof your home and watch your kids.

The key to surviving at home is to think of it as dangerous and take the time and steps to eliminate as many risks as you can.

Luckily for those who won't, over 80 percent of the population is covered by the 911 emergency number. Unluckily, when the American College of Emergency Medical Physicians conducted a survey a few years back, they discovered that almost half of the adults could not identify 911 as an emergency number, or confused it with 411, the directory assistance number.

Be afraid, be very afraid.

· 6 ·
driving

Roadkill and the Duke of Hazards

hen just under half of all accidental deaths in this country are caused by motor vehicle accidents, it pays to learn how to shave the odds. Frighteningly, 80 percent of the deaths of Americans between sixteen and eighteen years old are caused by automobile accidents.

There's about a 33 percent chance you'll one day be involved in a car accident. If auto accidents were a lottery, a good chunk of us would be rich. Though a lot is made in the press about the 40,000-plus people killed on U.S. highways each year, you don't hear much about the more than 3 million people who are injured in these accidents. That's a much scarier statistic.

According to the cops, car accidents are caused by alcohol, speeding, running red lights, not concentrating, aggressive driving, and tailgating. They forget to mention that people making mistakes hit people who aren't. Because you're not at fault doesn't mean you'll walk away. Excellent drivers get clobbered all the time. It can take one peabrain little navigational error to ruin a lot of folks' day. Perhaps the worst road accident in history occurred in Afghanistan in 1982. A Russian fuel tanker was rear-ended in a 1.7-mile-long tunnel. Some five thousand people were incinerated in the resulting blast. Only one guy made a mistake.

Realistically, most accidents are fender-benders at intersections or rear-enders. They can ruin your day, but not your life.

Rule of Three

There is a rule of three when it comes to car collisions. When there is a collision, there are three crashes. First the car hits the object, then the person hits something inside the car, and then the organs in the body hit the inside of the body cavity. All three impacts smash and damage and can result in a medical emergency or death to the driver. You can eliminate one of these traumatic impacts by utilizing the primary survival tool: the seat belt.

Seat belts were invented during World War II for American pilots and have become the single most important safety device in a vehicle. A lot of people object to them, bleating that they will be trapped in the car if there's an accident, but the fact remains that if you are thrown out of your vehicle in an accident, you are three times more likely to be killed, and your seat belt will keep you from colliding with your dashboard and windshield.

Size Matters

There is one other thing that can save your life: the size, height, and weight of your vehicle. If you take a bowling ball and run it into a Ping-Pong ball, the physics of mass, inertia, and impact becomes apparent. Survival in a vehicle can be determined by its height, since higher vehicles will slide up and over smaller vehicles, using the other vehicle's roof, hood, or trunk to absorb the impact. More than half of all traffic fatalities involve vehicles of dramatically different mass, and 80 percent of these fatalities occur in the smaller vehicle. So the first step to automobile survival is to drive a truck.

Speed Matters

Go ahead and run as fast as you can into a wall. Doesn't feel so good, does it? Now walk slowly and do the same thing. Not so bad, right? Onlookers may make a wide tack of you on the way to a phone to call 911, but you will have discovered the basic principle of death vs. serious injury and serious injury vs. minor injury. The chance of death or serious injury doubles each 10 mph you travel over 50. In any moving vehicle higher speeds tie in directly to reduced reaction time, loss of control, and collision. So your second lesson is to slow down.

Driving Safe

Driving is generally not a dangerous activity. If you are a middle-aged urban professional with a late-model, full-sized vehicle equipped with air bags, and you're wearing your seat belt, keeping the necessary escape routes open, and checking your mirrors and blind spots occasionally, you're probably spending more time bitching about your insurance premiums than getting serviced at the body shop.

On the other hand, if you are an eighteen-year-old heading back from the Dew Drop Inn in a jacked-up '65 Mustang with the carcass of a Bud Light twelve-pack in the passenger seat on Saturday night, things are a little different. In some areas, up to three of every five drivers on rural roads after midnight in the United States can be drunk.

Survival on the road starts with the right vehicle, the right attitude, and the right driving style. Drive for space, not for speed. Keep a buffer around you and keep your escape routes (in the front and to the sides) open.

Make use of the safety equipment provided. Seat belts worn, children in the back, ABS active and brakes checked, tires with the proper amount of tread, air bags activated, and no heavy or sharp projectiles in the car.

Know your car. Most people haven't a clue what their vehicle will do in a skid or an emergency situation. Most people don't even know how quickly their car will stop, and few understand threshold braking or realize that their vehicle will stop sooner by not locking the brakes. (Threshold braking is applying just enough pressure to the pedal just short of a lock.) Don't be shy about doing a little backroad racing to understand the limits of your car or truck or taking advantage of an empty parking lot to brush up on your skidding skills.

Drive into accidents. When accidents happen, people have their foot jammed on the brake, their mouth open, and a desperate hope that they will stop in time. Avoiding accidents requires active control of your car combined with a clear picture of what is going on around you and knowledge of the capabilities of the vehicle. Swerving, gently steering into a skid, and knowing the limits of evasive maneuvers are also important.

Know the statistics. Driving at night, on the weekend, during rush hour, and even driving on secondary roads double the chance of an accident or fatality.

When driving or traveling by road abroad, realize that a lot of things you assumed Stateside no longer exist. Accident and fatality rates can be up to forty times higher in places like Egypt—and ten times higher in South Africa—than they are in the United States.

Two-Wheeled Mayhem

Motorcycles are by far the most dangerous vehicles on the road—twenty times more so than cars, according to some studies. And it doesn't take a pathologist to figure out why. I enjoy racing motorcycles and have no problem sliding around a wide sweeper, my head a few inches from the track. Notice I said track, not road.

You may take comfort in seeing the gray-bearded bikers on their hogs and Hondas, but remember that you don't see the thousands of photographs of young kids who screwed up remembered in photographs on the mantels of their moms and dads.

Motorcycles have much different dynamics than cars. Use the brakes properly (more front than back), avoid the impulse to brake around corners (the bike will "stand up" and veer into oncoming traffic), and respect the limited adhesion motorcycles have in wet, dusty, and rough conditions.

Ride alone, wear a full face helmet and protective clothing. Being continuously prepared for an accident will help you think straight when things get tight. Before the deadly symphony of sheet metal and asphalt you have a few microseconds to hit the throttle, lean in harder, brake, or dump the bike. Having your best friend or hot date on the back will slow down the thinking process. Proper gloves and a helmet (most riders end up sliding on their hands and hitting their heads when they dump) are important even if they are cumbersome.

The best thing to do is to attend a motorcycle riding course, such as those conducted by the Motorcycle Safety Foundation. Or even a racing course. They're not required by law, but they should be. Simply having the ability to negotiate a serpentine laid out like mileage posts on an interstate highway in the DMV lot is not enough. The more comfortable you are with extreme situations and your machine, the greater the odds you will survive a little bit longer.

Pay attention. You can't jump on a motorcycle with the same mind-set as hopping in a car. On a bike, you can't talk on a cell phone, change CDs, chow down Big Macs, or smoke butts. You can't shave or put on lipstick. Aboard a motorcycle you need to repeat the biker's mantra: This activity could kill me today.

When an Accident Isn't

Accidents aren't the simple fender-benders they once were. Scam artists, impersonal insurance judgments, and cops that steer clear of fender-benders " 'cause there's too much paperwork" make the downside of owning a car a bummer. I was once hit while parked at the side of the road. After helping the errant driver change a tire, I discovered from my insurance company that he had to be carried back to his house and was passing blood. It was all a scam, but it would have been his word against mine if I hadn't had witnesses. Don't assume that an accident is an accident. It could have been by design.

What to Do in Case of an Accident

- When an accident is imminent, try to avoid a direct collision. Running into a field, the median, or a fence is preferable.
- After you are hit take a few seconds to look for oncoming traffic and then leave the car if you are able. If the accident is minor, move to the side of the road. Often pileups occur as people plow into cars blocking the road.
- It is natural for adrenaline to be pumping and people to be upset, but do not argue, discuss, or talk about the accident. Focus on organizing the matter at hand.
- Carry a disposable camera in your glove box at all times. If an accident occurs, shoot pictures from all four angles and note the hour, location, and weather conditions. Pace off skid marks and create a diagram. All of this will be invaluable in court or for insurance claims.
- When you get the name and address of the other driver, also write down the license plate number and ask to see some form of ID. If the person is drunk or belligerent, get names of witnesses.

- Call the police or ask bystanders to get help. Do not attempt to provide medical help in urban areas. It is important to wait for police to take statements, but remember that whatever you say will be introduced into evidence if you are sued.

Rugged Stuff

Most of what you learned in driver's education class can be thrown out the window when driving off-road in remote areas—along jungle trails, swamps, brushy savanna, and boulder-strewn deserts.

Driving off-road requires a different mind-set than traditional motoring. The emphasis isn't on speed but, instead, maneuverability and terrain. You can run across a number of adverse conditions when driving in remote regions. I rarely come across a situation where a local's description of the trail ahead is accurate. If you have to cross rough terrain, travel in convoy and be prepared to spend a lot more time than you originally estimated.

Here is a cheat sheet on how to deal with challenging conditions:

Soft sand: Deflate tires to about half their normal pressure. Apply power smoothly and consistently. The key is to keep speed up and stay on top of the sand. When stuck, do not rev the wheels, to avoid digging in. Soft sand dramatically reduces your fuel consumption and often leads to rollovers on dunes or slopes.

Slippery mud: Driving in deep mud can quickly high-center the vehicle, lifting the wheels off the ground and hanging up the vehicle on the frame or drivetrain. When driving through deep-rutted muddy paths, quickly flip the wheel back and forth to gain traction and break out of the ruts.

Snow: You can't drive on snow without a firm base underneath. If possible, go down to the parking lot and get a feel for just how much extra room you will need for braking, turns, and other, trickier maneuvers. When stuck, rock the car slowly by backing up and then rolling forward gently. Be aware that doing this too roughly can damage your transmission. Use dirt, floor mats, clothing, or anything else on hand to create traction.

Ice: When driving on ice, it is important to remember that rubber does have traction on ice but not down hills or during sharp maneuvers. Often black ice (frozen water on clear roads) and sheer ice are undrivable at any rate of speed above a crawl. Use engine gearing instead of brakes, and when you accelerate, do so gently. Use sand or salt to create traction. Often a slight push to get the vehicle going can stop wheel spin. Radial tires perform best.

Flooding: The most mundane form of flooding can cause hydroplaning. Your tires surf over the water surface, usually covering the windshield with the spray and removing any control of the vehicle. Slow down and don't assume that because the water is smooth the washed-out road beneath it is. If water is deep and you must cross, spray the electrics with WD-40 or coat with dipstick oil and fashion a snorkel for the air cleaner to raise the height of the air intake. Roll down the windows and open the doors, allowing the water to pour into the car. Drive slowly and with enough forward motion to create a bow wave and push the water ahead.

Descending steep hills: When faced with a seemingly impossible steep, slippery slope, you must remember to actively drive down the hill, even though your brain is screaming to brake, as it would be if you had just happened to jump off a cliff. This and all extreme maneuvers must be done in low-range four-wheel drive to provide maximum torque, control, and traction.

To descend a steep slope, you first have to pick the line you'll follow and determine what you will do at the bottom of the hill (turn, stop, slow down gently). Then, with your passengers out of the vehicle, engage the lowest gear in 4WD and gently (we use this word a lot when it comes to off-road driving) let the vehicle roll down the hill, allowing the engine to do the braking work. If the rear end starts sliding, gently apply a little gas. If you are generating an unsafe speed at a stomach-curdling rate, gently pump the brakes— do not lock them. In my experience it is best to practice this gentle pumping at the top of the hill.

Climbing steep hills: Attempting steep ascents seems like fun until the vehicle starts to stall and then lugs to a stop halfway up. Then you are left wondering what the hell to do as your truck starts sliding down the hill, wheels locked and heading for a backward flip. The answer is to practice doing the reverse slam.

On your way up a steep, muddy, or slick hill build momentum and make sure you are in the lowest gear that will take you over the top. Usually first gear. Shifting gears halfway up the hill will cause you to lose too much momentum. Coming in too quickly gives you too much wheel spin and the vehicle loses power. Know the highest torque range and drive slightly above it. If you lose traction on a slippery slope, flick the steering wheel back and forth to gain traction. Once stopped or stalled, quickly jam into reverse, start the engine, and drive down.

If you begin sliding sideways, blip the throttle to straighten out. Vehicles with ABS may perform this task automatically, but you should still pump gently to gauge how the vehicle will swing out. On overly steep hills the vehicle may want to go ass-over-teakettle, but this can be compensated for by forward velocity. Always approach hills straight on, and for God's sake know what's on the other side of the peak.

Crossing ruts, barriers, and bogs: Always cross ditches at an angle rather than head-on to avoid being hung up. Barriers can be crossed, but you need to build up the approach and exit with material. If you are crossing bogs, deflating the tires and keeping your speed up can help, but walk it first because if you can't walk across, you can't drive across. Hilly terrain provides a major problem, since most vehicles will roll if the angle of the vehicle exceeds 35° to 40°.

The best advice is to understand that off-road vehicles are not actually meant to go "off-road." Even tanks aren't. They just do a little better at handling off-road environments than do conventional passenger cars. Ignore those snazzy commercials starring high-speed, mud-spraying acrobats with macho, *National Geographic*-sounding names like Explorer, Expedition, Sierra, and Discovery. Instead, these vehicles should be driven, even off-road, as though you were driving your three-year-old to a dentist appointment—or as if you were driving home from the car wash with a cargo of nitroglycerin.

Engine Breakdown

In this era of black boxes and computerized, fuel-injected V-10s, the days of playing roadside mechanic under a shade tree are long gone. Sure, if you drive an old Jeep or Land-Rover, you can fix just about anything with a small tool kit and a cache of spare parts. But with today's automobiles, if you develop a problem or break down on the road, you may as well go fishing while waiting for a flatbed tow truck.

Gas engines work on the principle of injecting fuel and air into a chamber, which is ignited with a spark to push a drivetrain to propel the vehicle. Usually, a car will not start because it is missing one of the three primary ingredients to put it in motion: electricity, gas, or air. If an engine runs but won't "go," the problem is with the drivetrain.

Electrical failures can most likely be sourced at the battery. A starter needs a good amount of battery power and an engine that isn't frozen. If you hear a clicking sound, you are listening to a solenoid and a dead battery. Your options are to push-start it (not an easy feat for an automatic transmission), get a jump start from another vehicle, or get a new battery.

If the engine turns over but won't start, check for your three key elements of combustion. Pop off the air cleaner to check for clear air passage, disconnect one spark plug lead to see if it arcs, and then smell the carburetor to check for fuel. If your car has spark, air, and fuel, then it is the mixture that needs attention. Your plugs are probably fouled and need to be removed and cleaned.

Many people flood their stalled cars by pumping the gas pedal. Modern fuel-injected cars need no extra help. In cold conditions push the gas pedal to the floor and then turn the key for ten seconds. If it is warm, don't push the gas but turn the key and then slowly push down on the gas. If there is no spark on any of the leads, then your problem is in the ignition. If there is no gas, take the gas cap off and wiggle the vehicle to see if there is gas in the tank. If you still can't get your vehicle going, leave a note and start walking. If it's snowing, hot, or you are halfway across the Sahara, stay with your vehicle. It is now your new home.

emergency car kit

- ❏ Spare gasoline (2.5 gallons), water (1 gallon)
- ❏ Cell phone or CB radio
- ❏ Chains
- ❏ Flashlight/compressor combination
- ❏ Jumper cables
- ❏ Spare radiator hose, fan belt, headlight
- ❏ Reflective triangle
- ❏ Tool kit including tubeless tire patch kit
- ❏ Gloves
- ❏ Old parka
- ❏ Old blanket
- ❏ Disposable camera (for accidents)
- ❏ First-aid kit
- ❏ Fire extinguisher
- ❏ Shovel

· 7 ·

crime

Could You Lend Me $20 Until I Hock Your TV?

There's a whole chapter coming up on self-defense. Essentially it tells you not to waste your time, your teeth, or your life on learning how to kickbox a drunk at 3:30 in the morning.

Hopefully, you'll understand that the point is to not get into trouble but to run away if you do. Good.

But what about surviving crime that doesn't necessarily involve self-defense? Those dumb "I feel so stupid" crimes that happen to all of us? Car break-ins, pickpocketing, minor thefts, petty muggings, and maybe even more serious stuff that we hope will happen to other people.

Crime All the Time

The first major lesson in surviving crime is to expect it. Not just in bad neighborhoods or late at night but anytime, anywhere. In the pinball-like confluence of criminals and victims the chances are good that you won't run into criminals today, but with enough time and travel you will. In general, you can safely assume that there is crime in bad neighborhoods when the bars close on Friday nights, and there is also crime at nine in the morning in nice neighborhoods, specifically because that is when people don't expect it to happen.

On the heels of expecting crime to happen follows the next advice. Don't act like a victim. Criminals cue in on folks who carry themselves like they're frightened of the world. Body language is everything. Darting eyes, head cast low, a meek posture and stride—all these suggest to some guy lurking in the shadows that you're an easy mark. Instead, walk confidently and purposefully.

Be Vewy, Vewy Cawfool

Elmer had it right. Many crimes require a willing victim. Someone who stops to help someone, give directions, or tell the time is someone who entered into an evil appointment with all the best intentions. When they see a cheap pistol pointing at them, they can't believe the nice man is, in fact, a thug. When it comes to attacks on women, almost 90 percent begin with some type of ruse to gain the victim's trust.

Your Home

Despite spending thousands of dollars on security devices to make homes burglarproof, many people still open their doors when the bell rings. Go figure. A simple intercom is ideal in most cases, but it also provides access to impersonators who then rob your home. A coded access is ideal, since only people who have your code can dial in. Most homes are cased before they are robbed, so be suspicious of people who cruise by looking too intensely or too many times. And don't leave your garage door open: You're providing an inventory of goods for a lazy thief.

Put a block on windows and doors so they can't slide open to allow access. Plant plenty of nasty bushes around your house. You can use lots of lighting, but if nobody's watching it won't help, so install motion detectors at the sides and back of your home.

When you sell something in a classified ad, arrange to meet the person at your office or next door. What better way to have something stolen than inviting a "buyer" into your home to show him how it works?

Your Car

Make sure you lock your car doors, keep everything inside hidden from sight, and have enough insurance. If a thief wants your car, he'll get it. You can install an alarm, have a safety trip, use a steering wheel lock, and even install a tracking device, but chances are he'll know more about those devices than you do and how to disable them quickly, or he'll resort to carjacking. (If you really want a surefire antitheft system, install a homemade direct disconnect system to the battery.)

Carjacking is popular due to the success of antitheft devices. When I was driving through Johannesburg (the carjacking capital of the world) with the Flying Squad, they explained that there's no reason for a thief to smash up a nice car, jimmy the ignition, and then scream down the street with the alarm wailing when he can invite you to hand him your car and convince you to throw in your wallet for some spending money too.

Carjacking is a very organized and predictable crime. Syndicates put in orders for certain cars, either for parts or resale. Typically, the most popular cars are not the flashy ones but models that have been top sellers for the last three to five years. They are in high demand for parts and repairs.

Once a carjacker has an order for a specific model, he will typically wait where traffic slows down to make a turn or at a stoplight. When the traffic light changes to green, he can make his getaway.

The most popular method is to bump the car to feign a minor traffic accident. Carjackers want you to get out and leave the keys in the ignition. They'll also watch to see if you pocket them. After you rudely inquire where they learned how to drive, they will knock you down, grab the keys, and make off with your nice car. They will often carry a gun to intimidate you, and will use it if you take too long explaining that the car belongs to you and not them. If there is a baby in the backseat, don't worry; they'll toss it out when they're clear of any chase cars.

How do you survive car crime? Take the bus. (Sorry, couldn't help myself.)

Probably the most dangerous and cleverest crime combination is carjacking plus home invasion. Thieves look for commuters with fancy gold watches and flashy cars heading for nice neighborhoods. They follow you right into your garage, rob you and your house, and drive off with their loot in your car.

Preventing a carjacking may appear to be paranoid behavior, but it can be rather effective. Drive with your windows up and your doors locked. Leave enough space in front of you to avoid being boxed in. As you roll to a stop at a traffic light, adjust the rearview mirror so that it covers your blind spots. Keep your eyes on blind spots on both sides of the vehicle. Stay in the lane closest to the center of the road.

If you think you're being followed, make two to four right turns in succession. If the guy is still behind you, head for a police or fire station. If you are rear-ended or the person in front of you brakes suddenly, causing you to run into that vehicle, remain in the driver's seat. If possible, signal with your hands to go to a nearby full-service gas station, or some busy store or parking lot, to exchange license and insurance information. If you need to speak with the other party, crack the window and explain where you want to go to file a report or exchange information. Choose a location with as many people as possible. Keep the engine running. Carjackers normally work in pairs or teams, but don't assume that if the other car has a single occupant the situation is safe. Install a car phone; many can be programmed to dial 911 with a single button.

Other Danger Zones

ATMs: Thieves don't like crowds and they don't like crowded places. A good rule of thumb is to do your business in daylight hours, take out more money at once rather than less money more often—and do it when other people are around. Lots of people. That usually means Friday evenings or lunchtime during business days. The worst time is late at night, stumbling out of a bar to get more beer money. Often the crime occurs after you leave and get in your car. When you leave the ATM, check to see if you are being followed and lock your doors. If you lose your card, report it immediately and be skeptical of callers posing as bank managers or cops who want to verify your PIN. Never reveal your PIN to anyone.

Phone booths: Telephone booths are an ideal place to rob people. Bad guys love 'em, because you can't run, there's only a single entrance, and no one can hear you scream. Often, you've pulled out your wallet or purse to get your change, revealing precisely where you keep it. The deterrent is to use open, wall-attached public phone booths or busy phone banks in well-lit places. Popping in to a telephone booth to make a call is also an ideal way to have your car ripped off. Many people jump out of their cars to make a quick call, and leave their engine running.

Elevators: Elevators make an even better venue than telephone booths to get jacked up in if the thief is looking for uncompromised discretion and privacy. There's no way out and, again, there's no one to hear you shout for help. Most elevator thefts happen on the lower floors, where the thief has readier access to escape routes. A good way to avoid being pickpocketed in an elevator is simply to face others in the elevator with you, away from the door. Sociologically curious, perhaps, but effective.

City streets: The MO for many pickpockets is to distract and grab. Someone spills something on you and tries to brush it off. In some cases they offer to hold your purse while you wipe it off. Duh. Hey, do you have change for a twenty? If you do, I'll figure out where your money is kept. Did you drop a fiver? Maybe you'll pull out your wallet to check. Purse snatching is not even worth going into. You carry your valuables in a purse, you deserve to lose them. Same goes for gold Rolexes and nice jewelry.

Often beggars put on a half-assed entertainment show and then send kids to shove their grubby little hands into your pockets. While they are entreating you to donate to the cause of the impoverished, the smart ones are lifting your possessions. Don't bother chasing the laughing one, because he's already passed it off to the cherubic but snot-nosed little girl. Oh, and if they hand you a baby, you're probably being jacked up. As the kid runs off with your weekly pay packet, you're wondering if babies bounce when they're dropped. You quickly pat your money belt to make sure your cash is still there. That's okay, chump, they expected that and Pops is waiting to lift it at knifepoint around the corner.

· 8 ·

self-defense

Never Bring a Knife to a Gunfight

There is a general sense of foreboding before something dangerous happens. Trust it. It could be an odd electric smell or something that raises the hairs on the back of your neck. But learn to look for these primal signals your gut is feeling and try to escape. If you are distracted by music, talking, reading, rubbernecking, or preoccupied with a map, you will find yourself in the middle of these situations instead of peering into them able to change direction or break off.

If you can't escape, then your next step is to keep your distance and defuse the situation. Often people are accosted because crooks want their money, their car, or some other possession. With women, they may wish to shorten the courtship part and violently rape. If they want your money, hold it out and use it to maneuver to an exit spot. Throw the money down and break for it. If you feel you are in for a violent personal attack, try to buy time and space and then run like hell.

If the bad guys grab you, this is not good. You then need to weigh the advantages of striking quickly or pretending to be terrified and then striking when they lower their guard. The British SAS training school figures it takes over 2,400 repetitions of practicing an action to successfully take out an unsuspecting soldier or sentry. In most scenarios, your attacker is ready for action long before you can react. Once again, the goal here is to run away to safety. If the attackers order you into a car or to another place, resist and make your stand. Situations never get better when you leave the point of first contact.

Just what do you do when you feel you need to defend yourself? Well, if you have put yourself in a position where a mean person wants to do mean things to you, you've already screwed up.

There's a section in every bookstore on the subject of self-defense. Like weight-loss books or guides to operating computers, books on self-defense speak to our basic fears. They all have colorful titles written by even more colorful experts, often with outlandish names like Wun Hung Lo, Master of Dood di!, or Stone Kipling, the Green Berets' Green Beret. It's not unusual to also find the words "dummy," "idiot," or "stupid" in the title, like *Kung Fu for Idiots* or *Martial Arts Even Dummies Can Master*. Often they're written by ex-navy SEALs, buffed kickboxers, and steroidal-type people with necks thicker than their heads.

Although I can almost hear the air being rent with thousands of piercing screams as insulted self-defense experts do backflips and break concrete blocks to scare me off, they don't. Self-defense books always pick up the story when it's too late. Like trying to teach passengers how to swim in the last twenty minutes the *Titanic* is afloat.

When it comes to self-defense, there are only three things you need to know:

- Awareness: Watch out for nasty things.
- Avoid: Stay away from nasty things.
- Counter: Turn a nasty situation into an even nastier experience for your attacker.

If you can master the first step, you'll never need to remember the other two. If you practice the first two, the third is useless. If you find yourself at the third stage, you've screwed up again.

It's one thing to read *How to Pick Up Chicks* and then get lucky, or watch *Fishin' with Billy Bob* and then catch that musky, but quite another to read a self-defense manual and then get yourself sucker-punched by a foul-breathed punk brandishing a smashed Budweiser bottle on your way home after a night at the opera. Books that purport to tell you how to overpower and render an attacker helpless are worthless, simply because they forget to mention the absolute overpowering effect of surprise and/or sudden trauma and/or a large weapon stuck under your chin. So don't expect me to chain an illustrator to a desk and have him draw thousands of pictures of stances, flips, blocks, thrusts, jabs, strikes, and other moves, as all they will do is get you killed faster than if you just simply ran like hell.

When in Doubt, Run Like Hell

Most of us have been scared, intimidated, or threatened by another person. After the episode, we feel stupid, vengeful, or victimized—exactly the way we're supposed to feel. Sensing intimidation through projection or threat is how we learn to avoid bad things. Alpha males, pack leaders, and pregnant animals do it. Apes, chickens, and even caterpillars do it. It is an aggressive posture that announces you intend to do someone harm. Self-defense is not an art, but simply an ability to identify these vibes and then avoid them.

When we mentally relive an embarrassing incident as a victim, we reconstruct the scenario—usually imagining ourselves as some type of Jackie Chan or Jean-Claude Van Damme, springing into action and knocking the bad guys silly with a series of blurred kicks and triple punches. This, of course, is pure fantasy—unless your attacker is a blind quadriplegic geriatric. Instead of the comic-book heroics, simply be thankful you did exactly what you were supposed to do when confronted by folks intent on doing you harm and/or stealing your possessions: be victimized and survive the episode.

Why do victims seemingly always emerge from personal attacks as losers and the aggressors as victors? Because that's the way it's supposed to play out. Your attacker has previsualized and planned his attack. He knows the response of his victims, and he's got more tricks up his sleeve than you do. Watch a few security camera videos of robberies and you'll notice the bad guys are always on a knife edge; they look coiled up, tight and springy, ready to lash out at any second—exactly the way you are taught to be poised in those self-defense videos, but aren't.

To the contrary, you're like a rat checking the cheese out in a trap—curious, bemused, and slightly edgy as you try to figure out why a man with a large crowbar seems to be rapidly headed in your direction. As an attack becomes imminent, the right and left parts of your brain may hit the adrenaline accelerator, but it takes the naked-eye part of your gray matter a good twenty to thirty seconds before you figure out just what the hell is going on. You will still be in the denial stage by the time your attacker has head-butted you, shot you through both kneecaps, and is trotting away with your new Nikon.

Self-defense is linking that initial cerebral tickle to an evasion or avoidance tactic. Does it feel dangerous? Then slow down, turn around, change direction—just get away. It changes a villain's game plan and also buys you time.

Most crime victims have the same look as a deer before it gets pummeled by the front end of a Chevy pickup. People are simply amazed the event is unfolding. Those who try to fight off their assailant usually end up in a schoolgirl cuss 'n' grapple. The unlucky fool who decides to really mix it up with the perp with an $80-per-hour boxing stance will undoubtedly be the beneficiary of a crowbar across the bridge of his nose for his stylish efforts. Often these Cyranos believe they have one more chance before they black out and crumple to the sidewalk, but after attempting one last misaimed kick to their assailant's groin, the villain swings his tool like it was a nine iron, ensuring that you will wear dentures, as well as walk like a bird, for the rest of your life. Which at this point, if you still resist, will last about twenty minutes.

Feel the Pain, Smell the Sweat

Yes, you can sign up for a year's worth of Hai Lo, No Dough lessons and spend your evenings in a sweaty bathrobe practicing grappling and flips. You might even get one of those recycled stock car trophies with a lumpy-looking judo guy on top. It's still not going to help you when you wheel around at the ATM, crouched in your Angry Tiger Leaping from Laundromat Crouch, and catch a .38 slug in the face. Oh well, maybe you can get your money back from your self-defense lessons and pay for your long-term medical care.

Now, if I was to be mildly fair, I would mention that training can develop a proficiency in using your body as a weapon and defending yourself against sticks, knives, weapons, or even flamethrowers. You will get a sense of confidence that maybe you could hold your own in a bar brawl. But people only bar-brawl in John Wayne and Bruce Lee movies. The last bar brawl I saw involved a man methodically having his nice white teeth repeatedly smashed out on a frozen sidewalk. I never bothered asking what the fight was about because it never matters. Fights hurt and kill people. I've also been in fights involving pool cues, handguns, machetes, steel chairs, plate-glass windows, many large angry people, and even an AK-47 on full auto. Until you've actually felt the pain and smelled the fear and sweat, you are underestimating the long-term effects of getting involved in self-defense or fighting.

Because there is one element that is difficult to learn: You need to be able to kill people.

Killing Strangers for Fun and Health

When you take those self-defense courses, they treat bad guys with a certain delicacy. You are supposed to "disable" or "neutralize" your opponent. You are not supposed to drive a Fairbairn/Sykes into his carotid, jam a radio antenna through his nasal passage, or even empty a full clip of .44-caliber slugs into his still-jerking head. It's gross, and besides it might leave an ugly stain on the bedroom carpet.

The fact is, most people don't have the basic killing instinct. Sure you may be "mad as hell" and you're "not going to take it anymore," but could you really smash someone's nose into his brain matter, choke the life force out of him, bite off his ears, or snap his neck while smelling what he ate an hour before? It takes a lot of work to kill someone and then a lot of paperwork and police station time to convince the authorities that the skinny third-world kid wasn't just asking you for directions when you twisted him like a Gumby and pummeled him like Mr. Boffo's Giant Beanbag.

If you want to join the military to learn how to defend yourself, they'll probably ask you to call in an air strike before they recommend choking the enemy to death with his newly stretched testicles. So get your exercise, hang around to meet buff guys or girls, watch the Chuck Norris movies, but when push comes to shove: run like hell or pack a weapon.

Passive Self-Defense

The best method of self-defense is always passive. That means defusing the situation by talking or walking. If that doesn't work, just give the bad boys what they want (i.e., handing over your wallet) and expeditiously remove yourself from the scene of the crime (i.e., run).

If you decide to get into it with your new friend, you begin a process of escalation. If you smack a thug in the nose and he doesn't crumple, you can expect a bigger smack back. Remember, he wasn't looking to brush up on his boxing skills when he decided to go rob people tonight. He might accommodate you in a little one-on-one, but remember he's got places to go and other people to rob.

If you grab for a gun or a knife using that rusty commando move and you don't time it quite right, the chances of the bad person blowing you away are very high. Even if you adopt your best NAVMC 1146-A03 Hand-to-

Hand Combat Stance and Movement, your new friend might just blow you away on principle. So when your body screams fight or flight, pick what's behind door number 2 and haul butt.

Active Self-Defense

If you really do fancy yourself a brawler and need new bridgework, there are some key survival tips. Keep in mind these tips provide no guarantee that you will ultimately triumph, but they are the building blocks for getting whupped in style.

- Be aggressive in look and posture.
- Never take your eyes off your opponent or blink.
- Think of ways to distract your assailant.
- Attack, never defend.
- Try to use any weapon, any opening, or any trick to conquer.

There is a specific stance that gives you that "You want a piece of me, punk?" look. This may dissuade you from being called names by a twelve-year-old kid, but it may remind professional thugs to make sure the safety is off before pulling the trigger. Still, if you feel you must try, make your knees springy, your hands up in front of your face (left higher, right lower), and lead with your left foot. Some folks feel more comfortable switching left to right.

Your hands can be kept in a fist (second knuckle in nougie mode) or chopping karate style to deliver a knife-edge blow. The heel of the hand or foot is also a hard striking weapon. If your opponent has a knife, club, or gun, make sure you have put in some quality time at the gym or in self-defense classes before you try defending yourself instead of fleeing.

The idea is that the appropriate hand will block whatever blow, and the other will strike a deadly smack to a vital spot. You need to keep in mind that this stance has been developed to make use of the energy created by an attack. So if you attack your new friend, he may direct your energy into a neck-crushing flip.

Pain Zones

Let's say you really don't have a choice and your attacker is not going to let you run away. One clue might be a knife stuck in your arm when he was aiming for your chest, another might be two slugs in your legs with another chambered and ready to fly for your forehead. There are two things that could help you.

First you need to be prepared to strike your fist (or foot, head, knee, etc.) through your attacker (not just bitch-slap him), causing him death. I know that sounds severe in this era of rehabilitation of career criminals, but if your new friend has a weapon in the U.S. of A., you are now allowed to attempt to homicide him (i.e., kill him).

Most people's first thought is to grab the weapon and wrestle it away. Dumb move, since in the dim light you probably didn't notice that the knife had its sharp end pointing toward you or, if it was a gun, it probably had a grip attached to someone's hand, not yours. Do not focus on the weapon but rather on the attacker.

Your goal is to strike a blow that can kill your opponent. You must hit in an area where a blow can achieve a deadly or incapacitating result.

Where?

The best shot is pushing the nose into the brain. This is a hard one to practice without actually killing someone, and you'll find few takers as sparring partners. But in principle, the maneuver involves first flexing your knees and then pushing up with the palm of your hand under the bridge of the nose. The action pushes the cartilage into your opponent's thinking spot. There are no other frontal areas that can cause death. If you are behind and to the side, you can hit the perp on the side of the head just above the ear, or jam a pipe into the back of his head on a line equal with the ears. Both of these blows cause the victim to see stars (like in the cartoons) and can result in death. Do not close your eyes, flinch, or pull back. You must previsualize the result of your short, sharp blow and focus your energy on a spot past the impact point. If you can find an impromptu weapon like a pipe or a two-by-four, then by all means tee off as if trying to cut a dogleg on a par 5.

The eyes are also a good area to inflict some nasty damage. Though a jab to the eyes may not inflict death, it'll certainly cause the villain to pause a moment for a personal inventory assessment—certainly long enough to effect your own getaway. Simply poking a clenched fist with a pointed thumb at the villain's eyes will start his new career auditioning for Long John Silver commercials. The "SEAL Blitz"—quickly jabbing your extended fingers into your attacker's eyes—is the simplest and most effective way to deter an attack.

If you are not up to killing someone that night, you can simply try to hurt him.

Due to the prevalence of women's self-defense videos, the groin has become a popular striking area if you are up close or being held from behind. A jab from a heel or knee to the perp's groin causes him to involuntarily bend over and heave for breath. The throat is also an excellent spot to strike. And a sharp blow to the nose causes the eyes to water and the person to back off. Finally, a strike to the solar plexus (in unsuspecting victims) will cause the victim's diaphragm to involuntarily expel air out of the lungs, knocking the wind out of him. None of these blows can kill but will afford you the chance to get the hell out of there.

Trickier and less vulnerable areas include the collarbone. It can be snapped with a direct blow but may not incapacitate an attacker. Closer to the ground, a sharp kick down on a foot arch or to the shins or knee joints can cause sharp pain but won't necessarily induce your assailant to release you.

Some folks will get carried away and continue their repertoire of moves. You may get a sympathetic hearing at your arraignment, but beating to death an unarmed thug will put you in the pokey. (It's also not really very cool to be jumping around the limp body of your assailant doing a Rocky Balboa when the cops arrive.) Keep in mind that until you practice these basic moves and successfully deliver the first blow, you put yourself at greater risk by playing tough guy than by bolting. If there is a group of attackers, you are out of luck. Your best bet is to protect your head and roll up into a ball for your whupping.

How to Hit

When I talk about a blow "going through" a victim, I'm referring to a punch or kick whose target is behind the actual strike zone (the same concept as hitting a golf ball or baseball). The classic fighting stance is fists in front, legs apart, bent at the knee, and one foot ahead of the other. The real-world stance in stress conditions is hands outward, eyes wide open, body rigid and backing up quickly. As soon as you shift into a fighting stance, you send a clear message to your attacker that may provoke him to attack first.

When you strike with your hands, you want a closed fist held back and rotated directly into the person but aiming for a spot behind his body. This way your brain doesn't let your muscles stop until the force of the punch does. The same goes for your upward knee strike and downward kick. Does it hurt? You bet. Both you and your assailant. It is best to practice this in a class or a gym to understand the effect.

Extreme Defense

A lot of people want to know what I carry for self-defense in war zones. I tell them that I carry a sense of humor.

In very dangerous places I have an armed escort supplied by the local commander, warlord, or bad guy. Even if they can't shoot straight, they at least provide a nice squishy barricade around me when the bullets fly.

The point I'm making is it is fruitless and self-destructive to carry a weapon in a war zone. Although Gunga Dan (or Dan Rather) was famous for packing a pistol in Afghanistan, it isn't really much use when you come to a roadblock manned by twenty people with tanks, RPGs, and machine guns. More often than not it gets you arrested and interrogated (in which case you'll quickly learn that you're not supposed to carry guns in war zones unless you are actually in the military or militia).

Knife Fighting—a Losing Battle

Probably the worst tool for self-defense is a knife. To properly attack or kill an attacker, you need at least a six- or seven-inch blade as well as the skill to do it quickly. Knife fighting requires you to be way too intimate and close enough for your knife to be knocked out of your hand or used against you. Even soldiers would rather use a rifle butt or a rock than a knife to fight with. A blade will only be intimidating if your attacker is unarmed and alone, or you sneak up on him in classic commando style. But even then you can find it shoved in your rib cage once your assailant takes it away from you. Using a knife to protect yourself usually means things get slippery real fast—and it will probably be with your blood.

If you do carry a knife, make sure it can open cans, clip toenails, whittle whistles, and do more mundane things before you try to use it to kill people.

Better Ideas in Self-Defense

The Kubaton

One good weapon is the kubaton or yawara, a small six-to-eight-inch rod that can be used like a key chain or carried in a pocket. It looks like a fat, unsharpened pencil, but when wrapped in the fist with the ends protruding, it can amplify your strike force with crippling consequences. Having a small hard object in your hand can also focus your strike and cause sharp, surprising pain in your attacker. Once again, hydraulically hopping Monte Carlo homeys are not going to be too impressed, but a sad-sack mugger might pause long enough to let you dash off.

Pepper Spray

The ideal self-defense weapon looks like Binaca but packs a much nastier punch. Many people swear by nasty irritant sprays and promote them as a nonlethal deterrent for attacks. Our warm and friendly post office introduced pepper spray as a way to control unruly dogs, and now there are about two hundred manufacturers of this deterrent. Pepper spray has quickly surpassed Mace and other sprays due to its 95 percent effectiveness in stopping perpetrators (compared to only 60 percent for tear gas or Mace).

For what it's worth, pepper spray is also touted as being "all natural," avoiding long-term chemical effects. It is available in tiny key-chain-sized canisters and will spray a stream of nonlethal irritant at your attacker. If you hit the face (affecting the mucous membranes), the 10 percent concentrated derivative of hot peppers called oleoresin capsicum (with 2 million scoville heat units, or about six hundred times hotter than cayenne pepper) kicks into action. Your attacker will begin to choke, close his eyes to stop the burning, and probably run around like he's just been lit on fire. Pepper spray lasts between thirty and forty-five minutes and will definitely change an attacker's mind. It is also ideal to deter aggressive dogs or bears.

In a far-off location you'd probably be okay employing pepper spray as a deterrent, but here in the civilized and litigious U.S. there is always the backlash of being charged with unreasonable force. There have been about sixty deaths in the United States from pepper spray, and there is a current concern about its overuse as police forces spray more pepper spray than cheap perfume at the Macy's cosmetics counter. Keep in mind that it will be hard to prove that the nice man in court wearing a suit (covering the tattoos on his neck) was about to rape and fillet you in a parking lot instead of returning the purse you dropped. But if I was to choose a weapon in an urban situation, I would go for pepper spray. It gives you distance, the ability to warn off an attacker or groups even within pistol range, and makes it almost impossible for a sprayed thug to come after you.

I guess I should warn you, though, that it is highly likely you will get a whiff of your own pepper spray. Many people fumble around and end up spraying themselves or breathing the fumes. There is no magic antidote for pepper spray. If/when you are hit:

- Do not rub the face. This will aggravate the pain already being experienced.
- Flush the affected area with cool water and get into a breeze (a fan will also help).
- Use cold cream or a nonoily soap to wash the area (grease and salves will trap the particles).
- Remove any clothing that has been sprayed and discard.
- Any handling of a sprayed person will transfer irritating materials.

Stun Guns

You can get a four-inch stun gun for less than $20. These cigarette-pack-sized buggers lay out 60,000 to 300,000 volts of electricity from a 9-volt battery. Proper application turns a raging attacker into whiny, drooling jelly. The stun gun short-circuits the nerves and causes the muscles to spasm and your attacker to collapse. But remember, a stun gun is only useful in close combat and when you have a modicum of surprise and skill in deploying it. Although the ads sound appealing the stun gun is a very tricky tool to use.

Restraining

Let's say that for some insane reason you have managed to momentarily overpower your assailant and now you want to play bounty hunter and hang on to your new friend until help arrives. Most survival guide writers will tell you to make sure you have handcuffs ready. Well, you don't, and your victim is now writhing on the ground, looking for his teeth, and you need to act quickly. First make sure your friend is out. That means a good kick to the side of the head, a rabbit punch to the neck, or sitting on him while you tie him up. Then use his shoelaces to tie his thumbs together behind his back and his belt to secure his legs. A shirt can do in a pinch, and if you want to donate any of your clothing, you can bind his legs or gag him. Gagging people requires that the cloth go into the open mouth and be tied behind the head.

You can also reverse this by using a belt for the wrists behind the back and the shoelaces to tie his shoes together.

But wait, I saved the best for last: If you did your job well and incapacitated your attacker, bystanders will now render first aid and scold you for beating him up!

Pleased to Beat You

You may be fooled into thinking that you are liked by others and that people just need to get to know you better in a dark alley. Usually, a violent attack is premeditated, and getting the trust of the victim may be part of it. If forced to accompany someone, you are always better off determining the outcome of your situation where you stand, because you will soon be deprived of escape or defense options. Screaming and running are good; just running is better. If your attacker chases you, then you can scream.

Violent attacks and rape are a danger in any aspect of normal life and travel. Your best line of defense is to prevent situations and stay out of locations that are high-risk: traveling alone, late at night, in countries where rape is endemic, when drinking, on dates, and anywhere you cannot control your movement or departure.

So the key elements of self-defense are:

- Don't get into situations that force you to fight for your life.
- Defuse, avoid, or leave situations that make you nervous.
- If confronted, run, don't fight.
- Give the aggressor(s) what he wants.
- Practice self-protection before attempting it.
- Use a low-intensity weapon (pepper, stun, kubaton) in worst-case scenarios.

· 9 ·

disasters

Toto, I Think We Are in Kansas

There's a saying in the TV business that a sunny day is weather but a snowstorm is news. And so it goes with disasters. The very word is designed to scare or get attention.

The truth is a little different. Most television-style disasters are reported by some guy conveniently dressed in designer disaster apparel standing in front of a burning building or collapsed pier (often the only burning building or collapsed pier) doing a stand-up "live" to the studio. Viewers are then fed with a backfill stream of shaky home video, bedraggled victims, blurry camerawork, bending palm trees, and lots of flashing red lights. The fact is, according to official statistics, in America only three hundred to five hundred people die each year from weather-related disasters, even though the United States has the most violent weather patterns in the world. The casualty figures, though, are much higher if you lump in temperature-related deaths and natural disasters.

Now, there are many disasters such as famine, pestilence, epidemics, war, and plain old misery that never make it to the seven o'clock news because there are no muddy puppy dogs to be saved, and these disasters don't really affect wealthy countries (some may say that AIDS does, but not on the magnitude of Africa's epidemic).

Despite our lack of coverage and interest, however, each year over 160 million people are affected by disasters triggered by floods, earthquakes, or drought, and the trend is for this number to rise 10 million a year. Warfare may kill about 55,000 combatants a year, but it affects millions of civilians who end up as refugees, starving, injured, or dead. Well over three-quarters of the world's humanitarian spending goes to house, feed, and assist refugees.

No Farther Than Your Backyard

Having been through a number of disasters (riots, earthquakes, flooding, war, famine, and even giant hailstones), I can tell you that people's first reaction is to run like hell. Not anyplace specific, just run away from where they are at that moment.

When earthquakes, terrorists, or tornadoes strike, our animal instincts take over. Those who remain calm stand a better chance of surviving, but most people don't remain calm. How do you stay calm in disaster?

The solution to this is training. Not three months at Fort Bragg, but taking the time to walk through the various actions that should be taken if an unforeseen calamity strikes. This really works if you keep it simple, localize it, and make it a game with your children.

You should "disasterproof" your residence to the best of your ability. This means understanding the aftereffects of typical disasters.

Here is how to deal with disasters.

Medical Emergencies

Not a disaster per se but one that can put you into a tizzy and may be part of a disaster. Keep the phone numbers (day and night) of your physicians written out & programmed into the speed-dial system on your telephones. Buy a good-sized first-aid kit (they also come with a small manual) and screw it to the wall so you know where it is. Drive at a normal speed from your house to the hospital and time how long it takes. Then draw a map of how to get to the nearest medical center or emergency room. Tape the map in your glove box and keep a copy under the phone.

Ideally, each member of your family should attend a first-aid course and actively discuss what to do in case of different medical emergencies. This should include mundane things such as children knowing how to dial emergency numbers or using preprogrammed color-coded speed-dial buttons (red for fire, green for Mom at work, etc.).

Fire

The next most likely disaster is fire. Fires normally occur in the kitchen, in rooms where portable heaters are used, in areas where cigarettes are smoked, near overtaxed electrical outlets, and in the yard (for a variety of reasons). Candidates for fire hazards can be as innocent as having a Christmas tree too close to the fireplace or a hot bulb next to a flammable drape.

In most cases fires start at night, begin small, and then spread quickly. Although much is made of smoke detectors and fire extinguishers, you should start at the beginning.

Fireproof your house. Walk around it with your fire inspector hat on and write up your own violations. Give yourself a serious demerit point for allowing smoking in your home, having a heat-producing item next to a synthetic item, using candles, storing flammable liquids inside, using a gas range, having a fireplace, or doubling up on electrical outlets. Although there is nothing inherently unsafe about using a gas range or keeping hair spray, they do provide the basic building blocks for a major screwup. Even keeping a dish towel close to the stove could induce someone to throw it on burning fat, creating a nice little fireball. So, in fireproofing your home, you need to look at each object and see if it can contribute to ignition.

Protect your house. Now that you have removed fire hazards, build in some protection. Use wool throw rugs or blankets to decorate your bedroom or living room, as wool has a low ignition point. Install large, rechargeable fire extinguishers (not the toy ones that go blip and die out) in every room. (Ugly, yes. But they will be worshiped the first time you use one.) Install smoke or ionization detectors wherever you like. Make sure they are hardwired into your home's electrical system, with battery backups.

Install door and window locks that allow a panicked child (or you) to exit in complete darkness. Small, low-wattage night-lights are ideal in hallways and near exits.

Next, rehearse how you would leave a darkened, smoke-filled house. Try it with your eyes closed and see if others can do it. Think about the situation you're in when you go charging out of the house and the phone is inside. What about the family pet? What about valuables, heirlooms, and other "oh shit" items that can cause people to go back into a house to retrieve them? Should they be stored in a fireproof vault? Kept in a case close at hand? Thinking through the process can make the event less traumatic.

Fire Drills

- Clothing on fire: Don't run. Wrap arms around shoulders to protect face, then stop, drop, and roll.
- Oil or fat: Cover with metal lid. Do not spray with water or the fire will burn hotter and higher.
- Electrical fire: Kill power. Start with fuse. If that's not possible, cover hands and pull plug. Use extinguisher.
- Furniture: Smother with nonflammable rug or blanket (wool). Use extinguisher.
- Carpet: Smother and cool with water.
- Drapes or wall hangings: Use extinguisher or knock down and smother.

Exterior Hazards

Once again it's prior planning that will make the difference. Fireproof your property. Keep a zone around your house free of grass, flammable brush, or dangerous trees (like coniferous trees that can explode and burn from crown to crown). Is your roof flammable? What would burn first? Change it.

When Caught in a Fire

At home: Your first responsibility is to remove yourself and your loved ones from danger. That means outside the building or to a safe spot. If you cannot initially find your way out because of flames or smoke, wet a blanket and a facecloth or handkerchief, cover yourself or at least your mouth, and crawl along the floor to see if you can access a door to the outside. If you can't, you will need to exit out of a window or skylight. Gather the people in the room farthest from the fire, seal the door with a wet blanket, and begin to make your way out of the window. If you're above the first floor, use sheets, blankets, or clothing to make a rope. Sheets can be ripped into halves or thirds to provide more length. Throw mattresses and pillows out to cushion the jump. If you have to break a window, open it, then break it inward with a sharp heavy object; pushing the glass outward sends it right to the spot you'll want to drop to. If there is no window, it is often only drywall and external plaster or sheeting on eighteen-inch studs between you and freedom. Use a bed frame or other heavy object to smash in the wall.

When you jump, do not try to push back against the impact or break the fall with your arms.

In a large building: Although most commercial and tourist buildings have fire escape signs, posted evacuation notices, and emergency lighting, they can be surprisingly ineffective in a fire. Smoke quickly blocks out the lights, while stairwells fill with panicked people shouting directions. Remember that smoke rises and the stairwell is designed to withstand fires. Running up to the roof may limit your options later. If a stairwell is crowded, think about using another stairwell.

Fires at hotels and motels account for less than 1 percent of all building fires, but they pose the greatest threat to travelers because you will be unfamiliar with exit paths. Most hotels and chains in this country were brought up to federal standards that include smoke detectors and sprinklers in high-rise hotels. Overseas there are few standards and less safety enforcement for hotels. Try to stay in the bottom five floors and ideally pick the first floor that is not on the street (for security purposes). And always take the time to locate your emergency exit route when you get to your room.

Forest fires: When caught outdoors in a fire, things are likely to be a little tougher. Fires can explode across forests, sucking out the oxygen and creating firestorms that move quicker than any animal.

If you see the flames, your best bet is to get to a low, wet, open space. Do not climb upward, as the upward draft from fires moves them faster up hills than down. Wind direction is important and it can shift quickly. Typically, fires are heading in the direction of the smoke. If the fire is moving away from you, you can be a little more relaxed. If the smoke is overhead and coming toward you, you had better think fast.

If you can't find a large clearing, lake, creek, or firebreak, get as low as possible (crevices in rocks, creek beds, or cliffs are ideal). In worst-case scenarios find an area with as little fuel as possible (thin sparse trees) and create your own firebreak by lighting a long line of fire that will offer a dead space for your safety. You can also try to bury yourself in at least a foot of earth, keeping in mind that in an intense fire, there may be no oxygen.

Car fires: Often a badly maintained or defective car will catch fire. Having seen a few of them and been in one, I can tell you there is little you can do except get away as fast as you can. Fires are usually started by greasy engines, electrical shorts, or gas leaks hitting hot manifolds. Unless you have the proper extinguisher at hand (something that is common in Europe but largely absent here), don't bother being a hero. (I once pulled over to help some dufus put out his flaming car and he grabbed my extinguisher, emptied it into his $200 wreck, and said "Thanks, man." What I got for being a Good Samaritan was a bill to recharge my extinguisher.) Cars don't explode as dramatically as they do on TV or the movies, but they can incinerate curious passersby.

Earthquakes

You hear it coming like a freight train, preceded by an orchestra of car alarms. If you are asleep, you will think someone is trying to shake you to wake you up, or you'll hear the rattling of the windows. In your car you'll feel like you have a flat tire as you wobble side to side. In a high-rise office building you will feel the crazy whiplash as the scenery outside seems to be moving back and forth. Having been in several earthquakes, I have to say it gets easier the more you go through it, but everyone's first earthquake is unsettling. The ground below us is not supposed to feel like a carnival ride.

Earthquakes are unpredictable despite some assertions that there is "earthquake weather" during hot, still days where you think you can feel the earth creak and groan.

The chances are 40 percent that you will be at work or out of the house when it happens. If it happens when you are at home, you may take comfort in having spent twenty minutes on preparation.

Preparing for an Earthquake

There is not a lot you can do to prepare for the physical effects of an earthquake, but often older homes can be retrofitted with earthquake-safe features like better attachments to the slab or concrete supports, wall supports, and safety glass for interior mirrors and exterior windows. Water heaters need to be strapped to the wall.

Throughout the house, heavy or top-heavy objects should be fastened with straps, glue, or Velcro. (Often TVs will rattle off stands and injure children.)

Remove all glass-framed pictures, objects, or shelves from above beds.

Attach safety locks to cupboards to prevent the contents from pushing the doors open.

Have a source of fresh water and food (usually sold as earthquake emergency kits) in case roads to the nearest store are blocked. Your water heater and toilet tank (not the bowl) are good sources of emergency water.

Buy a battery-operated television, a radio, and a large flashlight and keep these items in a handy place. Keep a supply of new batteries in their original wrapper; don't put them in the battery-operated devices. It is also wise to keep gas and kerosene on hand if you have a Coleman stove or lanterns.)

Keep a large first-aid kit fastened to the wall for any cuts and abrasions that may occur.

Also keep a supply of plastic garbage bags for lining the toilet bowl in case you lose water pressure. If you have to use them, be sure to dispose of them daily.

Hurricanes

Every year about a hundred tropical storms (winds above 39 mph) form around the world. Two-thirds of these accelerate into hurricanes (winds above 74 mph). Just under a third of these brutal storms form off the coast of China and the Philippines in the Pacific Ocean.

Between June and December, the Caribbean, Mexico, and the southeastern United States wait to see what havoc Mother Nature will stir up. The most likely time for a hurricane to hit the States is September, followed by August and then October. Hurricanes do more damage than any other form of natural disaster in America. (The bean counters figure that our average annual allotment of 3.5 hurricanes causes an average of $5 billion in damage.) The worst hurricane was an unnamed one that blew through South Florida in 1926. Eighteen hurricanes have resulted in a death toll of over two thousand since 1775.

Hurricanes grow from a nice puffy white cloud into a monster and piddle out after between one and two weeks of fury, depending upon the amount of open water they cross. Beginning in 1953, they were given old-lady, Tuesday bridge game names like Camille, Agnes, Hazel, and Gloria. Innocuous male noms de guerre—like Andrew—are now included to add a little more personality to their wrath. If a hurricane's lucky and causes a few billion dollars of damage and kills a few people, its name is retired like Magic Johnson's jersey number. The letters "k," "q," "u," "x," "y," and "z" are not used in naming hurricanes, and the Greek alphabet is used if it's so bad a season that the storms outnumber the letters in the Roman alphabet. Hurricane names are localized depending on the storm's origin. So Hurricane Maria might be hatched in Nicaragua, while Joseph starts huffing and puffing in Senegal.

Hurricanes are large weather centers that radiate outward thirty to eighty miles from an intensely calm "eye" to a nasty tropical fringe. The eye is typically about twenty miles across with a large, dramatic "wall" surrounding it.

Hurricanes spin counterclockwise in the Northern Hemisphere and clockwise in the Southern Hemisphere, where they are typically called cyclones.

A hurricane's weapon is a ring of high-speed wind and rain that huffs and puffs and blows down large buildings and the ubiquitous trailer parks that lie in its path. Some have had wind speeds of over 190 mph. In the West Pacific Ocean the same type of storm is called a typhoon. These occur between December and April. In Australia they are known as a Willy-Willy, and in the Indian Ocean they are cyclones, which develop with the onset and retreat of the monsoon winds (April to June and September to December).

Hurricanes last between a day and a month and peter out when they hit cold water or land.

Surviving Hurricanes

The first step in hurricane preparedness is knowing when hurricanes and tropical storms are most likely to strike. The Caribbean, Florida, the Gulf Coast, and the Yucatán peninsula in Mexico are prime targets during the peak of the hurricane season in North America, which runs from June through October. Usually, there is plenty of advance notice through the media, but still a lot of folks in Central America and the Caribbean try to ride these things out in low-budget bungalows on the beach and they get clobbered.

If you live in a hurricane zone, you already know the drill: down to the local Home Depot to load up on plywood for the windows; then lawn furniture inside; and then the family gets packed into the minivan for a stay at a motel near Grandma's. Some of the crustier old salts ride the storms out at home, with a camcorder and a bottle of Jack's.

If you are visiting a tropical locale and you get stuck in a hurricane, you had better upgrade your accommodations from that grass shack and hammock. Large concrete buildings do just fine in hurricanes. Stay away from the boarded-up windows. Typically, there will be a lot of flooding, card playing, and drinking while the storm howls.

Don't be fooled by the storm's eye, or the calm period of a hurricane (if you are in its direct path). It might take a few minutes or two hours (hurricanes travel at an average of 10 mph) before the other side of the spinning dervish starts blasting away as an encore.

Tornadoes

Tornadoes can be considered minihurricanes that form, strike, and disappear with a lot more capriciousness. Wind speeds are often twice that of a hurricane and up to 300 mph with an updraft of up to 200 mph in the center. Tornadoes are so powerful that their dark funnel contains everything from farm animals to tractors. The funnel may rise and fall, causing a vacuum-cleaner-like effect that destroys everything within a narrow path of 50 to 150 feet across. Tornadoes may be large or small, lasting for fifteen minutes or less than a minute. They typically travel between ten and twenty miles an hour but can be much faster. The average life of a tornado may be short, but there can also be multiple tornadoes in a single hour.

Tornadoes in the United States are caused mainly by southerly winds coming up the Mississippi Valley, bringing humidity from the Gulf of Mexico, which collide with dry, westerly winds coming across the Rockies. The area affected, which extends from Mississippi up to Minnesota, is called Tornado Alley. There is also thunder and lightning, heavy precipitation, and a loud screaming roar to send a shiver of fear into a prairie boy's heart.

The only way to get out of the path of a tornado is to get into a cellar that is belowground or into a strong building away from the windows.

In a house, close all windows and doors that face the tornado and open those on the opposite side. Since the real damage is caused by the roof lifting (in the case of flat and gable roofs) and the walls blowing down once support is lost, a few open windows will actually exacerbate your problems.

If there is no shelter, get as low to the ground as possible. A culvert or ditch is preferable. Cars are often picked up and tossed because of the air gap underneath.

Floods

Floods kill a lot of people every year but not that many in developed countries. In North America the average toll is around 140 people a year; most victims drown in their cars when trying to cross flooded areas.

I had the misfortune of being caught in a flood in the desert and almost drowning when I dumped my motorcycle and it pinned me in a rapidly flowing river that had moments earlier been a road. I have also crossed a raging stream safely that took the life of a family a few hours later. The difference between life and death is knowing the dangers and preparing for them.

Floods come in two kinds: flash floods and seasonal floods. Flash floods are typically a desert phenomenon where hard-baked earth is the recipient of localized torrential downpours. But you also get flash floods in the jungle where mountaintop deluges collect and thunder down small creeks.

In the desert, clouds will build up into magnificent cumulonimbus formations until they become thunderheads. Then, in the afternoon, they release their moisture in short but intense downfalls. The water typically rushes down ravines and arroyos, flushing everything in its path. This means don't camp on riverbeds or arroyos even if everything around you looks parched and dead. The farther down hillsides you are, the more at risk you put yourself. In my case, rain more than two miles away completely flooded the secondary road I was on.

It only takes about two feet of water and a mild current to float your car away. Every foot the water rises puts five hundred pounds of pressure on your vehicle. If crossing flooded roads, roll down the windows, open the doors, and walk the area for washouts. In most cases you are safer leaving your car or returning via the way you came.

Remember that after a flood there can be a high danger of electrocution caused by flooded electrical equipment and wires.

Blizzards

Cold snaps, snowstorms, and ice storms are a part of life for most of the United States and Canada. Usually, they provide a respite from school, a chance to make snow angels, and maybe an evening in front of the fireplace. In the worst cases your heater will quit, power will be cut off, your car battery will freeze solid, and your engine will make a couple of speculative groans before it stops. But surviving blizzards is easy.

Don't freeze. Maintain an independent source of heat (separate from your gas or electric lines). Items like burst pipes, sagging roofs, and flat tires (yes, it can get so cold that all your tires go flat) can be fixed later. Your first priority is to provide heat.

Don't die. The second priority is not to kill yourself by staying warm. Space heaters and other temporary heating sources pose an extreme fire hazard around clothing, furniture, and other flammable material. Oxygen can rapidly be depleted and toxic carbon monoxide can be generated from heating devices. Even cars become death traps with all the windows rolled up, the heat on, and exhaust leakage. In most cases, if you do use unrecirculated air and keep the air intakes free of snow, this is not a problem. Another danger of blizzards is the increased stress from exertion that leads to heart attacks, slips and falls, and injuries.

Don't starve. Chances are you have enough food in the fridge to last a couple of days. You can also use your fridge to keep things warm if you get creative. Often power cuts will make the refrigerator an ideal place to store things you don't want frozen. Just put heated stones or pots of heated water in the fridge to raise the temperature and you'll have an instant hot box.

Don't drive. Many people try out the four-wheel-drive feature on their new sport utility vehicle and then discover that four-wheel drive doesn't transform their vehicles into yuppie snowplows. The greatest hazards in winter driving are not your vehicle's shortfalls, but your own ability and, of course, the idiot in the Chevy Chevette sliding down an icy hill on his bald summer tires.

If you are trapped in a car, as I have been a number of times, you should stay put. I was once stranded on the top of a very high mountain pass in Tajikistan wearing tropical clothes in a car with a dead battery. I made it because I prepared for my long evening and used every trick in the book to stay warm.

If your car works but is stranded by snow or icy conditions, find a safe place to turn off. Look for shelter from the wind. Keep close enough to the road to be noticed by passing motorists but not close enough to be rear-ended in the blinding conditions. If your car is going to be your hotel for the night, prepare for the hours ahead. You can provide some relief from wind-chill by stacking branches, cardboard, or snow on the windy side. Attach something bright, shiny, or reflective to the top of your antenna, fashion a road sign to attract passing motorists, or put down branches leading up to your car starting about fifty yards back.

If you are tempted to leave the car, consider that you may never make it back. What looks like a road could turn into a vast snowfield, and that light you saw in the distance could turn out to be exactly that, just a light—but no farmer around with a steaming mug of cocoa, a half-pint of schnapps, and a cell phone with Sheriff Billy Bob's home number on speed dial.

If you are going to run your engine periodically, make sure the exhaust pipes are free of snow or obstruction and block the radiator from the front with the trunk carpet. Make sure the intake vents are clear and pile snow on the hood to provide an insulating blanket.

If your engine is dead and you will be spending the night watching ice crystals form on the windshield, gather what you need to keep warm inside the passenger compartment. Use insulation from under the hood, the trunk, or, in extreme cases, the headliner. Your greatest source of insulation will be the car seats. (If you are by yourself, think about how you can use the seats to make a sandwich.) Stuff any extra clothing inside your jacket and pants until you look like the Michelin man. If you don't have a hat, make one, and fold over insulation to make stupid-looking gloves and booties.

Try to exercise every fifteen or twenty minutes to promote circulation. Rotate clothing to avoid moisture buildup. For example, turn your socks inside out or swap them with your mitts to dry them out. (Hey, whatever works.)

If there are two of you, sit together in the backseat to reflect or conserve heat.

Run the engine enough to heat the car and then turn it off. Don't bother running the fan, as the thermostat will open, sending hot air into the heater core. Turn the engine off when it has reached operating temperature. Often you need to keep the rpm a little higher than idle to charge the battery properly. Don't bother with the lights, wipers, or defrost, since it just drains power and affects gas consumption. Use the radio sparingly—only on the hour to check weather reports.

To gauge how long your gas is going to hold out, estimate time and fuel consumption as if you were driving. For example, at 60 mph you would get 240 miles on a tank, or four hours of gas. This gives you a sizable fudge factor but will help you conserve enough gas to take you through to morning.

When is it okay to leave the security of your stranded car? If you are far off in the woods or at the bottom of a ravine, maybe it's time to build a fire and attract some attention. But if you have a radio, lots of gas, and no major emergency, stick with the car, since major and secondary roads will most likely be plowed.

Avalanches/Landslides

About six hundred people die every year due to landslides, between twenty-five and fifty in the United States. Slides are a function of gravity, friction, and often precipitation. Earthquakes and temperature extremes can also trigger slides. The two slides that should concern you are dirt and snow.

Dirt and rock slides can be brought on by heavy rain, liquefying entire hillsides and creating brown torrents. They account for few if any deaths each year in North America.

An avalanche is typically fresh snow that sits on slippier old snow. Avalanches are the result of three factors: slope, precipitation, and human triggers. About 90 percent of all avalanches start on slopes of 30°–45°, and 98 percent of all avalanches occur on slopes of 25°–50°. Avalanches occur most often on slopes above the timberline that face away from prevailing winds. Leeward slopes collect snow blowing from the windward sides of ridges and build up into danger spots and are the site of three-quarters of avalanches.

It is unfortunate that the average angle for an avalanche is between 35° and 45° of slope, the same degree range found on Black Diamond and Expert ski slopes. Over 85 percent of all avalanches occur during or within twenty-four hours of a snowfall. Few people die during the storms but shortly afterward, when the snow is fresh and recreational activity is highest. Most deaths occur in Colorado, followed by Alaska and Washington. The most likely months for avalanche deaths are February, March, and January.

Avalanches are triggered by skiers (59 percent), snowmobiles (24 percent), natural causes (14 percent), and cornices (3 percent). Victims of avalanches are usually climbers, hikers, snowboarders, and cross-country skiers. The majority of U.S. avalanche victims are snowmobilers, followed closely by climbers, then backcountry skiers. Deaths from avalanches are increasing dramatically.

Avoiding Avalanches

To avoid avalanches, understand that avalanches typically occur on an open slope, in a bowl or gully above the timberline.

The safest place to travel is along the valley floor away from large avalanche run-outs, along ridgetops above avalanche paths, in dense timber, or on slopes of 25° or less with no steep slopes above them. Although it may be sound advice to avoid cornices on ridgetops, often they are impossible to see when you are on top of them.

If you are forced to negotiate dangerous areas, climb, descend, or cross them one person at a time. That way, if misfortune strikes, there will be someone to dig you out. Also take the time to cross a slope at the very top or bottom. This also means climbing or descending the edge of a slope rather than the center. Weigh the risks of pushing onward in high-risk areas. Your best insurance policy is to carry the three basic tools of survival in avalanche areas: an avalanche transceiver, a shovel, and a collapsible probe. Only one of three victims buried without an avalanche beacon survives.

If caught in an avalanche, keep your mouth closed. The recommended method is to shed any equipment you are carrying and swim a backstroke, keeping your greatest efforts for when you feel the avalanche slow down, because as the avalanche slows, the powdered snow will compress into hard-packed ice.

Usually, you are helpless in the fast-moving wave until you come to a rest at a lower slope angle and the wave of fluid snow begins to slow down, settle, and compact. This is the critical point at which your survival is determined. When the snow is fluid, you can move your arms, legs, and body to create an airspace. There is no correct action other than doing the funky chicken to avoid snow packing down hard. Without this airspace you will suffocate.

Victims trapped under a heavy snowpack left by an avalanche usually don't live more than thirty minutes if they don't have some type of airspace. Even with air, you only have a 50 percent chance of survival in the first half hour. The chances of surviving decrease dramatically for victims buried more than four feet. The good news is that 86 percent of avalanche victims survive their entombment, although about a third of these die from trauma not associated with asphyxiation. Most fatalities from suffocation occur in the twenty-five-to-twenty-nine age group, and 90 percent are male. Two-fifths of avalanche accidents occur during a deadly window between noon and 2:00 P.M.

Lightning

By now you've learned that statistics are just well-organized lies. Let's lay a few on you about lightning.

There are over 16 million thunderstorms each year around the world, about 100,000 in the United States. Roughly a tenth of these are considered severe. In the United States an average of eighty-nine people are killed by lightning each year and seven hundred to eight hundred are injured. Florida, Texas, and North Carolina have the most victims, and despite the popular myth that golfers are a favorite target, lightning can strike anyone anywhere: open spaces and ballparks (29 percent), under trees (13 percent), while boating (6 percent), near tractors (3 percent), and then golf courses (4 percent). (Maybe people think lightning is just nature's way of getting rid of ugly pants.)

Tricks to avoiding a lightning strike are few but important. Stay low and avoid conductive devices like steel golf clubs, fences, telephones, indoor appliances and pipes. Trees often conduct the electrical charge down to the base.

The best place to be is inside a building or inside a car with your windows up.

To get an idea of how rapidly a storm is approaching, remember that sound travels at three hundred meters a second. To calculate distance of lightning, count the number of seconds from the time of the flash to the sound. Multiply by 3 to get the distance in hundred-meter increments. For you meter-phobics, a meter is a big yard (39 inches versus 36 inches).

If you feel the hair on your head rising during a thunderstorm, you can assume the position: The "lightning-safe position" is a low crouch on your tiptoes with your feet together and hands on your ears (to provide protection from acoustic shock). Since your head is down there anyway, kiss your nether regions good-bye.

· 10 ·

flying

It's a Long Way Down

I t's neither natural nor comforting to be suspended five miles over the earth with your body hurtling at 500 mph and the only thing between you and your maker is some recycled aluminum and a silly seat belt.

According to Boeing, flying in an airplane scares the hell out of some 25 million Americans, or one in six adults. And the fear factor isn't helped by a string of books and films portraying or documenting disaster in the skies, ignoring the reality of the fact that you've got a slim one in 11 million chance of dying in an air crash in the United States.

I have done a lot of flying in all manner of winged and rotored craft and had my share of rough landings and one crash. I can tell you from experience that survival is both out of your control and within your grasp. If a jumbo jet chooses to explode at cruising altitude, there's not much to do but enjoy the ride down. But if you're flying coast-to-coast and hit some severe turbulence, wearing your seat belt can prevent you from wearing the overhead bin as a beanie.

What should you fear the most? Air safety statistics.

Let's learn a little about safety and hooey when it comes to aircraft.

The growth in air traffic has prompted Boeing to say that there will be a major air crash every week by the year 2010. Journos went foaming at the mouth over this ominous sound bite but never bothered to mention that this would be a *reduction* in air crashes. A dramatic statement, but the truth is that by then there will be only twelve more accidents a year at a time when there will be twice as many airliners in operation.

This means that air travel is probably the most regulated, highest-tech, best-inspected, and safest form of travel in the world.

Flying's well-earned safety statistics make perfect sense if you stand back and look at the big picture. There are twelve thousand airliners in the sky making over 15 million flights and carrying 1.3 billion passengers annually. With all that activity, worldwide there are only about fifty to seventy accidents that destroy commercial aircraft (including jets, small turboprops, and cargo planes) every year. Not too shoddy compared to the carnage on the highways below.

So why bother even dealing with flying in a survival book? Well, as you guessed, that was the good news. As we start our statistical spiral into worst-case scenarios, things get a little hairier.

Although today's airline pilots are among the workforce's most level-headed, seasoned, and trusted employees, they still get blamed for about two-thirds of major airline crashes. I take some issue with this, since I have never flown with a pilot who decided he was going to have an accident, nor have I found anyone in economy class who could fly any better. Pilots live for emergencies and they are a lot better prepared and trained for emergencies than, let's say, the school bus driver you entrust your kid's life to twice a day on that aging, seat-belt-less yellow rust bucket. But let's not get off on a rant about who is better at safeguarding lives.

There are some things you can do to swing the odds in your favor.

Hop off a jetliner onto a turboprop and you just increased your chances of crashing by a factor of four. Commuter flights (flights with thirty or fewer seats) carry about 12 percent of all passengers in this country. These small planes fly lower, take off and land more often, and are piloted by less experienced, more overworked pilots. Often they are not subject to the same safety standards as large airliners. (Commercial airline pilots have a one in 1,100 chance of dying on the job.)

If you like to charter planes, your odds look even worse. About seven hundred people a year die in small private planes or charters. The accident rate for a small plane is about 11 for every 100,000 aircraft hours compared to 0.8 for commercial jets. There are two fatalities for every 100,000 hours of operation for small planes.

Surviving Arriving

So maybe it's okay to grip that seat rest on takeoff just a little bit. Well, maybe a lot when you realize that well over half (68 percent) of accidents happen during the 6 percent of time spent taking off and landing an airplane.

This is the time the crew is strapped in, facing the opposite direction, with two seat belts. More bad news. Each crew member has to look after forty lost souls if you pile in or pancake. If you thought you had to wait a long time to get off the plane when people were being polite, just imagine what it's like when everyone wants to get out *now*. It makes the last scenes of *Titanic* look like a BBC drawing room comedy.

Most things that can go wrong in a flight usually occur at low altitude. Even so, the pilot typically has a chance to wheel around and make a landing. Crashes can occur because of bad landings in limited visibility, tire blowouts, bad brakes, slippery runways, or, in the case of an ill-fated flight I was once aboard, the pilot mistaking a soccer pitch for a runway. What saved my life in that accident was a forest of giant bamboo that slowed our plane down after our crash. Luck, not survival skills, saved me.

It Does Matter Where You Sit

There are many theories on where you should sit to survive a plane crash or hard landing. About half of the people involved in crashes survive, though four-fifths survive the initial impact. In the 1960s only 10 percent of passengers survived air crashes. But even with today's safety advances, 30 percent won't make it out the exits.

If you want some general commonsense tips, here they are. Ask for the first seat in from the aisle in the second-from-last row. This gives you a clear shot for the rear exits, puts you near where the crew hangs out, close to food and drink, gives you a full row in light flights to stretch out and sleep, and lets you see the entire length of the plane. It also sticks you next to the toilets, chain smokers, and the place where people wander back to get more booze or exercise their kids. But I have put in enough miles on third-world airlines to cherish this low-budget motel space and to appreciate the overwhelming safety position it affords.

Crashing with Style

Okay, so you can probably cruise for a few decades from this cherished safety spot, but what happens when your pilot does a Stuka dive into the nearest crop-dusting strip and manages to get the thing down in a selection of pieces?

What's it like to crash? Well, there are really two crashes. So don't practice your brace position only to jump out of your seat after the first hard slam. The flight attendants will be screaming "Brace, brace, brace" as you are torn between staring at your crotch and sneaking a peak out the window. The first bang is the plane hitting the ground at flying speed, followed by a period of what seems like weightlessness. Usually enough to gently launch projectiles in the air above your head and dislodge overhead luggage. The second crash is the doozy. That's where structural damage usually occurs and all hell breaks loose. It might be a solid object that stops you, or your plane may decide to do flaming cartwheels through a cornfield. It's all in somebody else's hands now. When a plane crashes, all that snazzy carry-on luggage takes on the characteristics of a missile. Food carts slice off passengers' arms, and even people flying through the air can kill people.

In more serious crashes the aluminum frame seats and shell turn into razor blades, cutting people into small pieces. And the impact of a crash can decapitate you, leaving your lower mandibles still attached. Hey, I didn't say it was pretty. A good doctor friend of mine had the unenviable job of snipping the fingers off crash victims and putting them into baggies so they could be fingerprinted.

If you have a survivable crash, you need to get out of the plane. In most cases people do a lot of screaming and huddling down in their seats. That's okay, just let them. People freak out on airplanes because they are not used to fighting for their lives when seconds earlier they were having a second Bloody Mary and watching their favorite movie. Don't be shy about crawling over people and remember that seat backs can fold forward for more room.

One tip. Most people surge toward the front of the plane to get out, and that is where most people are seated. In an emergency head to the back exit. If you think you are doing anybody any good by staying in your seat and being calm, think again. You are better off getting to an exit, opening the door (which will activate the slide), and then directing people to exit in an orderly fashion. Often the cabin crew will be doing this but not if they're dead or incapacitated.

Folks who die in less-than-catastrophic crashes tend to die from smoke inhalation. It didn't matter where they sat but where they didn't get to.

More tips: Don't wear synthetics, since they burn or melt. Wool and leather can save your life. Crawling low in a smoke-filled cabin can get you a better grade of oxygen but it can also get you trampled. You're better off leaning forward or crouching. It's odd that the supplemental oxygen above each seat deploys automatically during decompression (they fall out a lot during rough flights or landings) but often not during fires. Go figure.

There is nothing else you can do on a crashed plane but get out. There is no firefighting equipment, no heroic deed list—not any reason to stay inside. Once outside you can regroup with the crew to figure out Plan B.

It Does Matter Where You Fly

Aviation is a first-world luxury but it is a third-world necessity. Often you have to fly across forbidding terrain, vast deserts, or stormy oceans. This means that airlines in third-world countries have to do a lot more with a lot less.

When having lunch with a former Aeroflot pilot in Uzbekistan, I asked him how he flew around the world barely knowing a single word of English, mandatory for pilots of commercial airliners. He replied, "Many same vords used all da time."

Seventy-five percent of all air accidents happen in countries that account for only 12 percent of world air traffic. The only good side to this is that typically their roads are equally or more dangerous.

Flying anywhere in Africa is a relative crapshoot. Your odds of smashing into some grassy plain increase twentyfold. When Ernest Hemingway crashed in Africa, the plane that rescued him also crashed. Fodder for cocktail parties, you think? Perhaps, but the odds of your plane crashing in Africa are one in 50,000, compared to one in 1 million in industrialized countries. Taken out a life insurance policy lately?

Somewhere in the middle of the statistical scale are Latin America, the Middle East, Asia, and Eastern Europe/CIS (that's the old Soviet Union). Here you hope you link up with an airline run by an outside Western operator. In the United States the fatality rate can be expressed as 0.5 for every million miles flown. In Russia it is ten times higher (5.2) and twenty times higher in China (10). This is changing rapidly as the Russian- and Chinese-made copies of our aging airliners are gracefully being retired by design or by being totaled on the side of a mountain—and are being replaced with shiny new Boeings and Airbuses.

The most dangerous airlines to fly are local carriers in China, North Korea, Colombia, all countries in central Africa, and pretty much any airline that has a flying goat for a logo.

Flying in the third world, though, is a lot less terrifying than taking a local bus. If you are given a choice of taking a clapped-out airliner over a mountain pass or a clapped-out bus, take the plane.

· 11 ·

travel

Death Takes a Holiday

hy do you find life insurance vending machines at airports and not next to condom dispensers in Hollywood motels? Why do you get an airsickness bag on an airplane and not in the back of a cab? Why do hotels put those little sanitary bands on toilets, but not on your mattress?

The media love fiery plane crashes, celebrity kidnappings, billowing hotel fires, disease-ridden sex tourists, druggings, muggings, ferry drownings, even knockout drugs spread on the nipples of hookers. It's enough to make you stay at home. Damn, it's dangerous out there. Or is it?

Well, being somewhat of an expert on dangerous travel, I can tell you that there's only one problem with this picture. Your home is a far more dangerous place than those exotic countries featured in the news. Statistically, traveling is 40 percent safer than staying at home.

Think of your last vacation.

You researched a number of options, discussed them with friends, travel agents, and your travel partner(s). You read travel articles and guidebooks, watched TV shows, read the newspaper for tips and background.

If you were like most serious travelers, you bought at least two books about the activity or region. Maybe you even checked for State Department warnings, took classes, and went to lectures.

Then you put your trip together, carefully choosing reputable and federally regulated airlines, hotels, car rental agencies, ground transportation, lodging, and restaurants. You even went to get shots, prescriptions, first-aid kits, sunglasses, specialized clothing, and comfortable shoes.

You went down to the bank and bought American Express traveler's checks, bought a money belt, made copies of all your credit cards, bought travel insurance, checked with your neighbors, went over your pack list twice, and then headed for the airport.

In a licensed cab or bus you entered a federally inspected airport (complete with security and medical staff), climbed aboard an FAA-inspected aircraft staffed by a safety crew, and then flew through internationally controlled flight lanes until your arrival at your destination.

Prepare for the Worst

As you can see, preparing for a trip is often far more nerve-wracking than the actual vacation. Here's my routine for heading out:

- Call your insurance company and make sure you are insured for whatever items you will be bringing. You can also buy travel insurance (for canceled rooms or flights), repatriation insurance (in case of medical emergency), medical insurance (to pay bills incurred overseas), and even kidnapping insurance (called KR&E, for "kidnap rescue and extortion"). You can even buy flight insurance. Believe me, the insurance industry plays off your fears very profitably.
- Call your credit card companies; ask them to review your current balance, jack up your credit limit, and advise you on what to do in case of an emergency. Ask about any useful benefits they might have for premium cards (rental card insurance, frequent flyer miles, flight insurance, purchase insurance, loss insurance, health or airline club membership, etc.). It might be worth getting a premium card.
- Make sure any ATM cards have numeric passwords and order any new cards you want as extras.
- Check your passport or driver's license. Make sure it won't expire while you are on the road.

- Make three photocopies of the front and back of all your ID, medical cards, tickets, ATM cards, visas, passport, and so forth. Leave one copy with someone you can contact back home, leave one at home, and take one with you. If you are traveling with a partner, make another set of copies for him.
- If you are going overseas, make sure you have your passport, visas, shots, and paperwork (prescriptions, letters of introduction, business cards, etc.).
- Have a conscientious friend swing by your domicile to collect your mail, pick up the junk flyers, and see if everything is still there. You should tell as few people as possible that you will be gone, and even when you cancel the maid service, give some lame excuse. Having your mail held is fine, but it doesn't stop the barrage of pizza flyers and "tried to deliver" notes left on your door. Yes, you can call the police and tell them you will be out of town, but if you live in Los Angeles, I'm sure they'll be thrilled and let everyone know. If you live in a smaller community, it helps. Leave a number and a key with the neighbors.
- Turn down your water heater, do a double check on the taps, close all windows and drapes securely, put sticks in the sliding glass doors, disconnect the phones (so they don't ring all day), and have your calls picked up by an answering service. Unplug all your lamps and appliances. If you have valuables, stick them in your safety-deposit box. Lock any garage doors from the inside.

If you travel more than three or four times a year, ignore all of the above and have a good time.

Travel Light

You can carry an incredible amount of stuff without checking a thing by doing the following.

Use a soft legal-sized carry-on bag. Wear a larger-than-normal waist pack with heavy items, use a correspondent's vest to stuff in other heavy items, clothes, and fragiles. Carry a second soft laptop bag (without a laptop, of course) filled with reading material, CD player, and whatever. Carry a third purse or front waist pack with more stuff and carry or wear a jacket packed full of even more things. If you travel like I do with a reasonably sized backpack, shift as many things as you can into a scammed plastic duty-free bag.

Many folks swear by wheeled carry-on bags, but the new designs are almost always above legal check-in dimensions and will get checked in on busy flights. In poor countries, wheeled luggage screams, "Hey, tourist bag with valuables inside," and these are always left standing ready to be snatched, since there is no strap to wrap your leg around.

Write your home contact phone number, address, and a note to call collect for the reward on large sheets of paper and put them in your luggage.

Long-Haul Survival

It is not unusual for me to be on planes for two days at a clip, sitting in airports, sleeping in my seat, just getting from small charters to regional feeders to big carriers, skipping from continent to continent. When going around the world, I find it easier to go from east to west, picking up time and daylight as I travel. Going the other way seems to eat up your time and jet-lag you more. There are some benefits to flying on dirt-cheap, third-world airlines vs. big-name carriers. The third-world airlines usually have lots of empty seats, especially empty back rows. Airlines that have had recent crashes, hail from war-torn regions, or have prestigious but money-losing routes are ideal. Check for add-ons that national carriers offer that can give you stopovers or additional legs for little or no charge. My favorites are South Pacific–based carriers, Middle East carriers, and new airlines. Often airlines will fly more cargo than passengers on long-haul flights to Europe and America and are almost empty.

Ask the desk person to block out the seat next to you with some heartbreaking story about a sprained leg or not sleeping for five days. If you get bumped or need to catch the next flight, use a pay phone to call the 800 number to book a seat and get a seat assignment. It beats waiting in line. Watch out for airports that use shuttle buses to take you from the gate to the plane. If you are not at the gate a good thirty minutes before departure, you will miss the plane. If you are too late to check your bags, go directly to the gate and they can check your bags from there. Most airlines demand photo ID and/or passport, so have it ready with your ticket. (I've used the cover of my *Dangerous Places* book to get on in a pinch.)

Departures can be a zoo. Everyone is in a hurry to either get somewhere or help someone else get somewhere—and most lapses in airport security occur in the departure process. Your bags may not get checked. There are delays at security checkpoints. Crooks grab your valuables while an accomplice slows you down at the metal detectors. Try to focus on security before boarding an aircraft. Once you are on the plane you can relax.

On most non-Muslim international flights drinks are free and you can scam them two at a time. They make great gifts and tips later. Tear the world map out of the magazine to show your new friends where you are from. The airsickness bag makes a great waterproof carrier or emergency drinking device. The blankets on airliners are perfect for picnics, and if you get the long-haul toiletry kit, ask for extras—they make great gifts at your destination.

You can order seconds on flights, so take the opportunity to load up on free food. And the utensils make excellent camping cutlery. When the drinks come around, ask if you can have a full bottle of water each time the attendant comes by. On very long flights the crew hangs out in the galley and it's a great time to get to know them. Chances are they can give you tips on where you're going and will be happy to slip you an extra meal, beverage, or toiletry kit.

All your carry-on bags and waist packs should be carabinered together to discourage theft and to remind you to take everything when you leave.

The Starting Gate

When the plane arrives, don't be shy about darting up to the front to be the first through customs. Always be a tourist, never a writer, business executive, etc. Never chit-chat about anything. Just smile, look tired, and answer the uniformed agent's questions. Always go through the "Nothing to Declare" line with a focused look ahead. If you are pulled over for a thorough search, bear the scrutiny politely.

Bringing in cardboard or hastily wrapped boxes or cargo automatically gets you searched, as does carrying generic electronic or mechanical devices like two-way radios, tripods, too much of anything (for expeditions), or large bottles full of unmarked fluids. Having *no* luggage is asking for a full body-cavity search.

If authorities give you a hard time about the kiddy porn, sniper rifle, or fifty kilos of cocaine you happen to have in your bag, don't say anything other than to deny ownership and knowledge of it. Since everything you have is carry-on (remember?), it is completely possible that somebody planted these items on you and is waiting outside the airport as a friendly cabdriver. Remember that you have no rights outside of the United States and you could spend ten years just waiting to go to trial.

Many third-world customs officials will find irregularities in your visa or luggage and will hit you up for a fine. Often they will just tell you that your camera is not allowed in and they are confiscating it. Keep your cool and don't get indignant. Offer to work out whatever the problem is but tell them your money is going to be sent to you once you contact someone from the hotel. Don't flash your secret stash or tip them off as to how much money you have. Arrival and departure at airports provide the best opportunity for thieves.

In many impoverished regions, baggage handlers rifle through pockets and openable suitcases before they arrive on the conveyor belt, so it is wise to check the contents of your bags as they come off the belt. You won't be able to file a report, but you can make a stink and demand to look for your goods. It's also a good time to check your inventory to see if you left anything on the plane. If you lose something, you have to find an airline employee or cop to file a report. Your insurance company will usually demand that you have a stolen-goods report, no matter how poorly made out.

It's best to buy standard dull-colored backpacks or suitcases. Keep your gear on your back or with a strap wrapped around your leg.

Carabiners can be used to click baggage handles together, making it awkward for thieves to walk away with them. Get used to fastening your bags together so that you never lose track of anything, even your camera. Use yellow tape to identify your bags to porters who don't speak English; simply point at the same yellow tape on your carry-on. Number your bags 1 of 3, etc., so that you force yourself to do a count.

Be aware of well-dressed, polite local people who want to engage you in conversation. Touts always work the airports in foreign countries. They will gain your trust and then offer to help you. It's best to ask airline representatives how much it costs for a cab into town and if this smiling gentleman is a con man. Often he isn't, but anyone who hangs around an airport makes his money from tourists either by directly charging or by getting kickbacks from all the shops and hotels you will visit.

Mr. Toad's Wild Ride

In a strange town there is one place where tourists always get rooked. It's your first cab ride into town. If you have avoided the touts, you need to bargain with the cabdrivers. Since you have already asked an airline employee what the fare is, negotiate your best fee. Once you agree on a price, write it on a piece of paper and show it to the driver. Watch out for instant surcharges for airport pickup, extra bags, nighttime, etc. Also make sure you change enough money in the airport for the cab ride so you don't get stiffed on the change or exchange rate. Keep your bags in the backseat with you so that, in case of a tiff, bags locked in the trunk don't hold you hostage.

Often you'll be hit up for a tip. Remember, you don't have to tip anyone anywhere for anything. Just keep smiling and thanking the person even if he follows you into the hotel yelling and screaming.

If you decide to cheap it out of the airport and take a bus, be prepared for some serious luggage hauling and don't even think about it unless you have a backpack or ruggedly wheeled luggage. Those itty-bitty rollers are no match against a third-world city street. Carrying luggage to save a few bucks on a cab also makes you a marked victim in the city.

The "Up to You" Fare

Of all the things that give me grief and lead to knock-down-drag-out fights, it's when a local's concept of remuneration disagrees with mine.

The scenario is simple. You're in a hurry, you jump into a cab, and along the way you notice that the only thing used to gauge distance or cost is a bent St. Christopher medal and the grinding sound that comes from where the speedometer used to be.

When you ask the fare, the driver replies, "Up to you," with a warm, sincere smile and you shake your head at his naive trust in you. When you get to your destination and hand him a couple of guidos, however, his twinkling eyes turn into steel-gray BBs. He pushes the money back in your hand as if you had called his mother a prostitute (well, she probably is but this is about money not honor). You, shocked that a warm, smiling native has been insulted by your imperialist, colonial assumption that a cab ride would be cheap, roll off another gaudy, just-printed-yesterday bill. Suddenly your cabdriver looks like the guy that fits the noose around condemned killers' necks. He's dead-ass serious about this money. You ask what the fare should be. It's outrageous. Now he throws your money on the ground and starts looking for a cop. To your surprise he actually finds one, and now, according to the cop and the driver, it seems you are cheating him. You end up paying enough to repaint his cab twice, and, as you storm away, you don't notice the driver splitting his take with the cop.

Now, what are you supposed to do when you get in a cab? Write down the agreed price and point to your piece of paper if he gives you a hard time. If a driver pulls the "trust me, my friend" routine, bounce out of there and watch him wave you back in, this time with a firm price. You will soon get used to being followed by hordes of gesticulating, insulting cabbies. Strangely enough they're all lined up outside your hotel the next day smiling and eager for your business.

Home Away from Home

A number of robberies, rapes, and nasty things happen at hotels—more than the "hospitality" industry would like you to know. Hotels are the second place that touts and con artists hang around. You'll also find petty thieves, prostitutes, and conniving maids and dozens of minimum-wage and part-time workers with master keys to your room floating around.

The swankier the hotel, the better the security. Gated resorts are safer than downtown business hotels. Small out-of-town hotels are safer than inner-city behemoths. A lot in choosing your accommodation is common sense. Cheap highwayside motels where drooling pervos can stare through faded curtains are not as safe as the cabana on a private island. Hotels are safer in safe countries. That means that you should spend a little more money when visiting Joburg than Geneva. You should also look into hotels in satellite or suburban areas of a city rather than central or tourist areas. You'll need a smart travel agent to know the right suburb to search for instead of an online service that will put you right next to the airport or the bus station.

Most hotels will put valuables in a safe and look after your bags; many offer in-room safes. If you use your room safe and something gets stolen, don't bother trying to hit the hotel up for reimbursement. You didn't read the fine print. Your biggest fear should not be from the maid or plumber but from professionals who case hotels and know which rooms they are going to hit. Leaving the Do Not Disturb sign on the door, the lights on, and the TV on is a great idea. Until, of course, the maid barges in and turns everything off.

Most hotel door locks are useless. Every room has a master key. The dead bolt inside the door is the only thing that will keep unwanted visitors out. Unfortunately, a good shove can pop most dead bolts open. If you stay in hotels that don't have door locks, use a chair wedged under the doorknob as a deterrent or go out and buy a rubber door wedge.

Men will often follow women travelers to their hotels. You can also expect a number of phone calls from amorous admirers. In rough-and-tumble Africa, expect women of ill repute to be waiting in your room. Hookers—male and female—canvass virtually all third-world hotels save for the most upscale and some backpacker haunts, particularly in the provinces. Once you've checked in, expect a knock on the door—or several—throughout the evening.

Your watchword should be prudence. The fewer the people who know where you are staying, the less reason anyone should have to come and visit you. This will keep you safe.

Feeding the Locals

It's wise to choose an expensive hotel your first night in-country. You will have a phone in a centrally located area, and the hotel staff can watch your things, provide advice, and make arrangements for you. Once you have your bearings, you can head out into the boonies. Hotels will store your gear while you wander around. Often you can walk from your fleabag into a swank hotel, tell them you just checked out but you want to store your stuff, and they are happy to oblige.

Keep in mind that once you are "out there," there is no safety net. Customs, laws, economic and social mores can range from odious to criminal. In some countries people pilfer things from tourists. In other regions a thief can be beaten to death in front of you by the locals for attempting to steal your watch. In all cases the mind-set is to bring only what you expect to lose or give away. Usually, the most valuable things will be your money, your camera, and documents. Strangely enough, the item that is hardest to replace is your airline ticket. In most cases you will have to buy a new one (at a heart-stopping price) and wait a year for a refund for the lost one. Your money, in the form of traveler's checks, can be instantly replaced, your camera should be insured, and your clothing should be well worn, dull looking, and hopefully of little interest to thieves.

When you walk around, you should know full well that you look like a tourist. Choose a backpack in a dark or neutral color. You can also "antique" your pack so it doesn't attract attention. Just spray-paint those god-awful blue, red, or green ones with black paint to knock down the color and newness. You can wear a waist pouch but don't stick your money in it. Your money should be in an inside pants pocket, not in one of those money belts that other tourists carry. Make sure it has a zipper or Velcro fastener. Your camera should have the logos taped over with black or gray tape and be tucked under your arm in a purposely scuffed case.

Do not wear tight clothing, since a thief can easily see where your cash and possessions are. Do not wear clothing with logos, bright colors, patches, or Pacoima Bowling Club embroidery. You want to remain neutral, almost enigmatic, so that touts and thieves focus on other tourists.

As a matter of style and survival, avoid tourist restaurants, major sites frequented by bus tours, lining up for museums in the morning or for evening cabaret shows. All these places are frequented by thieves and con men and you learn less about the country than you would at EPCOT.

Stranger in a Stranger Land

Try to learn a few words in the local language. Even if you unwittingly order a chocolate cat in a restaurant (as I once did), the locals will find you charming but stupid and will bend over backward to help you.

The mind-set should be to make friends and listen. Even if you don't speak a word of Urdu, you should smile and wave like a freshman senator as you walk the streets. The locals will think you are a capital fellow and will watch your back.

What you should avoid is the classic "louder is clearer" syndrome that most westerners adopt. The idea that people who don't speak English can be taught immediately by increasing the volume of your voice is insulting.

My advice is to find a guide. They can show you around a city or region, and you'll learn a lot more than out of a Western travel book. Travel becomes much more efficient if you know where you are going, what things should cost, and where all the cool places are. If you don't want a guide, then you will need to do a lot of chatting and talking to people who will give you directions and advice, most of it marginal, or simply wrong.

Sex, Drugs, and Rock and Roll

After you've learned to check your bags and your wallet, you might want to learn to check your libido. The most dangerous place for tourists is bars and nightclubs. These neon-drenched snakepits are full of every kind of species of leech and vampire. Fresh-scrubbed Rotarians and bus tours attract transvestites, B-girls, and hustlers like fleas on a dog. In exchange for their amorous attentions you can expect a hangover and an Optima bill bigger than your monthly house payment. Tourist bars are places where fake fights can break out, locals stick you with phony raps and their cousin the policeman can make your troubles all go away, including your money.

If those scams don't work, there are colluding taxi thugs waiting outside to roll you, nasty women/boys to drug you, cops to rob you, and streetwalkers to lure you into dark alleys where their boyfriends await you. If you are dying to try the local funny weed, assume that a drug transaction will be followed by a visit to your hotel room that night by the local police (who have been tipped off by your entrepreneurial new friend).

Drugs are probably the quickest way to misery. Around six thousand Americans are arrested for a variety of infractions in ninety countries every year. About fifteen hundred Yanks are doing hard time in foreign prisons, 70 percent of these cases are drug-related. You'll be happy to know that Mexico and Jamaica are responsible for three-quarters of these drug-related arrests involving gringos.

Beating a drug rap is expensive and you hope to God the country is not trying to impress Uncle Sam with how committed they are to drug enforcement certification. In places like Saudi Arabia, Malaysia, and Singapore they'll slice your head off your neck with a big Sinbad sword or snap you like a rag doll for smuggling drugs.

Giving in to the local sirens can result in nasty diseases from broken cheap condoms, violent demands for marriage from three-hundred-pound cousins, requests for cash payoffs from bigger older brothers, or being carved like a Christmas turkey by a jealous boyfriend. Best case is you find your possessions and cash permanently gone and a burning sensation where there shouldn't be one.

Can Justice Be Served?

If you've been the victim of a crime, often there are tourist police ready and waiting to help. Their response might range from rolling their eyeballs if a hooker overcharges you to sputtering indignation if your grandmother had her girdle tweaked. Can they do anything to help?

Sure, if you want to spend the rest of your vacation filling out crime reports, having photographs taken of your bruises, hiring a local attorney, and flying back eight months later just to testify in a trial where you learn that the slimy perp who jacked your wallet and peed on your shoes is now a model citizen, a devoted seminarian, and a credit to his criminal community.

If you are the victim of a crime, stop and think about the pros and cons of reporting your little run-in. In some countries the police can magically arrange to have the thieves sell back your possessions. This often happens when everything you own gets lifted from your hotel or car. The cops make you spend hours filling out funny-looking reports that get filed away forever. The more valuable the object, the less chance there will be of retrieving it. If you lose something really important like your plane ticket, check to see if your new friends have tossed it into the next alley. As I write this, I read that a Danish tourist was pulled over by police in Mexico City, asked for ID, robbed, and then forced to give up his ATM code. Now who you gonna call?

You can forget about getting your passport back. They are worth a lot of money on the black market of all countries. U.S. embassies around the world replace over a thousand lost or stolen passports every year.

Survival tips include sticking to the main routes and sidewalks, no late-night jaunts alone, keeping a little space between you and people who seem to be overly interested in your activities, watching out for groups of young teens (thieves tend to be a lot younger than you think), and not attracting them with stealable items hanging off you. Carrying a kubatan or pepper spray gives you a vital first jump (unless of course you find out that those thieves you just sprayed and thumped were actually concerned kids pointing out that your passport was sticking out of your pocket).

Get on the Bus, Forget About Us

Often travel involves buses. Not those sleek stainless U.S. Greyhounds, but those rusty, smoke-belching death traps that look like monkey bars held together with soccer tickets. The minibus or combi or matatu or bus-taxi caters to the working poor as they hustle and weave from ghetto to sweatshop in the world's bustling cities. The drivers get paid for the number of people they can haul in a short period of time by owners who view maintenance as unnecessary overhead. Minibuses kill thousands of people in third-world countries but, hey, they're cheap and colorful. Your best survival tip? You figure it out.

Next step, the city minivan buses or killer combos that commuters jump on and off like trainees at stuntman school. The only reason these multicolored, multiklaxoned death traps are safer is that they can't get up the speed to do a good job of killing the passengers or other drivers around them.

Next on the evolutionary scale is the flying coach or long-distance intercity bus. These are usually dysfunctional, formerly air-conditioned buses with ear-shattering cassette players, chattering drivers, chatty chickens, and long dusty routes enlivened by roadside pee breaks during roadside breakdowns. These buses travel at heart-stopping speeds, usually to avoid rebel roadblocks or to get the driver to his girlfriend's house before her husband comes home. These intercontinental missiles hurtle down country roads and highways dodging cows and spraying rickshaw drivers in their wake.

After seeing dozens of these buses splattered on the back of slow-moving fuel tankers, launched over cliffs, or robbed and burned by rebels, I cannot think of a single survival tip except to sit up front on the engine, very close to the cracked windshield, so that death will at least be quick and merciful.

Cranky Trains, Creaky Planes, and Curious Conveyances

Travel in a foreign country requires a number of conveyances. If you have made arrangements beforehand, the chances are good that you will be transported by clean, fairly modern vehicles driven by sober, attentive drivers. If you like to do things on a whim or on the cheap, be prepared to experience just how deadly rickshaws, mopeds, old taxis, Russian-made planes, leaky ferries, and Soviet-era trains can be. Survival tip of the day is plan a little, spend a little, and you can be gawking at the horrendous accidents you pass by instead of being gawked at.

Customs and Cautions

Oftentimes we carry our safe little world around with us in our heads. The sterility and boredom of a plane ride usually do not come with any indication that we have entered another world where things are viewed very differently.

I once ran across three gals who were dressed Madonna eighties style with bustiers, low-cut blouses, tight ripped jeans, and jingly-jangly jewelry. No big deal except I was in West Africa and they bubblegummed by me on their way to the market to do a little shopping.

Though Mali is a former French colony, it's also very, very Muslim. I warned the girls that dressing up for a wet T-shirt contest in Koran land was an invitation to being tarred, feathered, and stoned, but they gave me that blank Valley Girl look and skipped out the door of the hotel. It didn't take long for the locals in the street to start hurling insults at them, and a moment later, small stones. When they became bricks and rocks, I hustled the shell-shocked lasses back into the lobby. For my troubles I was attacked by a group of men who thought it would be a good opportunity to rob me while the rest of the crowd was playing Sandy Koufax.

We send very different messages by way of dress and action in different cultures. Now, you can toss most of the cultural sensitivity books in the trash because most foreigners know that Americans are a little weird and culturally insensitive. You're not going to get stoned for picking up the wrong fork, just as a Frenchman won't get pummeled for lighting up a Gauloise in an L.A. art gallery. Sure people will get miffed, but your gaucheness is not a life-threatening faux pas. There are, however, certain things you should remember.

- First area of concern is hand signs. We may not think too much when we form a finger gesture to signal "OK," order two beers, or wave good-bye. But you just flipped off somebody in Germany, Britain, Brazil, or Greece. Bottom line is keep your fingers in your pockets.

- Dress conservatively and cleanly. The vogue for funky or tattered clothing is not that popular where there is poverty.

- If you're male, always introduce yourself, offer your right hand in a handshake, shake politely (no bone crushers), and say "thank you" a lot. Don't be surprised if your host gives you a buss on each cheek. Don't respond by giving him tongue—he is just extra-delighted to meet you. This is common in the Middle East.

- Western women should be more demure and only shake hands if a man offers his hand first.

- Don't use slang, since you will confuse the hell out of your new friend, who will be too polite to tell you he doesn't have a clue what you're saying.

- Bring a small gift like chocolates or candies when visiting a home. Don't flatter a specific object in your host's home or he may present the object of your affection to you as a gift.

- In Muslim countries the left hand is considered unclean (yes, they do use it to you-know-what with). So eat and pick things up with your right hand. It is considered rude to point the soles of your feet toward your host. Women eat in separate areas, ride in the front of the bus, and in rural areas should have a male companion with them.

- When you get around to chatting, remember that devout Muslims do not eat pork, drink, or talk about sex. And be prepared to remove your shoes when you enter a home. Friday is the Muslim holy day, food is often eaten with the hands, and men eat separately from the women.

- In Latin America you may find that people stand too close, grab you a lot, and are somewhat formal in how they address each other.

- In Asia don't be surprised to hear people farting, belching, picking their noses with great relish, and eating like a Hoover vacuum cleaner.

- In India men shake hands, but women do a slight bow. Men should not touch women or strike up a conversation with single women on the street. Hindus do not eat beef. When you arrive at an Indian home, you will often be given a garland of flowers. You should not make jokes about getting lei'ed.

- Don't rub little kids' heads (although Asians like to rub the heads of blond children for good luck).
- If you get into a disagreement, don't raise your voice; forcing someone to be embarrassed or lose face is the worst thing you can do.
- A good general rule of thumb in any foreign country is not to talk about politics, sex, poverty, things you don't like, or comparisons between the United States and their country that denigrate the latter.

Ask what cultural differences there are between the United States and their country and you'll quickly learn what not to say around your host. Also keep in mind that your host is as worried about offending you as you are about offending him, so a little conversation in the beginning might loosen things up.

Coming Home

You know when it's time to go home: The sunburn is peeling for the third time, your coral cuts are infected, your stomach is finally used to the food, the hangovers are worse, you've finally figured out the local scams, and of course your credit cards are going out on you like lightbulbs on a cheap motel sign.

Although the party is over, there is still some business to attend to. When you get back, check your credit card activity. Someone could be using your card number without your knowledge and you won't want to wait until you get your bill to find that out.

Pay attention to your health. It is common to pick up bugs when traveling and not notice the symptoms until two to three weeks later when the incubation period erupts into a hellacious tropical disease.

If you're one of the unlucky ones, your house was probably cleaned out by thieves while you were gone. It seems they were wearing overalls and driving a rental truck. Your neighbor even came over to give them a hand.

Maybe you should take a vacation.

money

Money Is the Root of All Travel

A s a mildly renowned expert on adventure, safety, and extreme travel I am often asked what essentials people should bring on their trips. The answer is direct and dull. Money. Lots of it. If you are going to seek adventure, you'll need money.

The most sought-after man-made object in this world is money. Yes, some people stuff diamonds in their socks or tape bars of gold to Granny when they catch the last chopper out of a collapsed dictatorship, but for most normal travelers the U.S. dollar is still the mean green that fuels the tourism machine.

It is a cruel twist of fate that your most precious resource is also the one that dwindles the fastest through expenses, conversions, loss, theft, and just plain having too much fun. Navigation tips for this jungle lie ahead. Unlike odd socks, diseases, and bills, nobody ever comes back from travel with more money than they left with.

According to the World Tourism Organization, half a billion travelers spent $3.6 trillion, or 10.5 percent of the gross global product, every year. (That's a lot of drinks with paper umbrellas and ugly T-shirts.) According to Euromonitor, the average tourist spends $559 per trip. Obviously, Euromonitor respondents are big fans of Motel 6s and all-you-can-eat escargot buffets, because that budget wouldn't get me a lousy three days in New York or London, let alone a Broadway play or ten minutes at Disneyland.

The History Part

Way back in 1891, Marcellus Berry invented the "traveller's cheque" to foil those guys with masks and six-guns that they make so many movies about. It was a glorified version of a bank letter of credit, and it quickly caught on as the way smart travelers could carry large amounts of funds and not be afraid of losing them. Naturally, establishments who catered to wise travelers accepted these traveler's checks without question or argument because it was good for business. Thus began "cashless cash" for the traveler.

These days American Express sells $25 billion worth of traveler's checks every year to travelers and nervous expats. Traveler's checks have a host of new counterfeitproof gizmos like holograms and watermarks and still feature that funny-looking guy with the Mohawked bucket on his head (American Express tells me he is a Greek hoplite . . . they think).

The Horror, the Horror

Here are some real-life scenarios:

· After spending most of the afternoon successfully chiseling a fez-topped bandit for that moth-eaten Bokhara, you whip out a wad of Uncle Sam's finest financial instruments. You smugly point out the line where they are labeled "for all debts, public and private." Your once eager host tosses them back at you and spits in your too-sweet tea. Something about your mother, a goat, and being a thief.

· Even the banks shrug their shoulders when they discover that you have pre-1990 C-notes. They are useful only as gerbil bedding and toilet paper. You try to convince them that these aging hundred-dollar bills were once the property of your local priest, who got them from the mother of a Mormon bank president, but to no avail. They are declared bogus. Suicidal and desperate, you spend the weekend trying to get change by buying Chiclets from snotty-nosed kids, but even they know the scam.

· You check out after a week at the Casa d'Elegance to find that your massive Mega Platinum Card, the ultimate symbol of your wealth and power, registers only a damning "Declined" before the condescending smirk of an oily clerk. You, you pillar of the financial community, do not carry cash ("Cash is only for pimps and old women," you snorted back at the country club, "and traveler's checks are for widows and hippies"). It seems your jaunt across three continents in one week raised the suspicions of the fraud division, and your bank back home is diligently protecting your financial interests by asking that you call them before they approve any more charges.

Your premium, top-of-the-line, only-the-cream-of-society card company is very helpfully leaving messages at your home asking you to confirm that your cards have not been stolen. Meanwhile, you are trying to close that big oil deal in Baku but now trying to figure out how to use the local phone system to beg your ex-wife for mad money.

· Friday before the local religious holiday, the fish-stinking ferry only takes cash and you booked a week in a hotel that took your credit card deposit and won't give it back. Desperate for cash, you storm the streets looking for an open bank. You fool, it's siesta time. Suddenly, a familiar logo on a cash machine beckons. In slips your favorite high-limit credit card but it quickly spits back out. Feeling hurt and rejected, you jam it in again and angrily tap out your code again. It arrogantly spits it out with a generic excuse in whatever the hell country's language it speaks. Determined to prove your financial stability to the long line of swarthy locals that linger restlessly in line, you attempt it over and over again, only to find that the ATM (obviously in cahoots with the local Mafia) has decided to teach you a lesson by keeping your card somewhere within its cold, evil mechanical bowels.

You now swear you will become a Luddite and burn all your credit cards in revenge. A small child consoles you as you sob uncontrollably. Maybe somewhere along your journey that card lost its magnetic luster and now its one useful purpose as a coaster or a windshield scraper has been denied you. When you get home and read the fine print, you discover that you didn't even own the stinking card, let alone remember that your code shouldn't have letters in it.

These are not unusual scenarios. In fact all of them have happened to me, with the places, situations, and names changed to protect my innocence.

We have not even begun to touch on carbon copiers, shoulder surfers, card grabbers, and imprint bandits as we explore the world of electronic cash nightmares. The point is that all those fears you have about the newfangled cards and services are true. So it is best to understand the pros and cons of each method of carrying and using money.

Security: Theft Can Take a Load off Your Back

Although I have been to most of the world's most dangerous places, the only time I have been completely cleaned out by criminals was during a relatively tame visit to the Vatican. I had the misfortune of having all my luggage stolen from my rental car while visiting the Holy See. Silly me, thinking that doing evil to tourists was somehow under a higher jurisdiction there.

The end result is I ended up traveling in the most carefree fashion available. No luggage, only the clothes on my back, and thankfully with my wallet and passport intact. It took me a couple of hours in the American Express office to get my credit cards back and traveler's checks replaced (hey, they were kinda wrinkled anyway).

Looking back, I can truthfully say that it was fun to shop for a toothbrush, clothing, and a pair of spare socks. Luggage free, the homeward flight was a breeze, and back home, I am sure that customs officials thought I was the ultimate jet-setter, since it appeared I had just popped over to Rome for a cappuccino and a night out. All I was out was some clothing and cheap luggage (and I hope the Pope enjoys them). My insurance company replaced most of the items (minus my deductible), and I learned a lesson about what is important when you travel: money—which I had carried safely on my person along with my passport, cards, and expensive cameras. I learned firsthand that the most typical crime against tourists is thieves breaking into a car. Nowadays, I can watch the thieves patiently wait for the tourists to stick everything in their trunk and stroll away. Hey, I told you I was an expert. I just paid a lot more tuition than you did.

Don't Blame the Criminals

Let's not be alarmist, just how will you lose your money? Or will you? American Express says the main reason people lose their traveler's checks is that, er . . . um . . . they lose them only to find them again after they have been replaced. Visa coyly says four people in every thousand lose their traveler's checks or report them stolen. They won't separate the lost from the stolen. The point is that very, very, very few people are relieved of their traveler's checks (or credit cards) by thieves. According to an American Express study, the most likely way a tourist will lose things will be through a vehicle break-in, followed by pickpockets. So the excuse about losing all your money to gun-toting thugs in a back alley—after your misadventure with the Russian transvestite behind the Moulin Rouge—should be saved for your wife.

Carrying cash makes us feel rich, curbs our spending, and can be the only thing you can use when chartering the last camel out of Iraq or buying shrunken heads as souvenirs. But cash is becoming less and less attractive to travelers.

Cash's main drawback is that it attracts thieves. Tourists fumbling in their purse or flicking through crisp hundred-dollar bills might as well put up a billboard saying, "Steal my money now! Ask me how!" Pickpockets do not idly rummage through people's pockets or purses. They identify their victims when they open their wallet, exchange money at a Forex, come out of a bank, or use an ATM. The thieves then tag along until you are in an appropriate spot and blammo. You're a victim. Hey, you don't go fishing in a desert.

And then there are counterfeit bills, or what people assume to be bogus U.S. currency. This is a major problem in the Middle East, Africa, and Asia. Fifties and hundreds issued before 1989 are suspect (don't even bother carrying old, faded notes and don't be surprised if money changers throw back perfectly good bills because they think they're fake). According to the U.S. government and just about everyone I have changed money with in places like Pakistan and Afghanistan, the Iranians and Syrians made sure that there were a few billion extra C-notes during the bad old Reagan years. According to the Secret Service, there is even a new "supernote" in circulation that duplicates the new hundred-dollar bill perfectly. So how does Achmed the Egyptian hookah seller know the difference? He doesn't.

One tip is to have a wad of smaller bills to change when you first arrive in-country. American twenty-dollar bills (and smaller) are bulky but cause no problems when exchanged. When you arrive in-country, you can change a twenty or two and not lose too much until you find the best exchange rate. If you get into a squeeze, you can pay for most items (a phone card, taxi, food, etc.) with them, and if you lose one, it isn't the end of the world.

There is also a rule of thumb that is worth remembering. The more financial methods of payment an establishment offers, the more you pay. Traveling with cash allows you to save considerable money in small establishments and to bargain harder. When it comes to weaseling and chiseling, waving greenbacks can work miracles.

So the lesson is that cash, like all good things, is healthy in moderation.

Cash, the Unnatural Resource

It takes a brave person to travel with cash. Here are some tips:

- At the airport exchange enough currency to get into a city, taxied around, and fed. I plan on $50 in most cities (except Tokyo and Rome, where you'll need about $200). You can save more money negotiating with cabdrivers than looking at the various exchange rates at the airport (they are usually all the same). Also keep in mind that cabdrivers will have no change when they drop you off at the wrong hotel. So get your local money in small bills when you exchange your dollars.
- Get clean American bills in the new design only, in hundreds, fifties, and twenties (if you're a tipper, you may want a wad of ones and fives as well). Dirty and old U.S. bills are useless in more remote countries. The reciprocal works as well. Don't take grubby or torn bills from money changers or vendors. You won't be able to change them back. Don't have a heart attack as a crisp twenty turns into a brick of filthy rupees stapled together (which you twist and pull apart).
- If you travel to less developed countries, there may be a black market where you can get much healthier but illegal (aren't all good things illegal anyway?) exchange rates. There are better exchange rates for larger notes, and guess which currency gets the best rate? (Tip: The national anthem sounds like "José can you see.") Inquire with your hotel clerk, but be forewarned there can be some bumps along the way and you could be robbed for your troubles. For example, Myanmar taxi drivers will try to get newly arrived pigeons to change their money on the black market before they get to your hotel. But there isn't a black market anymore and you'll get a lousy rate from the little smiling guy at the food stall. This activity is illegal, so learn the rules (and penalties) in-country before trying it. On the other hand, I was going to buy a one-way ticket from Tashkent to Bangkok for $600 with my credit card when the smiling ticket agent sent me down to the central market with my greenbacks. I returned with a shopping bag of grubby Uzbeki soums, but the cost for the ticket paid with local cash was $300, or exactly half-price.
- Keep your excess cash (I love that term) rolled up tightly, wrapped in a blank piece of paper, and then inserted and hidden within various pieces of luggage and on your person. Some of my favorite

places to hide money are in flashlights, camera bodies, straws, rips in luggage, glove fingers, sewn pockets in my underwear. This way you have to be stripped naked, your hotel safe robbed, and your entire bus tour victimized to be bereft of funds.

· Carry a decoy wallet with one good card and many expired credit cards, useless foreign currency, and your day's spending allowance and be prepared to hand it over if you are accosted. Using this decoy as you shop and eat will identify where you keep your money to a thief or pickpocket and he will go for it first.

· Hide your money and credit cards. Simply carry them in an inside sewn pocket (or a zippered pocket) or an ankle holster, not a belly or neck band, where all the other tourists think nobody will look for their money. And, for God's sake, don't check or pat it every fifteen seconds or my decoy trick won't work. Nothing is more hilarious (or dangerous) than someone who has to reach into his hidden stash to pay bills.

· Using cash and traveler's checks instead of credit cards can be an excellent bargaining tool to knock enough money off a trinket to make up for exchange rate differences.

· Count your change. For every ten merchants that patiently pick the right change out of an outstretched palm there is at least one that will short you on the change or, worse, give you the last regime's worthless currency.

· Avoid giving street changers your money only to have them dart off and promise to come back with the rates. Yeah, I know this sounds hard to believe but it happens. I should know, I've done it. They will often swap your legit bill for a bogus one. (Remember the fake Iranian money?) Also watch out for the fake cops who demand to see your currency voucher and cash on hand. Surprise. They will claim it is fake, give you a receipt, and that's the last you'll see of it or them.

Finally, adventure travelers beware. I tried to exchange some U.S. money in Timbuktu to pay my hotel bill and was told that they didn't have enough CFAs to change it. When I asked them when they would have enough so that I could pay my bill, they said, "When you pay your bill in CFAs, then we can exchange your American money." I love the third world.

Real Money Except to Crooks

I am a fan of traveler's checks because they have some of the impact and lus-ter of cash without the drawbacks. I use them on my trips to far-flung places, and they are a simple but effective way to avoid major monetary disaster.

Here we get controversial, because many folks will say that ATM and credit cards are the next big thing. Well, remember, I am providing real-world advice for less salubrious destinations as well as well-trodden ones. If you are sticking to the main cities with a good range of plastic to choose from, then plastic may be the choice. But if you wander even slightly off the beaten path, you may be rudely surprised at the ineffectiveness of plastic.

Typically, today's traveler's checks (or TCs as they are called in the in-dustry) are purchased for a penny on the dollar and in many cases are free with premium cards or even auto club or credit union membership. Amex is the lingua franca of TCs, but you can get Visa and Thomas Cook checks as well as other brands. The other brands don't have the recognition of Ameri-can Express, but they work just fine in major tourist centers.

TCs are essentially a cheap insurance policy and really *are* replaced with-out question once they are lost or stolen. (I always expect a lecture and a wag-ging finger but I never get it.)

The Highway to Hell
Is Paved with Plastic

Plastic money is like laser surgery. It quickly removes things without any pain or suffering. If you travel with a credit card, you can reenact *Lifestyles of the Rich and Famous* and return to your mobile home park without the crème de la crème of European society any the wiser (although most folks need to have a couple of quick Scotches on their return before they can build up the courage to open their charge card bills).

Credit cards provide the fairest exchange rate (the bank rate on day of purchase) and easy replacement should they get lost or stolen. They can pro-vide a sense of security if a vendor doesn't ship you the right goods, rips you off, or provides shoddy services. More important, it has become almost im-possible to reserve a hotel room, book a car, or pay for an airline ticket with-out a credit card.

Plastic has two major problems. First, you have no control over the ap-proval process, and it is fairly common for problems to crop up with credit cards overseas, particularly if you have been giving them a hard workout. On my global jaunts I always have at least one of my cards go down only to find that "it should work just fine, sir" when I call customer service at great expense (those 800 numbers don't work overseas, don't you know, so don't be shy about calling collect). It seems there is a little pixie in the back office of each credit card company that decides exactly when you shifted from being a pillar of the financial community to a penurious profligate. I have had monthly bills in excess of $24,000 and then been dunned for an upcoming $25 payment. I have also been called over to the phone and been asked to explain how I planned to pay for the purchase I was about to make.

I once desperately needed a cash advance on two Visa cards, and after frustrating denials I picked up the phone and got in touch with the duty officer. He politely told me that they get so many requests for even-numbered cash advances on cards from Indonesia that they just ignore them. Oh. How could I prove to him I was the real McCoy? He told me to hang up and telex him (through the bank I was at) the serial number printed on the back of the card (something any minor criminal could do with ease). But hey, they don't need to explain when and why your card won't work, because you don't own it. They do.

The second problem with plastic is that countries have varying opinions as to what credit cards should be used for. For example, in South Africa gas station attendants just look at you funny when you whip out your Visa. They only take local gas cards. In central Asia you can wait an eternity while merchants sit on hold using the single phone line to get approval, only to remind you that you could have paid half as much if you changed your money on the black market.

The Savvy Traveler

Most people's idea of an exotic vacation still includes a few urban centers with electricity, phones, and banks. Since you will be passing through at least one urban hub, chances are it will have one of the 2,700 American Express offices as a backup to your profligate spending habits.

Business or luxury travel: If you do the grand tour, stay in large hotels, visit a handful of countries, and spend big, you probably don't worry too much about money. I would recommend using a quiver of credit cards, a backup stash of TCs, and about $500 in U.S. cash. Travel at this elevated level usually allows everything you buy to be billed to your hotel or to a credit card. Tip money is important, but Alfonso will smile just as broadly with a U.S. currency tip as he will with a suitcase full of lire.

Exchange only half of what you think you will need into local currency and always pull out your credit card when you buy anything. Europe and Asia are even more comfortable with you using cards for small purchases. You might find that the change you get when you use traveler's checks might provide all the local currency you need. Taxis, telephones, and food are the major reasons to carry local cash in large urban areas.

Organized or group travel: Cruisers, bus tourers, and package groups will find a plethora of financial institutions surrounding them, and most of the spots you will be visiting will be more than accommodating toward charging, accepting greenbacks, or even cashing personal checks. The penalty you pay is artificially inflated prices for those meals and souvenirs. Here again, credit cards are welcome, but thieves do prey on tourist spots and their nomadic ever-chattering hordes. I would strongly recommend financial instruments that are completely replaceable. Amex's policy of providing replacement cards or TCs within hours or delivering to your next port of call can be a vacation lifesaver. Another wallet drainer for the unseasoned package tourer is how much money can be lost by exchanging money every time you hit a new country.

Long-term backpackers: If you are a long-term traveler living out of a backpack, you have to do some careful planning. My years with a backpack (which haven't quite ended) have taught me that this mode of travel exposes you to the highest level of theft. Hostels, pubs, back streets, buses, and third-class trains are the ideal places to lose all your possessions. Many backpackers are young, just out of school, and have a credit history as in-depth as a self-serve gas station receipt. This creates problems. Credit cards are good for a Big Mac on the Champs-Elysées and maybe a museum or two, but then tragically stop working. ATM cards quickly clean out your meager checking account and then you are stuck working as a clog dancer at Euro Disney to pay your way home.

I advise a little financial discipline and planning. First, I strongly recommend sorting traveler's checks into monthly care packages. Get them in $50 units and use them as a budgeting tool. Second, get as many credit cards as you can (from your parents) and promise, promise, promise that you'll only use it for emergencies (ha, the fools). This gives you a rock-solid financial base with no risk. You can replace your TCs every time they are lost or stolen. You can buy that ticket to Marrakech with that credit card and you can figure out exactly how many days you can last before calling home for a cash infusion.

Socially, American Express centers are great places to meet other travelers, buy a minivan, or to hang your "Need money for ticket home" cardboard sign that might appeal to the pity of well-heeled travelers passing by.

Adventure bound: Adventurers and explorers go to places that don't have banks, where currency may be feather headdresses or stone wheels—places where the price of everything from gasoline to canoe rentals seems to match your desperate need to rent it. In these places, plastic is a curiosity, and even cash may be suspect. Once again, TCs come to the rescue because only a fool goes down a thundering river with thousands of irreplaceable paper dollars. You will need a heavier amount of local currency because the only "exchange rate" in these places is the number of cows local men pay for their wives with.

In all, there is no hard-and-fast rule for handling money when you travel. Security is the greatest concern that travelers have, and most respond by taking advantage of the products and services that companies like American Express, Thomas Cook, Visa, and others have created to cater to that concern. Overall, the amount these products cost is meager compared to the peace of mind and the increased relaxation they offer. And isn't that what travel is all about?

· 13 ·

kidnapping

Rob the Rich, but Eat the Poor
(They're Usually Fatter)

There is an ominous trend that requires a little more survival training than wearing two pairs of socks or adjusting the declination of your compass. In the last decade tourists have been kidnapped in Ecuador, the Philippines, India, Turkey, Kashmir, Cambodia, Colombia, Yemen, Russia, Pakistan, Indonesia, China, Venezuela, and many other countries including the United States. About two hundred foreigners or tourists are kidnapped every year.

Most lovers of the outdoors could not think of a single instance where kidnapping is a danger or a factor in safety planning. Bears, maybe, and snakes for sure, but other than a vague memory of the movie *Deliverance,* they can't come up with a single time they've worried about kidnapping. They're still wondering what all the fuss is about as they head off on their big trek to Costa Rica, Turkey, Mexico, Guatemala, Colombia, Yemen, and Cambodia.

Then one day while searching for a waxen-throated bird of paradise, a group of polite but raggedy-looking soldiers enters their camp, gathers up their passports, and informs them they are now prisoners of the Democratic Socialist People's Movement for the Liberation of Pedro Gonzalez or some guy that sounds like your gardener's brother. "So this is what kidnapping is all about," you mumble to yourself as you are led away to a remote jungle hideout. "Shit, I wish I'd brought something to read."

You don't even have to be heading out on vacation. It could be a big promotion and transfer to Eastern New Squalidstan. Here in this hazy concrete shoebox hell, those Aryan chiseled looks, healthy glow, corporate position, and even your bevy of blond-mopped, rug-rat children can make your life a living hell. On your way to work one morning in your chauffeur-driven Suburban, suddenly you watch your driver's brains splash against the windshield as he is midway through explaining the nuts and bolts of goat's head polo. Before you can think, you've been fitted with a trash bag on your head, you're being kicked, gaffer's tape has been slapped across your mouth, and you can smell the dog shit on the floor mats of the Russian Volga that's zipping you away to some hillside barn an hour out of town. Looks like you've been kidnapped.

Kidnapping is not romantic or pretty. Affluent families and expat businessmen are prime targets. Latin America is the hot spot for kidnapping, with ransoms running in the millions.

Maybe the most famous kidnapping (after Paris grabbed Helen and started the siege of Troy) was the abduction of the U.S. embassy staff in Tehran in 1979. There have also been a number of spectacular but little-publicized private kidnappings that generated ransoms in the tens of millions of dollars.

Kidnapping statistics are misleading. Worldwide there are between three thousand and thirty thousand kidnappings for ransom annually, depending on who you talk to. Only a small fraction of all kidnappings are actually reported—simply because the families or businesses of most kidnapped people don't much trust the ability of the police to execute a happy ending to hostage situations and prefer dealing with the abductors directly. Kidnapping victims like to keep their little vacation quiet to deter further kidnappings. The true number of abductions each year is probably over seventy thousand, not including minor tribal tit-for-tat stuff.

The number counters can give you a "typical" kidnapping scenario these days. The place is likely to be somewhere in Latin America. The victim is an employee of a corporation or a member of a local wealthy family. Ransoms vary by the size of the fish caught, but the bigger you are, the bigger the bill. After being kidnapped 66 percent of the victims were released after a little back-and-forth and a bag of cash, 20 percent were rescued, 9 percent died in captivity or were killed, and a hardy 5 percent escaped. About half were guests for ten days or less, 25 percent stayed a little longer, and the other quarter stayed more than fifty days.

The most likely place to be kidnapped is Colombia (three thousand to six thousand kidnappings a year), followed by Mexico with a piddly fifteen hundred to three thousand a year; the most likely time to be kidnapped is during your morning commute; the most likely ransom will be $2 million; and the most likely outcome will be a reduced payment of ransom and a quick trip to the GMC dealer to buy a bulletproof Suburban.

The underlying motive for kidnapping is money, but if your new hosts wear red stars or hold a lot of press conferences, publicity might be more important. If you work in an office and live in a home or compound and travel between those two points, you are at risk. If you appear in the papers or are known as a captain of industry, the risk meter is notched up a bunch. If you work for a major corporation, you can bet that your name (and your family's names) are on a list somewhere. What can you do?

- Try to stay out of local papers. Do not discuss financial success or specific monetary details with journalists or friends.
- Vary your routine.
- Hire protection in the form of a driver and bodyguard.
- Get kidnap insurance.
- Discuss what should happen with your family should you disappear.
- Build a portfolio to leave with your family along with your itinerary, with recent photos (full body, face, and profile), clothing sizes, blood type, medications you use, prescription for glasses, and a couple of phrases/questions that only you would know or have the answers to. For instance, how many miles were on your Lexus when you left on your trip?

Surviving a Kidnapping

Okay, so you screwed up. You've been gaffer-taped, thumped on the back of the head, and thrown in the back of a greasy delivery van on your way to a vacation in hell. Your captors appear nervous and don't find persuasive your entreaties to be untied and driven to the office to make your 9:45 appointment. You've been abducted and somehow you hope that your wife will forgive you for your transgressions and that your employer sees the financial incentives for coughing up a few million for your release.

Take heart in the fact that 80 percent of kidnappings are for money. Very few kidnap victims have kidnap insurance, but having this expensive insurance does increase the odds that you'll be back at home a lot quicker than if you don't.

The good news is that in the United States ransoms are tax deductible, and there are some things you can do to avoid a kidnapping:.

- For your kidnappers the ideal spot to be snatched is right at your front door. If you have a driver, they will wait until your vehicle can be blocked in.
- Your captors are on a mission and they will be told to grab you, secure you, and stop you from escaping. They may whack you on the head, drug you, or bind you (or all three) and stick you in a small uncomfortable place.
- Take a deep breath and expand your muscles when tied so that your bindings will be loose.
- Once you are trussed and stuffed, do your thinking as to how you can effect your release as quickly and effectively as possible. Your mission is to retain a positive state of mind, health, and determination.
- Despite what they do in movies, don't bother trying to memorize where you are being taken, since it doesn't really matter.
- They will know who you are, where you work, and about your family. They may not know who to contact, how much money you have, or whether you can pay the ransom.
- It is important to develop a frank and open rapport with your kidnappers. You will feel anger toward them, but being open and friendly can change their opinion of you. Ask them what they want, tell them that you want to help them get you back, but don't tell them anything that would give them an edge in jacking up your employer or relatives. They will not trust you, since your goal is to fool them and try to escape. But it is more helpful to maintain a healthy, cooperative state than a mute, antagonistic, or unhelpful state. Those victims who actively fight back, argue, insult, or antagonize their kidnappers are always the first to be beaten, killed, or singled out for retribution.
- Don't lie. The media will do a crackerjack job of providing your net worth, job title, and home address.
- Develop a routine that includes exercise and mental challenge and ask your captors for items that can occupy your time. If there are other captees, try to involve them in activities and discussions that maintain focus on physical and mental health.
- Your captors may lie to you to justify their position or elicit information from you. Stick to dull, defensible answers. If they ask how much money you have in a bank account, make up some excuse to explain why you are broke.

• If you are rescued by force, find a place to hide (from flash bang), get down as low as you can, and if you can effect an escape, run crouched over with your hands clearly seen. You can yell all you want once you are clear of your captors. This is the most dangerous part of being kidnapped, with random gunfire, pissed-off captors looking to kill you, and trigger-happy rescuers. Although 34 percent of victims are rescued from their captors, just under 80 percent of hostage deaths occur during rescue attempts.

Kidnapping should not be your major concern, but it is a growing problem in Latin American and central Asian countries. Read up on who is at risk and avoid providing travel details to too many locals.

· 14 ·

weapons

Things That Go Bang

You would be hard-pressed to find any mention of war zones in survival guides. Back in the fifties and sixties the idea of backpacking through a war zone sounded like a plot for a sitcom. But there is one very disturbing fact that should put everything in perspective. Wars don't kill soldiers anymore. Who's getting killed? Over 90 percent of all casualties in wars since World War II have been civilians. In many conflicts the safest place to be is in the military. I would much rather spend my time in a war zone surrounded by Kevlar, armored glass, and sandbags, with air, medical, and communications support only minutes a way. So since you are probably going to be traveling in a war zone as a civilian and not in the military, you had better read up.

I spend quite a bit of time in war zones and troubled regions, and even though there are front lines, most of the killing is being done by rockets, bombs, starvation, massacres, and land mines far from the front lines.

What are your chances of finding yourself in a war zone? Technically, none. Why? There are no more wars. I should explain. Since 1945, the countries of the world have been very hesitant to engage in declared warfare. Instead, we have between forty and sixty LICs, or low-intensity conflicts at any one time. When Russia invades Afghanistan or America sends farmboys to Vietnam, Grenada, or Panama, the countries involved are not technically at war. Instead, they're engaged in "police actions." That means that the troops are not there to save you. Just to make sure you get killed fairly.

There have been a number of other recent developments that should make the cautious person even more cautious. Wars can be fought by proxy on other people's soil. When our government supports another government financially, morally, or militarily, we incur the wrath of the people who are banging away at the regime trying to topple it.

Sometimes we call that terrorism, sometimes we call it an accident. When a 747 full of vacationers falls from the sky over Scotland because a North African country helped another country seek revenge on us for shooting down an Airbus full of innocent people, we could call that war but we don't.

When someone blows up a federal building or an office block because they don't like our government, we don't call that war.

Even when you visit a sunny mountainous country for a little hiking and picture taking and end up being kidnapped or buried in a shallow grave, you were in a war and on the front line but didn't know it.

How do you avoid/survive/surmount the various nasty things that conflict creates?

You need to know what is going on. Nobody can predict where an attack is going to take place, but you are ahead of the game if you know the players and the playing field.

If a fundamentalist group will bomb a U.S. installation overseas, then that narrows it down a bit. When a masked group mentions that it will kidnap all capitalist pigs, that could be a hint. When a Persian Gulf sandbox prides itself on having kidnapping as part of "the touristic experience" or when a South American country runs large ads telling people not to visit their country, you should pay attention. They are talking about you.

But people don't read such things before they go on vacation or travel. Hell, most people don't even read the warning labels on their hotel's synthetic pillows.

The first step in avoiding danger from current events is to read a newspaper, scan the Internet, or get involved with people who have been there, done that. Ask stupid questions if you have to, but at least understand the risks and the dangers.

For example, there are a number of companies that specialize in scaring the bejeezus out of you. Pinkerton, Kroll, Control Risks, and others track every bombing, kidnapping, action and reaction for big oil companies and folks who work overseas. The governments of Canada, Australia, Britain, and the United States all supply free travel warnings and in-depth booklets that can help you understand the dangers of everything from kidnapping to terrorism.

The Internet is also a great way to search for a certain subject (like "tourists" + "killed"), but sometimes you can get way too much information with way too little hard information.

Here are some of the basic and smart tips that I have learned from experience:

- If you are going to a place where you stick out, you are at greater risk than at home where you (hopefully) don't.
- Don't sit in outdoor patios frequented by expats or tourists visible or accessible to passersby.
- Avoid giving out your travel itinerary to locals, no matter how friendly they are. If pressed, just say that you are taking it easy and making plans day by day.
- Avoid corporations, embassies, restaurants, and other installations that are American or heavily populated with American expatriates.

Terrorist attacks are a tit-for-tat process, so know who's done what to whom and where.

Caught in the Cross Fire

If you are in a country that decides to decorate lampposts with its former government, there are some pointers that will keep you safe and give you a story to tell your kids.

The first indication that something is about to happen will be word on the street. Wildly hypothetical at first, it then turns into a crescendo of warnings before becoming an avalanche of gossip. If you feel that something is not quite right, ask the locals or the local embassy. The embassy may have a rather detached attitude at first and just tell you to leave, or they may completely deny any specific problems. (Don't forget they are out of the loop sometimes.) Most times, though, they err by being overly cautious.

If your government chooses not to have an embassy staff in the country you're visiting, it's usually for a good reason. If even these guys won't touch the country with a ten-foot pole, the next best option is contacting local NGOs (nongovernmental organizations). If anyone has the scoop about roaming around in hostile environments, these guys do.

Function Falling Down

When the stuff hits the fan, expect chaos. Lots of rat-a-tat-tat and muffled booms. Don't worry, it's just the rebels trying to reduce the amount of time the ruling government has to pack. Revolutions can take a few days, so do a little shopping while the stores are still open and then stay inside. Make sure you get batteries for your shortwave.

Most of the action will be centered around government buildings, palaces, military barracks, and sometimes the airport. The risk from stray shells, bullets, mortars, and tank rounds is pretty high, so don't spend a lot of time looking out the window. Your best bet is to move to a second-floor room away from the fighting (you can always watch the fighting from the rooftop bar).

There is usually a flood of incoming journos and a run on rooms, taxis, food, and water. Some journos (the ones with the familiar logos) carry Sat Phones and can be a good communications source. If you want to know where to find journos and their valuable satphones, try the bar of the most expensive hotel in town.

Most old hands sit these things out, whereas those with kids and better things to do hoof it. Remember that the rebels have probably blocked the roads in and out of town and that most evacuations are from embassies. It's hard to generalize but revolutions can range from quick Eastern Europe tank parades to brutal central Africa bloodbaths.

If things look nasty, try to get on a plane ASAP. This of course will be the singular thought of everyone else in the country, but if you are at the airport and you can convince the person behind the counter that *you need to be on the plane,* you'll get priority. (Don't bother phoning a travel agent to get a reservation. The ticket counter at the airport overrides such reservations.)

If you can't get on a plane, don't automatically dash off in a car. You could end up driving right into the fighting, looting, pillaging.

Your embassy or the one that seems to be the most helpful will probably arrange an evacuation. This can be as mundane as renting buses, or it could become high drama complete with marine helicopters, aircraft carriers, and machine-gun battles on rooftops.

Your best bet is to stay inside, send local folks out for food and supplies, and wait for someone to pick you up or tell you when to head to a collection point.

By registering with your embassy upon arrival, you put yourself in a much better position for a seat on an outbound chopper than had you neglected to do this. The United States, as well as other industrialized democracies, uses a warden system at its overseas embassies to alert travelers and expats when things heat up. Wardens are expats in the business community who are assigned to contact fellow countrymen in their particular region in the event of an evacuation or extreme security warning and/or travel alert or ban. If you haven't registered, you're at the back of the line, pal. Good alternates for back-of-the-liners are U.S.-owned businesses, especially hotels and airlines. Airlines are good because they want to get their people and property out. Find out where the air crews normally shack up when in town, and where they hang out.

If you are totally out of the loop and are stuck in the boonies without a phone or transportation, just hang tight. You might be better off than your big-city compadres. Urban areas suffer the most rioting, crime, looting, rape, and pillaging. In the country, where there is no military or political structure, things pretty much go on as before.

It usually takes about three to seven days for things to stabilize and the booze and drugs to wear off. But things will not be safe, because law and order will only be relative. Soldiers probably won't be getting paid, and checkpoints will be the quickest way to get their weekend beer money. If you are traveling, think about hiring a gunman (available from the local police or off-duty soldiers).

War Zone Wonders

Many times we end up working or doing business in nasty places. They don't have to be war zones to be dangerous. Ideally, you will be working for a corporation or aid organization that can handle all the details and ensure your relative safety.

If you are going it on your own, things can be hairy. In times of stability police are charged with the safety of the population and the smooth functioning of traffic, roads, and airports. In times of conflict things change dramatically.

In most cases the normal jurisdiction of police will be replaced by the military. Their job is to keep spies and the enemy out of certain areas and to check for unusual activity. Your travel itinerary will be one of them. Soldiers also know pigeons when they see them flutter by. They know that you have little influence and lots of interesting things, like money, your watch, and even your car.

When traveling in areas with military jurisdiction, it makes all the difference in the world to have the name of the commander or officer who controls the region. A written pass is probably the only thing that will get you through in most cases. And a driver who knows the lingo and is from the same ethnic/religious/tribal persuasion as the soldiers goes a long way.

Be patient, since each checkpoint will want to double-check who you are and the purpose of your travel. (You will be assumed to be a spy unless proved otherwise.) This can take a lot of time as you swelter in a tin shack or under a smelly canvas. Use the time to hand out cigarettes, show photos, or shoot the breeze. Typically, these small social favors build goodwill for your return trip.

Many times you will be stuck under the watchful gaze of a slobbering child soldier while your passport and pass are being scrutinized in a grass hut. It is best to have your driver handle the niceties, but if they take your passport, don't be shy about walking with the person to the commander's hut and leaving your possessions with the driver in the car.

Remember that you better have a good reason to be traveling and have someone waiting for you at the other end.

Once in-country or at your end destination, stay in close contact with other expats to keep informed of developments or news.

Carry a larger "survival kit" than normal. This may include hard-to-get medical items like IV drip, syringes, prescription painkillers, and other unusual goodies.

Soldiers at checkpoints will be eager to rummage through your possessions and try to siphon off one or two items. Explain that you are carrying them for an important person or as a favor for the commander whose name is on the letter.

Almost War Zones

There are a number of places where large billboards of mustachioed leaders grace every corner, shifty-eyed men follow you on the streets, and the newspaper seems to be full of glowing reviews of the newest regime's kind and just policy of hanging nasty intellectuals.

There probably isn't any actual fighting going on or any real crime because quite frankly the leader killed all those people last week. It is important to know that despite the presence of all those bristling guns, tanks, and barbed wire which give the impression of war, you are in one of the safest places in the world: a brutal dictatorship.

Here your main concern should be not screwing up. It is important to remember that even though your left-wing Berkeley-honed political sensibilities may be insulted, you are not in the land of the free.

It is tempting to discuss politics when people get thumped on the street, but once you do, you quickly learn you have no rights, no legal recourse, and it is only financial pressure from the oil company that pays the dictator's palace rent that might keep you from being summarily executed. Will our government come and save you? Other than a few stern letters, probably not.

When you find yourself in these places, your survival kit should consist of a candid understanding that you are a spectator and not a player. Should you cross the line, you will be prosecuted subject to that country's laws, or lack of them.

When you talk with locals, you can cause them more grief than yourself. So keep it light and chatty.

Being followed, searched, questioned, or detained is nothing personal. It's just how they do things there.

Real War Zones

If you travel or work in areas where opposing factions go out on turkey shoots, you should know a few things. It is quite common for regular folks to be going about their business in war zones. That's primarily because the front lines are often these regular folks' backyards. So, when the shooting begins, realize the fighters will not be blasting away at you. Still, your best bet is to find cover in a basement or bunker. If caught on a street, a doorway or just lying flat will keep you safer. It's often advisable to wave something on a flag and call out for safe passage. Wait for a lull and then wave a white cloth (or any cloth). In most cases fighters will tell you to get the hell out of there and let you pass.

If you are going into or through an active combat area, you better have something in writing from whoever runs the area or the local commander. It also better be the "chiefest commander," as they say in Kabul.

There are a number of dangers that will present themselves in areas of active combat:

Aircraft

Military aircraft are equipped with weapons that can stitch an entire village with very heavy bullets, rockets, or bombs. Bombs are designed to drop high explosives, napalm, or shrapnel-filled cluster bomblets, often on civilian areas. Traditional bombs make a whistling sound, missiles have an ignition flame, and tracers (every fourth round) will be your only visual warning. You will need to seek protection in a bomb shelter, which can range from a basement of a house to a buried cargo container. If caught in the open, get into the lowest depression you can find (to minimize injury from shrapnel) and cover your ears and open your mouth to avoid the effects of concussion. Bombs are dropped in clusters or, in the case of low-budget wars, rolled out the back of cargo planes. The typical five-hundred-pound bomb will cause more damage in buildings (due to collapsing structures and flying debris) than in an open field. Your chances of surviving are better in a slit trench or bunker than inside a target building.

If you get stuck out in the open you can always remember this guerrilla tip: To shoot at a jet fighter, aim 200 meters (650 feet) ahead of the target. If it's a helicopter or slower propeller plane, aim 50 meters (160 feet) ahead. Don't be surprised if your victim turns around and napalms you.

Tanks/APCs

Tanks have a blind spot in both firing and visibility of about 10 meters (33 feet) in front. This poor visibility means that tank crews are apt to spray anything that is in their sights from mounted machine guns. Be forewarned that the blast from the main gun can kill just with the percussion.

These lumbering vehicles are also not immune from antitank mines, shoulder-fired antitank rounds, and the occasional Molotov cocktail. Fighters seem to take special joy in trying to ace tanks and other armored vehicles. So don't be fooled into thinking that following a tank out of a firefight is a good idea.

Rocket Launchers

A rocket-propelled grenade (RPG) has a range of 500 meters (1,625 feet) but is used under 300 meters (975 feet). Many people confuse a light antitank weapon, or LAW, with an RPG. An RPG is used primarily against light weapons and the sides or treads of tanks. Rockets fired from multitubed launchers (or Stalin's Organs) kill with shrapnel and multiple launches.

Booby Traps

Many areas that have recently come under occupation can be booby-trapped. Often the retreating army has set up minefields to slow progress. Doorways, safes, liquor cabinets, even *Playboy* magazines may be attached to trip wires and mines. Areas of high danger are buildings and facilities used for infrastructure and communications (generators, radio, electrical, water).

Mines/UXO

Mines can be found in sixty-four of the world's countries and kill around fifteen thousand to twenty thousand people every year. Eighty percent of the casualties are civilians, usually villagers and children in rural areas going about their daily business. Unexploded ordnance (UXO) can be found anywhere somebody fought a war going back to World War I. Up to 20 percent of artillery or mortar rounds, bullets, rockets, bombs, and grenades do not explode after being fired or dropped. Often they lie buried just under the ground or debris waiting to be driven over, hit with a shovel, or picked up by souvenir hunters. But mines are not just buried in the ground ready to be stepped on. They are also set up with trip wires across paths, in buildings, under truck hoods, and even in latrines.

Mines range from small hockey-puck-sized antipersonnel mines to wheel-like antitank mines. And Claymores look like Granny's bedpan. There are also a number of diabolical permutations that listen for the sound of footsteps, bounce out of the ground, or even explode years later when the batteries go dead.

Most antipersonnel mines are designed to injure, not kill. For example, the U.S.-made 2.5-pound Claymore mine has a killing range of fifty yards in a 60° arc, but it can injure up to two hundred yards. These mines (and their Soviet-made counterpart) were often set up in hasty defensive positions using their long trip wire. Once tripped, they send out hundreds of steel ball bearings at crotch level. Not a pleasant thought considering the quality of medical care where land mines are still found. Small PMN mines are quickly stuck in riverbanks, around wells, and along paths to keep villagers and enemies away. They are designed to blow off a foot and incapacitate the victim.

If you see a mine or UXO, don't disturb it. If you can, mark it with something visible and inform local authorities. The skull and crossbones on a red background is the standard marking device, but a simple cairn will help people notice the spot. Most mines are located, identified, and (despite what you've seen on TV) detonated in place, because defusing them poses a risk of booby traps or accidental detonation. UXO can often be transported and then destroyed. Kids often collect mines to sell as scrap or to play with as toys. They will offer these to you as "souvenirs."

Guns

In any country where things are not peachy keen, you will run into people carrying guns. Hopefully, they will be police, but they can also be twelve-year-old kids, slack-jawed villagers, or testosterone-loaded teen fighters. Most visible guns will be carried by soldiers and guards. When you see bulky men with cheap safari vests and untucked shirts, expect them to be packing heat. In most wild and woolly places like South Africa, Mexico, Pakistan, or Colombia businessmen and affluent people also carry concealed handguns or have bodyguards. Don't be afraid. Just refrain from flipping people the bird in these places.

Westerners are not really comfortable with the idea of someone having a deadly weapon and using it to gesticulate or provide traffic directions, and you should know the following about people who carry guns:

Soldiers: A lot of soldiers in funky countries use guns as pointers, lethal direction indicators, and to make their points. It's nothing personal; it's just that they're lazy. Often their guns have no bullets and they couldn't hit anything if they tried. (Army cutbacks, you know.) There is also military intelligence and informers. It's possible you will find yourself being chatted up or followed by skinny young men. These are usually ex-soldiers keeping tabs on foreigners. Soldiers can hit you up for bribes, but always ask to see their commander.

Cops: There are three kinds of cops in the third world: the paramilitary, who look just like soldiers; the flatfoots that direct traffic and drink a lot of tea; and the secret police.

The paramilitary cops don't like tourists who are found wandering around with bad guys who are targeting tourists to screw up the tourist industry. Don't be surprised if you are told to get the hell out of Dodge by paramilitaries.

The flatfoots will hit you up for bribes and aren't above jabbing their rusty gun barrel in your kidneys to speed things up. Tell them you don't have any money in any language they don't speak and just keep smiling. If that doesn't work, demand to see their boss and march indignantly toward the police station. At that point they'll usually give up. Afternoons, nights, before weekends, and holidays are the worst time for bribe takers.

Secret police are usually rude, bullnecked men with gold chains and bald spots. I know it's an oversimplification but it's usually true.

Bad guys: Bad guys come in two flavors. There are those who look just like bad guys: bad teeth, bad clothes, beat-up guns, and a homing device on you like a shark after a mackerel. These guys are usually fighting some simmering conflict and think you are CIA. You'll meet these people at remote roadblocks in small rural villages and in back streets. They have a bad habit of kidnapping people for PR and money.

Then there are the well-dressed bad guys. They drive cars with too many gold accessories, hang out at clubs, and sell things that are illegal. They like to hit on foreign girls and impress them. They might chat up guys because it seems they have all gone to school in America or have relatives here. They won't harm you but they can get you into a lot of trouble.

Under Arms

If you travel with men with machine guns, it is okay to glance down to see if the safety is on. Most gunmen travel with their weapons on full auto. It's also okay to ask politely for them to take their gun from out beneath your chin. It's nothing personal.

Let us say that you do get into trouble and find yourself under fire. There are three basic scenarios.

Cross fire: Sometimes in botched robberies or firefights, nobody is aiming for you, but there can be a lot of bullets flying around and ricocheting. When this happens to "run and gun" journos covering street fighting, they instinctively dive for the ground but keep their heads up to see which way the action is flowing. Often combatants completely ignore you until you raise your telephoto or Betacam and then blam, you are immediately shot because your camera looks like a gun. Your best bet is to get low and crawl to hard cover. Leave the picture taking to the foolhardy. Usually, the inside of a concrete building is best. Wooden fences, car doors, and walls offer limited protection against small-caliber handguns but not against rifle fire. Always get down and never assume a bullet won't penetrate what you're hiding behind.

Sniper fire: Often snipers will be firing at people from upper-story windows or roofs. Snipers work and think in meters. They can be as close as 300 meters (975 feet) to over half a mile away, or 1,000 meters (3,259 feet). The sniper's job is to upset the equilibrium of an area, and these days, that means taking out civilians as well as soldiers. In some combat zones, like Bosnia, there are bounties on journalists or news crews.

If you are forced to cross an area with snipers, do not follow a group of people. A sniper will have an area zeroed in and may miss a single person but will have plenty of time to track members of a group. Wait as long as you can and then bolt in a zigzagging fashion. If it is a short distance, run as fast as you can; if it is a long open area, run like a football player, weaving and ducking. Keep a low profile and say your prayers. Wounds from sniper fire are almost always fatal due to the shock of the high-velocity bullet (almost three times the speed of a handgun bullet).

Direct fire: If you are being shot at, you will not want to wait too long to figure out a plan. If you were in the military, you might be conditioned to lay fire into the sound or direction of the gunfire. But since you are armed only with a camera and a pair of running shoes, you need Plan B.

Your first instinct should be to get down flat and roll for cover. You can roll a lot faster than you can crawl. Once behind cover, don't let your new friend zero in on you. Crawl or roll as fast as you can away from the shooter or toward better cover.

The good news is that studies have shown that in combat situations only 15 percent of conventional infantrymen fire in firefights and usually with poor accuracy. It may be heartening to know that in Vietnam our soldiers averaged 400,000 rounds fired per kill. So expect lots of noise but relatively few casualties. Most soldiers fire high, and modern bolt-action submachine guns tend to lift the barrel up, also making bursts go high.

Ambushes: You may be accompanied by a patrol or column or just minding your own business when caught in an ambush. Well-planned ambushes let most of the column enter the "killing zone," then pour in rapid fire to kill as many people as possible and then quickly escape before the attacked troops can muster a counterattack.

Often the victims will be pushed by the gunfire into predetermined paths that have been mined or booby-trapped, or they'll be channeled into another killing zone. You want to get away from the soldiers that are under attack and down into a ditch as quickly as possible. Ambushes rely on surprise and last only a couple of minutes. They happen at curves, areas where there are delays, and in valleys. If you are in a column where a vehicle is hit by a mine, bomb, or RPG, prepare for an ambush. Stay immobile and don't run down under cover.

Grenades: Grenades are thrown or launched and can kill out to one hundred feet. Grenades have a fairly short fuse time and can be thrown back only if you know *when* they were thrown at you.

What to do when someone chucks a grenade at you? In the vernacular, it's called "ass to the blast." Get flat and find cover. Fall on your belly, open your mouth, and cover your ears to protect against the concussion if you can't find hard cover. If protecting someone else, throw yourself on top of him, your hands over his ears. Hunch your head and keep your shoulders up. Hey, there's no time for lengthy introductions when a grenade rolls into the bar.

· 15 ·

pestilence

Dying for a Meal

There are not too many deadly things that you can pick up by breathing. Yes, there are airborne viruses, but most diseases are transmitted by physical contact, eating, or drinking. Touch a handrail, wipe your eye, grab a doorknob, eat a hot dog. It doesn't take much. Although the good old days of the Black Death are over, it was only a few decades ago that 20 million people died of influenza. And notice how every school year or summer vacation you pick up a cold when in a new environment . . .

Grimy cities with deadly pollutants will not kill you in the short term. (I thought it was humorous that folks in Pakistan told me to smoke menthol cigarettes in the stench of traffic because the filter would clean the air. They might have been right.) There are, however, areas where you must and should take precautions, not only on the road but at home. And if you're bent on traveling to the tropics, think of yourself as a sponge, your lungs as an air filter, and all the moist cavities of your body as ideal breeding grounds for tropical diseases.

Noah's Deadly Ark

You remember it from high school. Take a swab off your lunch and stick it in a petri dish. A few days later, *yeeech,* a new life-form. Bacteria are everywhere. Although most are benign, there are plenty of opportunities to bump into a nasty one. Food is an easy way to directly inject contaminants and disease into your system. Flyblown kabob, rancid popadums, and straight-from-the-ocean shellfish have sent me screaming into the third-world night. The rules on avoiding ingesting nasty bacteria are well known. Avoid buffets like the plague. Avoid tourist restaurants like the plague. Avoid steam tables, the special of the week, and any long-cooked food like the plague. Actually, getting the plague might be better than some of the nasties that await you at Manuel's Burrito Palace.

E. coli, Salmonella, Vibrio, and other teensy-weensy bugs live on much of the food we eat. Proper storage, preparation, and cooking prevent the spread of or kills these bacteria, but all bets are off when you pull over for a roadside taco stand in Tapachula.

Salmonella causes an estimated 2 million to 4 million cases of food poisoning each year. The most likely culprits are raw or undercooked meat and poultry, milk, and eggs. Cooking to a temperature of 165°F for at least fifteen seconds kills the germs. Washing hands, work surfaces, and utensils will also dramatically reduce the possibility of a problem.

Even the squeaky-clean supermarkets of America are suspect.

The U.S. Department of Agriculture Food Safety and Inspection Service's epidemiology branch says about 35 to 40 percent of marketed raw chickens are contaminated with *Salmonella.* When the USDA's Agriculture Research Services in Philadelphia sampled fresh meat products from four Philadelphia supermarkets, they tested positive for *Listeria.* Shellfish is a prime source of *Vibrio vulnificus.* These microbes do not multiply in extreme cold or heat but explode in room temperatures or when steam tables, refrigeration trucks, serving tables, kitchens, and so on are improperly monitored. Germs can be transferred when a cutting board used for raw chicken is then used to prepare a salad.

Food itself can carry a number of nasty things like worms, bacteria, and infectious viruses. Viruses like viral gastroenteritis are second only to the common cold in reported causes of illness in the United States. Norwalk viruses (found primarily in salads and shellfish) are responsible for about 30 to 40 percent of the cases. Norwalk infections usually cause nausea, vomiting, diarrhea, malaise, abdominal pain, loss of appetite, headache, and fever.

If you eat at Johnny SnotRockets, the hepatitis A virus can be transmitted through food, too, although this route accounts for only a small percentage of the total number of hepatitis A infections. These are primarily due to unsanitary food handling in restaurants and raw or undercooked shellfish harvested from contaminated waters. Hepatitis infections produce symptoms of fever, nausea, abdominal pain, and loss of appetite.

The fastidious and paranoid will be happy to know that there are eighty foodborne parasites. Sushi anyone?

When traveling (and at home), keep the following information in mind.

- Keep hot food hot (above 160°F) and cold food cold (below 40°F). In the bush that means no monkey carpaccio for you.
- Harmful bacteria are most commonly found in raw or undercooked meat and poultry, milk, eggs, fish, and shellfish.
- Overcook when in doubt, smoke for preservation, keep wrapped on ice to preserve. A cold stream won't do it.
- Keep raw animal products separate from other foods (especially produce).
- Wash hands before and after you handle animal products. Disinfect cutting boards, surfaces, countertops.
- Cook food to the following minimum internal temperature for at least fifteen seconds to kill bacteria: game and poultry above 165°F, ground meat or sausage to 155°F, pork to 150°F, beef to at least 130°F (medium rare), and fish or shellfish to 140°F.
- Remember that bacteria multiply rapidly when properly cooked food is left uncovered to cool off or warm up.
- Reheat leftovers or stored food to 165°F.
- Soft-boiled eggs are fine but not with runny whites.
- Use your nose to tell if food is starting to turn. Rancid or rotten food can be cooked to kill germs, so it won't kill you (although it will if you don't cook it through).

Nasty People

In 1861 Louis Pasteur had a bad feeling about germs. He figured out that people spread bugs to each other. Newcomers like *Ebola, Legionella, Hanta, E. coli 0157:H7,* and HIV have joined old-timers like bubonic plague and the flu. Since 1958, the flu has killed 750,000 Americans and put another 150,000 in the hospital, and the bubonic plague rears its ugly head in sporadic outbreaks. Although we downplay the mundane flu, back in 1918 it killed 21 million people worldwide, including half a million Americans. The flu mutates every year, making last year's resistance useless to the new strain.

There are many contagious diseases caused by overcrowding, bad sanitation, and lust, so we'll just go over the generals.

Typhoid is prevalent where there is contaminated food or water. Make sure you have your typhoid shots and kill those bugs through cooking and proper hygiene.

Encephalitis is passed on by ticks which proliferate in heavily forested, humid regions. Japanese B encephalitis is carried by mosquitoes in some areas of Asia. Both are preventable with a vaccine.

Measles, mumps, and nonparalytic polio are still found in poorer countries. If you skipped your childhood vaccinations, it is wise to have them. Polio has only occurred in less than two out of 100,000 travelers. A polio vaccination can prevent it.

Cholera, caused by a bacterium, can explode in epidemics in crowded areas with poor sanitation. Symptoms include abdominal pain, vomiting, and severe diarrhea.

Dengue fever is a mosquito-borne infection that can break out in waves, particularly in waterside villages or after heavy rains. It is rare to be affected by this, since it is considered a slum or refugee-camp disease.

Hepatitis A is a viral infection of the liver transmitted by the fecal-oral route, water, ice, shellfish, or uncooked food. It can knock you on your butt for up to eighteen months. Symptoms for hep A include fever, loss of appetite, dark urine, jaundice, vomiting, aches and pains, and light stools. You usually get hep A in third-world countries with poor sanitation. It is easy to prevent with one of the two vaccines available. For proper protection the vaccine requires an initial shot (good for three months) and then repeated doses to protect longer term. Proper food and personal hygiene are important.

Hepatitis B and HIV are largely preventable, since they are spread by exchanging bodily fluids through sexual contact, intravenous drug use, and blood transfusion. There is a risk in war zones and in hospitals where blood can be tainted and enter cuts or orifices. A vaccine is available for hepatitis B. Blockers are available for people with HIV, but although they increase the health and the resistance to viral attack, they do not cure AIDS.

Inoculation:
Gimme Some Old-Time Rehabilitation

Often the glamour of adventure travel takes us to mud villages with overflowing pit toilets, dead dogs, and even dead people littering the narrow alleys. Here is where you can bet good money that most of the diseases we warn against are available free of charge.

Many people are quite surprised to find themselves coming down with measles or mumps while traveling. Unlike the United States, which has eradicated much of the childhood and preventable viruses through inoculation, much of the rest of the world is more concerned with feeding rather than vaccinating their children. Recent outbreaks of plague in India and China are good examples of what you should watch out for. Whooping cough, mumps, measles, polio, and tuberculosis are common in third-world countries. (Measles still claims the lives of 1.1 million people every year.) Although some of the symptoms are minor, complications can lead to lifelong afflictions. Make sure you are vaccinated against these easily preventable diseases.

Wee Water

I would not have done you a service if I taught you how to fashion a drinking cup out of bamboo and then, as you enjoy your tropical Tang, gave you a case of measles. The fact that some rat is merrily urinating upstream from the spot where you dunk your cup is bad karma at its most virulent.

Every water supply in the world should be considered suspect. That does not mean that the water in the Ritz Hotel in Paris needs to be boiled; it just means that you should develop a mind-set where you think before you drink. Figures warn that 90 percent of all water supplies are contaminated. My philosophy is, just assume the other 10 percent hasn't been tested yet.

Water supplies in funky countries can be transported in old gasoline cans, stored in containers full of dead rats, and may be pulled directly out of the local river where they dump the dead. On the other hand, they may also have come from deep "bore holes" or wells in Africa and Asia put in by aid organizations, and have little chance of contamination. Hotels in second-world countries may look modern on the inside but can use big rusty cisterns to store the rainwater used to wash your salad greens.

Many streams are contaminated by naturally occurring minerals, mining tailings, dead animals, and fecal matter. They can also be fast running and fresh. You can buy bottled water in a third-world country that is stored in coolers full of sewer water and infected ice. My point is: Assume all water needs to be purified unless you have proof to the contrary. Keep in mind that locals can be resistant to (or afflicted by) waterborne parasites and show no symptoms.

Purification

Water can be distilled, boiled, and/or chemically treated to remove living organisms. The simplest method is to boil water at a rolling boil for at least ten minutes. Keep in mind that the higher the altitude, the longer you should boil water, about an extra minute for each one thousand feet. A more sophisticated version of boiling the water is to make a still that collects the steam, cools it, and stores it in a clean container.

boiling water at altitude

Altitude	F°	C°
Sea level	212	100
2,000 ft.	208	98
5,000 ft.	203	95
7,500 ft.	198	92
10,000 ft.	194	90
15,000 ft.	185	85
30,000 ft.	158	70

To kill germs in water using chemicals, the most popular agents are iodine, bleach, and potassium permanganate.

Iodine (2 percent USP) is the preferred method of chemical water purification. Iodine is not poisonous in small doses (you need to consume thirty grams for iodine to kill you) and is actually part of the human diet (as in iodized salt). To purify water, add ten drops to one liter of clear water or twenty drops to murky water. (In metric terms that's eight milligrams per liter.) One drop is the equivalent of 0.05 ml for those who carry those tiny plastic syringes for this purpose. Let the solution stand for half an hour and don't expect Evian. Since iodine in tablets or crystalline form can get wet and dissolve, it is better to use it in its liquid form. People with thyroid problems should be aware of their potential for negative effects of iodine.

Chlorine bleach (make sure that the active ingredient is sodium hypochlorite at 5.25 percent and that there are no detergent additives) is toxic and can cause serious burns if not diluted properly. For every gallon of water add eight drops of bleach (sixteen drops if the water is murky). Let the solution stand for half an hour. It'll taste like water from a swimming pool but it will be sterile. Be aware that chlorine can react with minerals in the water to create carcinogens, and can destroy clothing and burn skin if carried in a leaky bottle.

Potassium permanganate comes as deep purple water-soluble crystals. It can be used to dye shoe leather, start fires, and disinfect. To purify water, add until the water turns pink. (To use as a disinfectant, it should be a bright magenta.) Popular brands of water purifiers like PolarPure (one capful) and Potable-Aqua (one tablet) should disinfect about sixteen liters of murky water. If the water is particularly cold, double the wait time for any purification process due to slowed-down chemical action.

Filtration

Commercially available filters suck up water and then force it through a ceramic filter of about one micron. These filters need to be cleaned and in the process lose a little of their substance. They are also easy to contaminate and should be boiled to sterilize when required. Most manufacturers will tell you exactly what their filter will screen out. Look for filters with an ability to screen down to particles of one micron.

In the natural world sand is a good filter for sediment. The finer the filtration, the slower the water will pass. Filtration does not always remove the dangerous critters or contaminants but can make your morning tea less gritty.

Giardia

Giardia is a simple protozoan found in natural surface-water sources. It is passed by infected animals defecating in water supplies. According to the CDC, the number one vector for *Giardia* is the industrious beaver—hence "beaver fever." Birds and cattle also contribute their share. When you drink infested water, this one-celled bugger is ingested and then sets up housekeeping in your small intestine, where it multiplies fruitfully.

Symptoms include severe diarrhea, stomach cramps, and sulfurous egg-tasting burps that occur within one to four weeks after infection. About 30 percent of giardiasis victims do not exhibit symptoms but become carriers.

The commonly prescribed drugs are quinacrine hydrochloride and metronidazole over a ten-day period. Using coating antidiarrheal medications can mask the symptoms.

Giardia is killed in less than sixty seconds at 176°F, but since bacteria and human viruses need more time to meet their maker, it is best to boil all water for at least ten minutes.

Giardia is also killed by disinfectants (iodine or bleach for at least twenty to thirty minutes) and filtering through very fine ceramic or micropore water filtration systems. Iodine is considered more effective against *Giardia* than chlorine, and not all filters will filter *Giardia*.

Sex

Although the little red ribbons and quilts don't grab the headlines anymore, AIDS is still a major threat for adventurers and travelers. On the road we tend to seek a little adventure and comfort. Not always understanding, or caring, we may find ourselves in the company of someone we don't know, hung over and wondering what happened. Unlike Western countries, AIDS in the third world is a short quick death. In Uganda, Malawi, and Congo, HIV infection rates are between 20 and 40 percent. In some Asian, East European, and South American sex spots, prostitutes are using condoms so they can have customers still left alive.

Heterosexual contact is the main way for HIV to be transmitted in poorer countries. And unlike some, I don't advocate safe sex, I advocate no sex. Do you want to risk your life on a cheap condom that's been stored in a Chinese warehouse for ten years?

HIV is the preliminary stage of AIDS and can be detected by symptoms of fever, joint pain, and night sweats. These are also symptoms of other opportunistic infections, alerting you to the need of getting a blood test and, more important, not passing on the virus in its early, highly infectious state.

These initial symptoms can appear within three to four weeks after a person is infected with HIV. It then takes three to six months before HIV antibodies are found in the bloodstream. One method of early detection is looking for an HIV protein called p24 antigen, which appears within weeks of infection.

If you dodge the AIDS bullet, there are still plenty of STDs, like hepatitis B, the clap, syphilis, genital warts, herpes, crabs, lice, and so forth. According to the World Health Organization, 236 million people have trichomoniasis, and 94 million new cases occur each year. Chlamydial infections affect 162 million people, with 97 million new cases annually. Millions more have genital warts, gonorrhea, genital herpes, and syphilis.

Many travelers get hepatitis B without engaging in any high-risk activities, because the virus can survive outside the body for prolonged periods. Consequently, infection can occur when any infected material comes in contact with mucous membranes or broken skin.

The majority of people with symptomatic hepatitis B infection don't die, but spend a month wishing they would. One percent develop fulminate (Webster's: developing or progressing suddenly) disease and die of liver failure. (On the bright side, if you get back to the United States before getting sick, fulminate liver failure moves you to the top of the liver transplant list.) Five to 10 percent of people become chronic carriers, which means they can infect other people. For women this includes 85 percent of the children they carry who don't get treated. Thirty percent of chronic carriers have ongoing liver disease (chronic active hepatitis). Many progress to cirrhosis and require liver transplants (but start out lower on the transplant list). People with chronic active hepatitis develop liver cancer at a rate of 3 percent per year. The bad news if you get a liver transplant is that hepatitis B is usually still in your body and infects the new liver.

The vaccine for hepatitis B is 90 percent effective after three doses. See your doctor or a local health clinic for more information before you travel.

Insects

The World Health Organization figures that malaria kills about 2.7 million people each year, which puts malaria at the top of parasitic killers.

The term *mal'aria* comes from the Italians in the sixteenth century to describe a disease caused by what they thought was bad air in swamps and tropical places. Although it is considered a tropical disease now, it was once fairly common in more temperate regions. Malaria came to America with the colonists and slaves and was a major problem until it was largely eradicated in the 1950s. (Of course, the Indians gave Europe syphilis as their way of saying thanks.)

Malaria is caused by a parasite called *Plasmodium*, which lives in and ruptures the red blood cells. Animals also suffer from malaria. Humans can be infected with four different strains (*P. falciparum, P. vivax, P. ovale,* and *P. malariae*) through five different species of the *Anopheles* mosquito. The most lethal is falciparum, or cerebral malaria. The death rate in this strain is about 1 percent and is more likely to be lethal if not treated in time.

Malaria is spread when a mosquito that has bitten an infected person bites an uninfected person. Because of this continued transmission, there is constant mutation and creation of resistant types from undermedicated victims. At one time quinine (extracted from the bark of the South American cinchona tree and introduced by Amazon basin Indians to Jesuits in the seventeenth century) could kill or subdue malaria. Chloroquine was developed during World War II and eliminated many of the side effects of quinine (which is still effective in treating severe cases of malaria but not eliminating it from the system for good).

Now most malarial areas have quinine- and chloroquine-resistant strains. Travelers to Southeast Asia, Melanesia, and central Africa should be aware of the potential of getting malaria even if they are taking prophylaxis, or preventive medication. Malariachemoprophylaxis is the ten-dollar word to describe medicines designed to prevent transmission of malaria once one has been bitten.

It takes one bite to transmit malaria, and symptoms begin in about one week. These include fever, chills, headache, muscle ache, and malaise. Early stages of malaria may resemble the onset of the flu.

Steps to take:

- Avoid traveling in malarial areas.
- Take malarial prophylaxis and follow the instructions and full term of treatment. You can choose from mefloquine (Lariam), which is taken weekly; chloroquine (Resochin), taken twice weekly; or a daily antibiotic, doxycycline. (Having diarrhea or forgetting to take your medication on the right day can reduce the effectiveness of the drug.) There are a number of other options overseas such as Fansidar (considered to be unhealthy except in emergencies) and Paludrine (available in Britain). In many areas people mix a daily dose of quinine with another medication. New drugs like Malarone and Artemether (based on qinghaosu, a drug made from a member of the wormwood family or Artemisia annua and based on an ancient Chinese medicine for fevers) are on the horizon. In all cases consult your doctor and a local doctor for the latest recommendations.
- Report any signs of flulike symptoms (fever, chills, aches, pains, weakness) and mention your travel itinerary when consulting a doctor. Symptoms can occur up to three months after your return.
- Wear socks and shoes, long pants, and long-sleeved shirts at dusk, nighttime, and early morning.
- Use insect repellent.

- Sleep with a mosquito net and spray it with repellent.
- Use a fan, mosquito coils, room spray, or whatever secondary prevention is available.
- Avoid dark colors, don't use perfume or aftershave, swat mosquitoes if they land on you.

Worms

My least favorite foreign guests are the helminthic infections, or diseases caused by intestinal worms. Unlike more dramatic and deadly diseases, these parasites are easily caught through ingestion of bad water and food and cause long-term damage. Just to let you know what's out there, you can choose from angiostrongylosis, herring worm, roundworm, schistosomiasis, capillariasis, pinworm, oriental liver fluke, fish tapeworm, guinea worm, cat liver fluke, tapeworm, and the ominous-sounding giant intestinal fluke (who's eating who here?). All these little buggers create havoc with your internal organs, and some will make the rest of your life miserable as well. Your digestive system will be shot, your organs under constant attack, and the treatment or removal of these nasties is downright depressing. All this can be prevented by maintaining absolutely rigid standards in what you throw or breathe into your body. Not easy since most male travelers find wearing a biohazard suit a major impediment to picking up chicks or doing the limbo.

The Fevers

The classic tropical diseases that incapacitated Stanley, Livingstone, Burton, and Speke are the hemorrhagic fevers. Many of these diseases kill, but most make your life a living hell and then disappear. Some come back on a regular basis. The fevers are carried by mosquitoes, ticks, rats, feces, or even airborne dust that gets into your bloodstream. Coma and death can occur in the second week. There are so many versions that most are named after the places where you will stumble across them. Needless to say, these are not featured in any glossy brochures for the various regions. Assorted killers are called Chikungunya, Crimean, Congo, Omsk, Kyasanur Forest, Korean, Manchurian, Songo, Ebola, Argentinian, Hantaan, Lassa, and yellow fever.

· 16 ·

bush eating

You Gonna Eat That or Raise It as a Pet?

here are some important questions you have to ask yourself before you read this chapter. Is it cool to eat things you used to dissect in biology class? Will your newfound love of herbage make you race the gardener for the lawn clippings every Wednesday? How do I tell my neighbor's kid that I barbecued his hamster? Will the kids figure out those are deep-fried grasshoppers and not french fries? Will my fishing buddies get mad at me because I scarfed all the bait on the way up to the lake?

All these questions will be answered, but first you must understand two constants about bush eating. First: An aborigine will take a Vegemite sandwich over a baked wichiti grub any day. Second: The only thing grass will give you is green skid marks in your BVDs.

Survival eating is more about understanding what nutrition sources are available and overcoming cultural barriers. No, I don't mean learning to enjoy ballet; I mean forcing yourself to eat things you would normally squash in disgust.

Pass the Toad

A few years ago when I traveled in Borneo, I spent an educational afternoon in a longhouse playing with some recently captured baby fruit bats. As they desperately tried to hang themselves off my nose and fingers, I asked the assembled children what they thought of bats. They all rubbed their stomachs and said, "Mmmm." Lesson one: What to us are nature shows can be cooking shows to others.

The one skill that flowers when left alone in the wilderness is the ability to create pretty decent meals with a crackling fire and an unlucky animal. Gathering, preparing, and consuming the natural wonders that surround you can be an unpleasant descent into gastronomical horror or a great training to be a chef at a trendy BBQ joint. Cooking over an open fire is one of our last links to our Paleolithic ancestry. Now, I shouldn't say "fire," because nobody cooks over a fire unless of course you are Joan of Arc. Fire just blackens and burns food. Bush chefs build a bed of softly glowing coals to cook over. This deep red hearth provides a different deeper cooking heat than dancing, unstable flames. To get this quality of coals, you need to burn down high-energy fuel sources like hardwood. Burning green or light woods not only gives you ashes but also flavors the food with the amount of smoke given off, although this may be preferable if you are forced to consume some alien life-form you've dredged from the fecal muck.

As Hungry as You Wanna Be

Learning to live off the land requires some understanding of basic rules. Particularly when you are stuck without food in a remote place.

We all know (although sometimes it's hard to believe) that we're not going to pass out and die if we don't eat right away. So despite your growling stomach, it's a better idea to spend your energy getting rescued than chasing after mice. If, however, you know you're socked in for the duration, there are a number of sources of edible protein around you.

Don't just grab your birch-bark basket and start gathering salad fixings, though. You run the risk of getting very ill if you swallow the first edible foliage you see.

As Dead as You Wanna Be

You're going to have to balance desperation with restraint. Your brain is going to make just about anything within reach look like those free samples from Chic-fil-A. So before you dash around sampling everything that fits into your mouth, let's consider.

As a practical matter there is much in the wilds that can be eaten. The problem is, most of it is as palatable and gaseous as a reelection speech. You'd need to get your hands on five Quarter Pounders to meet your daily needs of 2,500 calories, but you're going to have to eat twenty pounds of vegetable matter to get the same calories. Just sitting around thinking about how hungry you are is going to burn 45 to 50 calories an hour. (Now you know why cows graze and people order in.)

Greens are great for a celebrity weight-loss/detox weekend at La Costa, but they won't get you three feet in the woods before you faint from hunger.

Even if you are smart enough to pack one of those blurry black-and-white plant guides, you still have major problems. Wild plants don't provide that much nutrition. Vitamins, yes. Fiber? Sure. But good stomach-settling dinners, no. The ground you're standing on may have grass sprouting, the trees around you may have inner bark, the bugs that pester you are edible, and even your leather gloves can be eaten after a little cooking, but you, my lost soul, need to concentrate your efforts on getting fed.

Many survival guides will tell you that 120,000 out of the earth's 300,000 plant species are edible. Mathematically, that means that 60 percent are inedible, and many will kill you. For example, there are about 700 plants in North America that are lethal, and none of them come with Mr. Skull poison labels. Everything from rhododendrons to rhubarb leaves offers you a short, painful way out of your predicament. There are also plenty of look-alike berries, fungi, molds, trees, and weeds to speed up your demise.

Eating High on the Bog

The trick is to choose things that are edible, not poisonous, and, most important, nutritious in comparison to the effort required to gather them. Anyone who spends more than a weekend outdoors knows that pine trees are completely edible (and almost tasty) and you won't go too hungry (but then again, you don't see many six-foot squirrels).

Realistically, for the first day you're lost you'll probably be okay. Hunger pangs come and go; there are crumbs in the bottom of your pack, an old stick of gum, and maybe even some chapstick that will go down after a little chewing. The second day you can probably get by doing a Euell Gibbons and nibbling on things here and there as you desperately wander around in your search for water. Then, stumbling upon a foul-gas-emitting swamp, you strain the bugs from the water and suddenly it hits you. Eureka! You've found the drive-thru window at Denny's.

Yes, you moron, water attracts animals (like you), supports fish and bugs, and is home to crayfish, frogs, snails, and other Gallic delicacies.

Swamps also support small mammals like raccoons and munchable greenery like tender twigs, shoots, and grasses. Rotten logs are equivalent in appeal, price, and nutrient value to a late-night Las Vegas buffet, but hey, it's free and it's at hand. Here at this swampside diner you'll find grubs, ants, earthworms, and the odd centipede or scorpion. If you like a little exercise before a meal, try digging in moist ground for grubs, slugs, and worms. Rooting around in swamps can be one of the most efficient methods of gathering protein.

Before you suck those earthworms like a *primi platti* with a slightly crunchy, slightly al dente texture, you might want to cook them. Making a murky mélange of swamp water leeks, pine needles, and mashed creepy-crawlers is a good entrée into bog cuisine.

Bug Basics

No survival guide would be complete without tips on entomophage, or bug gobblin'. Let's get the first step out of the way and admit that bugs are gross and that anyone who brags about consuming insects does not have a significant other or even a life. If God intended us to eat bugs, we would have a nose like an anteater and a tongue like a frog, great for killing flies and maybe for picking up checks in restaurants but not pretty. Actually, bugs are a big part of a person's diet in other countries. I've bought deep-fried grasshoppers from roadside vendors in Bangkok, and no visit to Australia is complete without a big feast of wichiti grubs. There are 1,462 known species of edible insects. Insects are excellent sources of low fat (7–9 percent) and high protein (up to 60 percent or even higher). There are a few drawbacks, however. They're small, the hard-shelled ones have parasites, they're ugly, and some (like brightly colored caterpillars) can be poisonous.

Cooking tips? Purge their gut first by feeding them something healthy and waiting for at least a day, then remove the shell and the head and smash them up in a stew. Don't eat dead insects, and remove any nasty jaggy things like grasshopper legs or beetle horns before munching. Ants in temperate climates can be eaten alive (they can be bitter, but tropical ants contain a lot of sugar). Bees can be followed back to their hives, and honey can be removed very gently. Maggots found on dead animals are tasty and nutritional once cooked. Soft bugs like moths and caterpillars can be roasted. Scorpions are yummy if you chop off the stinger and roast them. Cockroaches need a good enema and smell bad, wasps and bees need to be boiled thoroughly to break down the poison and soften the stinger, and don't forget to toss in the occasional tadpole, salamander, frog, or snail to liven it up. So now you know where the protein is, guess what's coming for dinner?

bug protein

	% of Weight
Earthworms	70.0
Moths	63.0
Fly larvae	42.0
Water bugs	38.1
Grasshoppers	24.0
Larvae	23.1
Termites	23.0
Ants	18.0
Crickets	12.9

Source: USAF.

Your hunger satisfied, you now seek a finer quality of food. Maybe a tossed dandelion salad topped off with strips of blackened squirrel. Well, if you're in the swamp, you're still in the right place. Rodents and small mammals are plentiful and can be found under or in dead trees or dug up in their burrows. Small mammals will come wandering into your camp at night to forage for scraps, making them easy to entice and trap. You might develop a taste for sushi and slurp down a handful of minnows. Better yet, try your hand at making a fish dam, or snares or deadfall to snag a curious animal.

Big Game, Small Chances

After about a week of shoving half the landscaping and fauna down your gullet, you'll want to try your hand at bigger game.

Yes, you can catch game in the wild, and with a little practice and timing you could probably kill every damn animal, bird, and reptile in the bush.

Your goal is to get to know your furry neighbors before you kill them. Every small area has its own rhythm, animals, trails, and territory. It is better to get to know the routines of the animals first. With enough patience they will come to you.

One of my great pleasures is watching a moose come down and drink in the early dawn before the drunk hunters show up on their ATVs asking if I have seen any moose. But even raccoons will visit camps, lynx will spray your tent, and porcupines think twigs soaked with dried urine are Mountain Dew. Careful observation will teach you to identify birds, fish, carnivores, and herbivores as they go about their routines. Then you can set your traps or make your move.

There are some basic rules to hunting:

- Large and small animals need water and will regularly walk between water and forage. They are most active early in the morning and late at night. Don't follow rodents to find water. Some mice get sufficient water from the food they eat.
- Don't interfere with animal patterns but pick a spot to observe. Make sure the critters are upwind so they don't smell you and change watering holes. After a few days in the bush, your scent will be a tad powerful.
- Since your scent will scare away many animals, think about where you relieve yourself and where you sit. The way to mask your scent is to cover it with the scent of a wild animal. This is usually done with the extraction of scent glands or urine. Good luck in collecting this.
- When you think you have a general idea of how things work in the animal commute, come up with a plan to trap them. There are a number of very tricky Merit Badge ways of catching animals, but they all boil down to pits, snares, and direct attack. More on this later.
- Once you have caught an animal, you must clean it. This means draining the blood out by hanging it upside down and cutting its throat, removing the guts, the skin, head, and feet. This should be

done immediately. Eating an animal that's been dead for a while can give you food poisoning.

- Keep in mind that other animals will get hungry smelling your catch, so clean it quickly.
- Meat spoils very quickly in the heat, so have a plan for how to store it. Typically, you should cut uneaten meat into strips and slowly smoke it over a fire. Those areas that have very high heat can dry it, and areas that are cold allow freezing.
- The skin should be stretched and any fat or gristle scraped off. Brains of the animal mixed in equal parts with fat are often used to clean hides. The hides should be cleaned thoroughly, soaked in water, and then stretched to dry over a smoky fire. If they stay damp, they will not cure.
- Don't eat all organs because some animal livers have toxic levels of vitamin A (shark, seals, polar bears). Don't eat brains or other disgusting stuff because you can get parasites. Blood is a great base for gravies and soups. Fat is needed for cooking and energy storage. Intestines can make great binding if cleaned out, stretched, and dried, hooves make glue, horns make tool handles, bones make soup or knives, tails make fly whisks, and so on.

Bigger Game, Smaller Chances

Before you make BBQ plans, you have to actually catch the critter. Animals have not evolved this far by thinking of you as Dr. Dolittle. Through the ages low biomass has been God's way of telling us to move on. For example, jungle floors have low biomass, despite having plenty of trees around. Open oceans also have low biomass, but reefs have a high biomass and lots of animals. African savannas, too, have high biomass. My point? Don't waste your time in places that don't have animal life.

Once you find the ideal place, and you think animals will be cruising by, set your trap. I say trap because actively hunting a large or even small animal can take days of hard walking. In primitive cultures the men go out in a group for a week or two at a time and often come back with nothing. Traps allow you to multiply your success rate and conserve energy.

Pits: A pit is simply a hole dug in the ground and covered with leaves and a crude mat. The animal is walking along minding his own business and crash. Sometimes hunters put spikes in the bottom to impale and kill the animal; other times they dig the pit deep enough to capture the animal alive.

You need to make sure the entrance to the pit is unavoidable and that the pit is deep enough. Obviously, you are not going to catch elk or moose this way, but pits are good for wild pigs and other midsize short-legged beasts.

Pits take a lot of time to prepare and should only be dug once you confirm the constant traffic of animals. You can also make a raised beehive-shaped pit of stones or wood with a very small opening at the top. The animal will jump in to get the bait but will be unable to climb or jump out.

Snares: Most survival guides provide you with dozens of diagrams on snares, traps, and other devious devices. They can range from Vietcong-style mantraps to thin threads that snag cute little bunnies. You will need the foresight to bring snare wire, usually a nonferrous wire. The snares are simply a loop of the wire larger than the head and smaller than the full size of the animal. The animal is directed along its normal path into the snare, catches itself, struggles to get out, which tightens the noose, thus choking or hanging it up until you come along to wring its neck.

The most successful snares should be spring-loaded to jerk the noose tight. They should be set along a well-used path with sticks or brush to direct the animal through it. A springy sapling, bent with a trigger device that explodes into action with a gentle tug, is ideal. Most trigger devices are a notched, ground-mounted anchor and a notched trigger. You need to make and set a lot of snares because you never quite know when they work or what will set them off. Baiting them helps.

The truth is, I have never met anyone who has lived off the questionable and minuscule bounty of a snare line. Often all you'll end up with is a lot of well-chewed furry animals (there are other hungry predators out there too, you know), a few gnawed-off paws, and the occasional unidentifiable rodent that stares at you plaintively in its pain.

Traps: These can be as simple as a big rock balanced on a stick fastened to a piece of food. The animal tugs the bait and blammo, Wile E. Coyote for dinner. You can be quite creative. The best ones have a perimeter that prevents the animal from jumping back once the trap is sprung. Once again, they don't always work, but what else do you have to do all day if you're lost?

Hunting: More fun but a lot more frustrating. It's a fantasy to think you'll lie in wait with a sharpened stick and then yell "yee haw" as you drive your fire-sharpened stake straight into the heart of a bull elk.

An animal's acute sense of smell, its hearing, and its nervousness don't mix with your less-than-delicate bush-refined skills. There's nothing to stop you from making bows and arrows, slingshots, spears, clubs, or even blowguns, but you're better off clobbering rodents with a fat stick than trying your hand at catching big game with a spear.

Keep in mind that in the old days it took a lot of brave men and even more arrows and spears to down dinner. That's why hunting has always been a male bonding thing. There's a lot more talking and bullshitting about hunting than actual killing. I could tell you to bring a rifle, but if you were smart enough to get lost with a decent hunting rifle and enough bullets, you probably won't be stuck long enough to need my advice.

Fishing: Fish seem far more amenable to being caught than mammals or birds. Finding a stream, lake, or ocean that has fish is your first challenge. After that, blocking off waterways, setting fish traps, and making nets are the way to go. Fishhooks and fly casting should be left for those trips to Idaho. Your best bet is to use a net, followed by leaving a number of baited hooks and checking them periodically. Don't forget the other slimy things that live in the water. Crayfish, mollusks, seaweed, and snails are all edible but cook them first.

Fish are attracted to light, so nighttime may be the right time to fish. Try anything and everything for bait.

Birds: A land-based survivor will not waste any time with birds. There is not much to eat and they are hard to catch. If you feel you must try, they can be shot at with slingshots, whacked with sticks, or jigged with hooks.

The following table gives you some comparative caloric benefits of various wild animals and insects. I have chosen the higher range but you can reduce the caloric and fat content by 10 to 15 percent for scrawny animals.

big and little wild game

GAME (3 oz/ 100 g)	CALORIES	FAT (G)	CHOLESTEROL (MG)	PROTEIN (MG)
Squab	297	25	100+	19
Pig	225	13	112	29
Rabbit	147	2.9	104	28.1
Quail	168	7	570	25
Venison	160	3	69	23
Pheasant	151	5	62	25
Buffalo	140	3	45	36
Antelope	127	2.2	107	25
Deer	134	2.7	95	25
Squirrel	116	3.1	80	20.5
Duck	102	3.5	—	16.5

INSECTS (3 oz/100 g)

Grasshoppers	200	8	—	24
Mealworms	250	13	—	20
Termites	350	28	—	23
Water bugs	220	6.1	—	38.1
Moths	265	15	—	63
Crickets	121	5.5	—	12.9

Source: USDA, Iowa State.

The Poison Test

So you ignored my advice and spent the day running barefoot and loin-clothed after large land mammals. Now you are hungry enough to eat just about anything. The course of last resort is just stuffing the scenery into your mouth—it's a good way to kill yourself.

If you are going to become a human hedge clipper, you need to know that what you're eating won't kill you or sicken you. The first step is to learn about the local landscape from an expert. The second best way is to carry and use a plant guide. The third and most desperate way is to do a homemade and highly dangerous poison test.

The only reliable way of avoiding toxic flora is by never eating any dead or sickly-looking plants (seeds can be considered live). It's not exactly like sniffing the cork of a vintage wine or nibbling on a Chicken McNugget found in some dumpster, but try this: If you're not sure about a plant's toxicity, try rubbing a very small piece of the potential food against your wrist to see if a reaction occurs. If nothing itches, burns, or stings after twenty minutes, rub the plant food just slightly on your lips. Wait a few minutes and then try the corner of the mouth. Again, after a few minutes, if you're not yet doing the funky chicken on a rug of pine needles, rub the plant on the tip of your tongue, wait, and then under the tongue. Wait twenty minutes. If you don't drop dead, it's time for the next step, as the food is more than likely not poisonous. Chew a small bit. Then you must wait at least five hours to see if there are any side effects. Don't confuse the test by eating other things during the interim.

If it isn't safe, trying this test can kill you with some very toxic plants. (Even if the plant is not toxic, a massive amount of roughage can give you a hell of a stomachache and some explosive aftereffects.)

The general rule of thumb is to skip anything that:

- Smells like almonds or peach pits
- Has a sharp, bitter taste or a burning taste
- Has a milky, rubbery sap
- Has bright red coloration
- Is a five-segmented fruit
- Is an old or dried-out plant

Mushrooms: If you're really hungry, don't waste your time with mushrooms because there aren't enough nutrients in the good ones to risk being poisoned by the bad ones. In North America you'll find about five thousand to ten thousand wild species, of which 2 percent are deadly. Some of these poisons do not take effect until eight to forty-eight hours after you eat them. This means you could go back for breakfast, lunch, and dinner on the deadly *Amanita phalloides, verna,* or *virosa* and not even know you're killing yourself. Amanitin poisoning takes about four to seven days to bring a merciful death. There is no one caution or hoary old folktale to help in distinguishing poisonous mushrooms from safe ones.

You could also stumble onto a patch of *Psilocybe* and be discovered by your rescuers babbling away, happy and visionary in your own psychedelic world. Best survival advice is to have a little mushroom-gathering experience under your belt before you chow down.

Weeds: Although dandelions have a milky sap, they are an exception to the rule. In fact, dandelions are quite tasty and the flowers could become your favorite woodsy snack. (Remember to snick off the green base that holds the flower.) Even the root is a poor man's replacement for a carrot. The leaves make salads and when cooked you could pretend you are eating spinach. Just about anything that is newly sprouted will be tastier than older plants. The fiddleheads of ferns or "pakus" taste like spinach, but they are good only in moderation; eating too many destroys Vitamin B. Don't forget to look under the ground for leeks, lily bulbs, and other starchy roots.

Trees: Pine and birch trees have a number of elements that will nourish you. Although the outer bark is bitter and hard, the inner bark is soft and chewy. The sap of maple and sycamore trees can be tapped (by cutting a series of grooves through the bark but not all the way around). Depending on the season, out will come a drip-drip of sweet sap. The inner bark of birch trees makes a nice "tree jerky" along with small twigs. The acorns from oak trees kept a lot of Indians and wildlife fed and can keep you alive as well.

Bulrushes: The cattail is a great source of food in temperate climates. You can roast the tubers (scrub them first), make flour from the heads, and munch on the tender shoots. Flour can also be made from ground roots, seeds, nuts, and the inner bark of trees.

Nuts: The high oil content found in nuts means high energy. Acorns and piñon nuts are found throughout the Southwest. Nuts should be boiled so the flesh is more digestible, but you can eat them raw. They do contain a lot of calories in their oil and starch, and you can get an unforgettable stomachache from eating too many. The oil from nuts and seeds can be extracted and used for cooking. The starch can make a passable flour. Nuts also last a long time and are easily carried (along with your snake jerky and berry goo).

Fruits: Depending on the ecosystem you end up in, most large fruits are edible. They provide good short-term energy and great taste. Mixed with nuts, you've got an instant bush snack. Be aware that many smaller berries are poisonous, but those that are not can be dried, like fruit, to eat while on the trail.

Chances are you are going to be stuck in the woods without a comprehensive four-color plant identification guide. If you think you have eaten something that is poisonous or not agreeing with you, drink plenty of water and force yourself to puke it out.

Scurvy is a major concern for bush eaters. You need to vary your diet to include foods that contain protein, amino acids (both in meat and fish), and vitamins (fruits and greens). Eating naturally is rough on our wussed-out digestive system, so take it easy until you find the foods that work for you. Fiber will be the last thing on your mind. Pine needles make a nice tea and have plenty of Vitamin C, which is ideal for combating scurvy. A habit I picked up from my snowshoeing days is chewing pine resin (it drips from torn limbs and hardens) like chewing gum.

All in all, you won't eat that well, but you'll be plenty busy gathering and preparing the meager amounts of sustenance you do find. The reality is that most people are only lost for two to three days and will do just fine with available water and shelter.

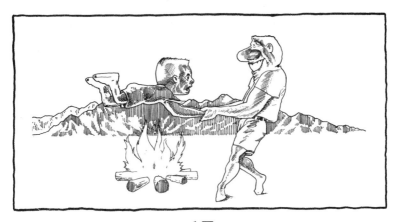

· 17 ·
fire

How to Make Cozy in Miserable Places

Cold, scared, and lost, the first comfort a human should attend to is fire. Being able to create and harness this mysterious phenomenon separates us from the apes and makes us masters of our domain wherever we are.

The act of building a fire does a number of things that are helpful. The action of gathering wood, picking a spot, and creating heat acquaints you with your new home, gives a focal point for further navigating, calms the mind, and gives time for reflection. A fire can be the only thing that separates you from despair, hypothermia, and disaster.

Fire also has a number of important uses, starting with heat, light, cooking, and a signal to anyone looking for you.

Later, as you nurse your sore feet, bewildered mind, and growling stomach, you will stare into the flitting sparks and hypnotizing dance of flames and tell yourself you will have at least one good story to tell your kids. Well, at least that's what I told myself when, after my companion had just survived a fall off a cliff, we got lost hundreds of miles from the nearest person, separated from our supplies, in a place unoptimistically named the Lost World.

I survived that night in Borneo—in fact, I enjoyed myself. I slept in a hollow tree on a bower of ferns and drank from larva-filled puddles. What made my disastrous predicament fun was my roaring fire on the edge of a cliff, drying me out, giving me light, and making me think that maybe this was just an extreme camping trip without catering or luxuries.

But building a fire when you don't have all the tools and supplies at hand can flummox some people. What if you don't have matches or a lighter? What if there is no fuel (only desert, water, or ice floes)? What if you are lost in a howling rainstorm, soaked to the bone on the edge of a cliff, covered in mud, it's pitch-dark, and your teeth are chattering so bad you can't even read your watch?

Well, the answer is you're screwed. So starting with that candid assessment, let's work our way out of this one.

The first lesson you need to learn is that you should always carry the basics of survival (fire starter, knife, shelter, water container, light). Failing that, you need to know what your options are for starting a fire. These are the traditional methods of starting a fire.

- Matches or lighter
- Friction
- Fuel and spark
- Magnifying glass

These methods and the right fuel (tinder, kindling, wood, grass, cloth, flammable liquids, peat, coal, plastics, etc.) can get you to the first step in survival in the wilds: building a fire.

Matches or lighter: If you need me to explain how to start a fire with matches or a lighter, you should probably put away this book now and sell all your camping gear. Actually, I am probably being too harsh or smug, since it's entirely possible to go camping these days and never build an old-fashioned fire. In a number of parks, and during peak fire seasons, it's against the law to build a fire. Stoves are much more functional for cooking food or boiling water. Lanterns and flashlights do a better job of providing light, so many view fire simply as a source of heat and comfort first and cooking and light second.

Regardless, you should always have a few cheap BIC or other disposable lighters in your luggage or pouch. Despite most survival guides touting waterproof matches as the thing to have, they really are your second choice. Matches are a finite source of ignition, and in the same space you carry twenty waterproof matches, you can carry one BIC lighter that provides thousands of lights. Plus, when it runs out of fuel, you still have a flint and striker. Zippos are great as fire starters, hand warmers, knuckle dusters, and collectibles, but you better have a tin of fuel and spare flints to make them work.

Friction: Ah yes, the ancient art of rubbing two sticks together. Don't believe a single thing you read about using friction to start fires. You can even try this pagan ritual with a portable electric drill to see what I mean. You need the right kind of wood (dry cottonwood is ideal), the right kind of weather (cold and rain are a bitch for this method), and the right tinder (pre-burned bark and cloth are ideal). If you have no other options, the simplest way to start a fire with friction is to find a fairly straight branch and a piece of wood with a flat surface. The idea is to rotate the branch between your hands, applying pressure on the flat spot to build up the friction and start the fire. You can also move the branch back and forth in a groove on a flat piece of wood. Other methods include building a bow that allows you to saw back and forth with the wooden drill looped in the middle. You need to press hard and work fast.

You will need very dry, very light tinder and you'll need to blow once smoke curls up. Remember to create your own tinder if you have to light fires this way. Shaved and distressed wood with lots of fibers, charcoal dust, and dry pine needles make a nice tinder, but anything from dried bracken to belly button lint can work. If you sprinkle in a little gunpowder (not too much), you won't even care about matches.

This method for starting fires is a method of last resort and is pretty much impossible to master without watching a pro do it. The good thing is that you'll get nice and warm just trying to start your fire. Lots of pressure, lots of dry kindling, and a firm determination never to be without a lighter again. It may be worth remembering that you can bring a fire kit that consists of clothes dryer lint packed in paraffin-soaked cardboard egg crates or even commercially available resin-impregnated, compressed sawdust fire starters. Hey, it doesn't have to be near impossible, it can also be made into fun.

Flint and steel: The only reliable and repeatable nonflammable method of starting fires is using flint and steel. The chances of having a flint supply at hand are slim to none in some parts of the world. If you bang enough different rocks together, you might get a spark, and just about any stone will spark against steel.

You can buy flint and strikers and you can also use just about anything that will make a spark: battery shorting, metal on metal. (An out-of-fuel Zippo or Bic is probably the ideal and cheapest flint and striker.)

The key with this method is the same with any primitive fire-starting method. You need absolutely dry and flammable tinder: tissue paper, very dry newspaper, twigs, leaves, etc. If this is your preferred method, remember to keep a storehouse of mouse bedding, moss, thin grass, fungi, bird's nests, etc., for future use.

Magnification: Camera lenses, water in a jar laid sideways, magnifying eyeglasses, and compass magnifiers can all be used to focus the sun's heat on a small spot to start flammable material smoking. Once again it's not as easy as it looks in the movies. You can't just start a fire with a magnifying glass by pointing. And the old saw about using ice to start fires is great in theory but pretty much impossible in real life. There is, however, a way to start fire with water. When I was in British Columbia with the Forest Service, we would regularly find half-filled jars of water laid on grassy areas by the Indians in an attempt to start fires (with the intention that they would then be hired to put them out). One tip with this method is to make use of the largest amount of light gathering possible: The bigger the lens, the brighter the day, the higher the sun, the better this method works. Obviously, the drier your kindling, the faster your fire will start. It is possible with great patience and extraordinary luck to start a fire by piercing a small hole in bark or paper and then adding or creating a water droplet. This will act as a small magnifying lens and will start a glowing ember with all the right conditions.

What survival guides don't remind you is that your need for fire is highest when the sky is overcast, at night, or when it's windy, cold, raining, and snowing (or all the above). The typical scenario will have your hands shaking uncontrollably, the woods squishy wet, and your snot dripping all over your nice dry tinder. So if you need fire, bring the right tools and save the Indian lore for summer camp.

Chicki-Chick-Boom!

We all know that the best way to start a fire is to have a road flare, a forty-five-gallon drum of flammable liquid, an old wooden hut and three months of trash as kindling. I know this from personal experience from the time I wondered if a road flare could bob in a fifty-gallon pool of freshly pumped AV gas and then woke up on my back watching bits of burning trash float down toward the ground. Yep, a road flare and highly explosive gas works mighty fine.

If you are abandoned or lost but have access to gasoline, diesel, thinners, or other flammables, they can make fire lighting a breeze. They can also turn you into a human signal torch as you hop around blazing brightly in the wilderness. So be careful (as all good guidebooks tell you) and remember that it's the mixture of fuel and air that burns, not just the fuel.

There are other, more mundane items that can turn your eyelashes and hair into a gooey black crust. Sulfuric acid (from car batteries) will burn. Some throat tablets contain potassium chlorate, which, when mixed with sugar on a 3:1 basis, burns brightly. Potassium permanganate is used as a disinfectant and when mixed 9:1 with sugar can be ignited when glycerine is added to it. Glycerine can be found in chemical stores, eyedrops, and antifreeze. Sodium chlorate (found in weed killers) and sugar (mixed 9:1) can be hit with a rock and ignited.

Plastic things like ballpoint pens, running shoes, plastic wrappers, and even your backpack can burn brightly and usually with a lot of smoke. Do you want to burn these things to stay warm or signal passing planes? I won't make that call. I'll just tell you that if something you've found burns and you need a fire, go for it. But there's also the fire you'll need tomorrow when you're naked, cold, and hungry.

Just remember Pelton's rule: The need for a fire is directly related to the time, difficulty, and desperate need to start one.

Wet and Wild

Can you start a fire in a rain forest or in the pouring rain? Only if you are out of the rain and your tinder is dry. How do you get dry tinder? Believe it or not, I wasn't kidding when I suggested belly button lint. Think about fabric lining or unraveled threads (cotton thread from your sewing kit is a suggestion) or shavings from rubber boots. How about flammable glue, deodorants, mosquito netting? You can also check out the flammability of hard plastics: first-aid kits, flashlights, pillboxes, and so on.

There are many things that will burn fiercely in the rain once you get that first small bit of wood burning brightly. Typically, even in the wettest environments you can carve away the outside of the wood until you get to drier inner wood. Look for hardwoods, since softwoods contain too much water. Also look for grass under fallen logs, dried moss under rocks, the inside of dead trees, leaves, litter, twigs, and acorns that are out of the weather under large trees or underbrush. Once the fire is going, look for highly flammable plants like pine boughs or plants that contain oils (pinecones, nuts, and seeds).

To keep your fire going, build a fireplace to keep the rain off and to dry your next round of wood.

No Fuel

If there are no trees or fuel sources to burn, you'll need to be creative but not too desperate. Man-made products or trash can burn, and your own clothing, backpack, accessories, shoelaces, can burn. Synthetics burn hot and bright when wet and give off dark black smoke to signal your location. Sliced up or scraped, synthetics make good kindling if you do find fuel. To use gas as a fuel, soak sand or dirt and do not light your explosive mix directly but rather use a wick or piece of burning material. Fuels from downed planes, float bowls, empty fuel drums, or cooking stove fuel might be available.

Even dirt from roads that are oil-soaked burns well. Look around in abandoned logging camps or construction sites for great greasy patches·that will burn like smudge pots once scooped up and lit.

Rummage through your kit to check the flammability of aftershave, high-proof liquor, insect repellent, and even plastic containers. Lichens, coals, peat, shale, animal droppings, animal fat, carcasses—all provide long-burning fuel.

On the water your options are very limited, but fat from fish or birds can create fuel. Spare rubber, canvas, and supplies can also burn.

Always think the process through, because you may only get one chance to light a fire. Have your fuel gathered, fire spot prepared, and Plan B in place before you begin, because when your fire burns out and your kindling is gone, what will you do? Should a fire be conserved for heat, cooking, light, or purifying water, or should you save your precious fuel to signal passing ships or planes? These questions should be answered first.

A fire that is too successful can also be a danger. An uncontrollable fire could provide you with more problems than you started with.

How to Worship the God of Fire

Fires have burned on earth since lightning blasted the ground and volcanoes rumbled forth glowing lava. The fire should consume much of your time and be managed wisely. But just as important as learning the skills of starting fires is the skill of where fires should be given a home and how they should be worshiped and fed.

Make a Temple

Before you spend an hour rubbing sticks, smashing rocks, and shorting out flashlight batteries (before you found that lighter in your pocket) you need to create an altar for your fire.

Loosely built fires in open spots provide little heat and a lot of smoke and are a pain in the ass to keep lit. What you want is a hot, tight little fire that burns long and strong and provides you with glowing coals, a round-the-clock heater and cooking source, as well as a welcoming friend when you return from your forays into the woods.

Your fire should be in a place that is free from wind and water. This might require raising the base (if it's snowing or on marshy ground) or lowering the base (in windy, unprotected deserts or rainy jungles).

Under ideal conditions, a fire pit should be dug in the ground and a wall of stones built around and under. This prevents the fire from spreading via wind or ignition of grass, allows you to control the amount of oxygen and fuel, and can provide an area for cooking, roasting, or drying. The stones below and around create an ovenlike effect and long-wave radiation after the fire has simmered down. The stones can also be used to heat your bed, cook food, or boil water.

A fire should be close to where you sleep and cook but not close enough to ignite surrounding brush, your bed, or you.

Having a large overhanging and reflective rock is an ideal way to double the amount of light and heat as well as protect your fire from the wind. When there are no rocks, you can build a reflector from large logs, mud, or sand.

High winds and rain are your biggest enemies.

Fire in the Hole

In cases where you have very high winds, a lot of rain, or inclement weather you can create a fire hole. A deep, three-to-four-foot hole with an air channel dug in at an angle from the windward side is ideal. This type of fire burns slower, will not go out in bad weather, and is harder to see. A belowground fire does not produce any radiant heat other than upward but may be a better long-term type of fire.

If you build a fire on snow, you need to make a platform of logs or rocks. You can also build an A-frame-type temple out of green logs so the fire is sheltered not only from the wind but from snow and ice below.

Given a choice between making a log-cabin-style pile of wood or a teepee, go for the log cabin, since the wood will not collapse on itself or fall to the side in a crash of sparks and embers. Remember, you need airspaces and some reflectivity to retain heat and take advantage of the upward draft that fire creates.

Heat Sink and Windbreak

In addition to a reflector, a heat sink and a windbreak can help. A heat sink can be made from large rocks that absorb the heat and can be used as platforms for cooking or even a griddle to cook fish and game on. Rocks like granite, or ones that have been immersed in water, tend to explode and split violently as they heat due to unbalanced internal pressure, so be forewarned. You can use these explosive river rocks to make flat cooking surfaces or cutting boards. The best rocks are the hard granitic types, not soft sedimentary ones, but let's not get too picky.

A windbreak is usually made of branches, logs, earth, or snow and will cause the wind to miss the fire: a three-to-five-foot wall about six feet away should suffice. You don't need to be a meteorologist to figure out where to build the windbreak; you will naturally sit with your back to the wind, which is exactly where the windbreak should be built. The windbreak can also be used to dry wood and wet clothing or to hang kindling, but be aware sparks can ignite it. The law of the jungle says that wherever your windbreak is built will be the opposite of which way the wind blows when the break is finished.

A reflector is used to store and reflect the infrared (radiant) heat that comes from the fire and resultant coals. It will typically be on the opposite side of where you sit and sleep so it can reflect heat back to you (get it? reflector?).

A windbreak and a reflector can be one and the same. You can also back up to a rock wall or boulder, or make a wall by stacking logs or stones, so be creative. The idea is to preserve as much of the fire's heat as possible.

The ability of a fire to radiate heat can be worked to the max by finding large rocks that will absorb and radiate the heat (sometimes for days after the fire has gone out). You can even sleep above an area that has had a fire and feel heat radiate for the entire evening. If you find just the right spot, you can create the oven effect and reflect and tap into every joule of heat, using a minimum amount of fuel.

If you decide to build a fire in an enclosed space, think twice. After spending some time with an old lady who lived in a cave in Turkey, I couldn't help marvel at the black filth on the roof, the rancid stench of burned meat, and black soot rubbed into every pore and crack. (The fact that she lived with her donkey in an adjoining cave didn't do much for the ambience either.) Put your fire in the back of the cave rather than the front. That way wind will not blow smoke into your cave from the entrance.

Remember, too, there are greater dangers other than reduced social acceptability. (Hey, what do you care, you're lost in the woods by yourself?) Carbon monoxide is a by-product along with the blinding smoke and greasy soot. If something does catch fire, you have less chance of escaping and you will smell like a trapper, since you will have effectively smoked yourself like a piece of old jerky.

Maintenance

Keeping a fire going is like running a car. You need to maintain the three basic elements in the right balance: air, fuel, and heat. As each element is increased or decreased, so are the other two. What you will be looking for is the right amount of air, keeping as much heat in the fire as possible, and then adjusting the fuel to maximize your supply.

You need to maintain three kinds of fuel. These are well-sheltered and dry stores of kindling, light woods, and heavy woods. Spend a good part of the morning gathering wood and get into the habit of bringing back wood every time you go out for food.

You should also get into the habit of drying your woods as your fire burns by using your reflector. Then stack it to allow wind to pass through and cover it in case of rain.

The best fuel for a fire is dense, high-energy material that burns slowly with a high heat. Oak and other hardwoods are ideal fuels. Naturally, these are the hardest to find and cut into firewood. One survival trick is to build your campsite around a downed or upturned hardwood tree. That way one of your basic necessities is taken care of and the roots or trunk make an ideal reflector.

Restrain Your Fire

A fire will consume anything flammable thrown into it. That means you can go through a good-sized forest in about a week if you want a funeral-pyre-sized fire. The bigger your fire, the more wood it burns. After you get over the joy of starting your first bush fire, you will learn that you spend more time away from it than in front of it, looking for more fuel in the frigid night. The ideal fire is two large logs leaned against each other, feeding off each other's heat. Then you simply throw medium or small hardwood logs in the middle and use the tops of the logs as a platform to cook on. You don't want a roaring fire because you are, in effect, incinerating precious wood.

To reduce the amount of oxygen, you can bury a fire with loose dry dirt and find that it is still glowing the next morning, ready to be brought to life with the addition of birch bark, pinecones, grass, or small kindling. To get the most out of your fire, think of a barbecue grill with the hood closed; the fire uses less oxygen, smokes more, and gives off less heat. As soon as you expose it to air and the cooling effects, it burns faster and needs more fuel.

Signal Fires

If the purpose of your fire is also to signal for rescue, then visibility might override comfort. You will have to sacrifice that cozy cave deep in the valley for a more exposed higher location. You will need to weigh fuel availability, distance to camp, and a certain degree of comfort. Often it's better to have a fire ready to be lit at a moment's notice when you hear the drone of engines or *whup-whup-whup* of helicopter blades.

When it comes to signal fires, bigger is better. Make sure there is plenty of fuel in the form of dead wood, cactus carcasses, animal droppings, and medium-sized dry branches along with smoke-inducing material like leaves, green boughs, or pine needles. Remember, on a still day a large column of black smoke will be visible for a long time even if the fire is short-lived. On windy days you want to apply the smoke-inducing material less and longer.

You can maintain a long-burning fire by digging a channel and slowly pushing a large log into the fire. Common sense should tell you that green wood burns faster and brighter and hardwoods burn longer and slower. Lighting a signal fire quickly is preferable to leaving a fire burning, since an unmanaged fire poses a danger of forest fire and keeping it lit will consume much of your time.

Light Up Your Miserable Life

Fire as a source of light can be static (the fire) or mobile (a torch). It is wiser to develop a collection of homemade torches and candles rather than keeping the flames on a fire high.

An ideal torch is a length of wet wood with birch bark and pine pitch wrapped in layers. Another would be a homemade candle made from animal fat, drippings, paraffin wax, or grease and a string, cloth, or grass wick. You can also bundle thin twigs together and stuff them with longer-burning highly resinous branches.

Finding the campsite at night is often a problem. This can be partially helped by hanging metallic or reflective scrap items up high or in the trees. They can also be used to mark a path. These will reflect the fire or even moonlight when you're returning.

A fire is not the most useful light source, so practice, and get used to, navigating by the stars and moon. Adapt the fire for its specific purpose, and if you need to have light, keep highly flammable grass, twigs, or pine needles ready to pump up the light instead of adding more wood.

· 18 ·

shelter

Home Is Where You Left Your Dirty Underwear

You could say home is where you hang your hat. Others say home is where the heart is. I like to think that home is where you left your dirty laundry. A lot of hiking and travel is focused on covering distance. Campsites are just flat spots to cook some food, pitch a tent, and then move on. I think it's because of this approach that we don't really have any skills in adapting or building shelters. My education came in the jungle where two hours out of every day were spent cutting and gathering the raw materials for a bush camp. The rains would come every day like clockwork, but by then we would be dry and comfortable in our pandanus-leaf hut, sipping tea and listening to the rain hissing in the jungle.

The function of shelter in the wilds is to keep you warmer, cooler, or drier than you would be without shelter. Not a very ambitious goal and one that is easily achieved. A portable tent fits the bill most of the time, but there's more to shelter than just tossing up a tent.

Let's start with where you should build a shelter. You don't really need shelter in dry, warm, and settled conditions. If you prefer not to be the fast-food joint for insects, scorpions, snakes, or kangaroo rats, you can make a raised bed of dirt, grass, or boughs and throw a light cotton kaffiyeh sprayed with pyrethrin over your head. Or you can do what I do: sleep on the ground and just get bitten.

Here There Be Dragons

The first reaction of most novice campers is to stick a tent right by the river or in a cleared area. There is a beginners' concept that a thin wall of nylon will protect them from marauding bears, mountain lions, and crazed woodpeckers. The only place this works is in Africa, where elephants won't step directly on a tent and hyenas won't tug on exposed hands or heads if they are in a tent. Or so they say.

The rush to grab the most scenic and convenient spot to pitch your tent raises two problems. First, flooding is a very real danger, and it is easy to be drowned in an enclosed tent in the middle of the night. Second, why is the area clear? You may find out when the animals gather round the water cooler in the A.M. I managed to break both rules at once when I pitched a tent on a river sandbar and was awakened by a cattle stampede that ripped large holes in the tent. Luckily, it didn't kill anyone. I have also narrowly avoided being run over by trucks driven by drunken yahoos, attacked by Cape buffalo coming down to the river to drink, and even been bumped and shoved by elephants irritated at finding me sleeping on the roof of a Land-Rover parked in their path. I have also narrowly survived being crushed by a large tree that was hit by lightning and then went thundering to earth next to my tent. Needless to say, I now camp far from the river and up high and in the trees.

There is no one perfect spot for your tent, but some places are better than others.

In a survival situation it is best to take inventory of natural features. I have spent very comfortable nights in a hollow tree, caves, and overhangs. No tent to pitch, no shelter to build, and nothing to pack away the next morning. I have a perverse enjoyment in sleeping flat on my back and listening to lions cough, as it reminds me of my position on the food chain. Some people really don't like the feeling of rodents scurrying over their face or fleas feasting on their exposed buttocks, or elephants, monitor lizards, or crocodiles poking around.

I do, but then again, I hate camping.

Making the Best of a Bad Night's Sleep

A campsite or shelter will never be as comfortable as your bed back home, so often it's not even worth trying. One of my most comfortable evenings was sleeping in an early spring deluge and waking up with the bottom half of my sleeping bag under water with a half-inch layer of ice on top. It wasn't that it was warm; it was just warmer than what faced me when I built up the nerve to leave my waterlogged chrysalis.

Most normal people pack a tent, and old hands still use tarps. Modern tents are ideal. They are self-supporting, lightweight, and, if you remember to bring the fly, sort of waterproof. People also view tents as prerequisites for privacy, getting dressed, and to a small degree a security blanket. Personally, I find them damp, cramped, cold, a pain to carry, and deadly to cook in.

Tarps provide better rain protection, less buildup of humidity, and offer more versatility at a lower cost. They require rope, a couple of sticks, some setup time, and they don't protect against bugs, rodents, and large pickup trucks.

The ideal scenario in good weather is a tarp, a personal-sized mosquito net, and a sense of humor. If it's clear, you throw the tarp back and watch the shooting stars. If it rains, you can lower the tarp and hope the wind doesn't blow too hard. When you get up in the morning, you can raise the tarp for cooking and shade.

I'm not going to lecture you on tents (the salesperson can do that for me), but if you're going to spend all the time, effort, and money to enjoy the great outdoors, why not sleep in it?

Tentless and Clueless

I believe a shelter should only be less miserable than not having one. That means don't overdo it. In the rain build a sheltered platform above the mud; in the jungle use a hammock; in the desert build a trench to keep you cool (and warm); in the winter use a snow cave; and on a beautiful night sleep under the stars.

Let's say we didn't bring a tent and it looks like it's going to rain—a lot. We looked for overturned trees, caves, thick pine trees, overhangs, and found nothing. Looks like we are going to get wet.

In Africa, where trees are either very large or nonexistent, locals can put together a very comfy hut in about half a day. Once it is mudded and painted, it is one of the snuggest, coziest places to spend a day or night. We'll use the same concept, but we're not going to get too artsy. We'll assume that you can cut or break off small saplings and that you once made baskets and Frisbees out of Popsicle sticks.

We're going to make a pair of flat woven panels which will be mudded and stuffed with junk. First you need to gather saplings that are flexible and strong (about a half inch to one inch thick and as long as possible). Weave the sticks against each other to make a flat panel. Keep weaving in smaller sticks, grass, and whatever you find until your panels are long and wide enough to protect you from the rain. Now tear off branches, pine boughs, reeds, and whatever to keep filling up the gaps. Stick things in both ways and use the springy pressure to hold them together.

If you are in a hurry, just make one panel and then prop it up against a tree trunk or two poles you've stuck in the ground. If you are a budding Frank Lloyd Wright, try working mud, sod, or dirt into the panel to create a waterproof barrier. It will need to dry and you need to mix in lots of grass.

Prepare a bed on a high flat piece of ground that affords the best wind protection. To do this, stack up grass, pine boughs, leaves, and whatever dry insulating material you can find.

Lean the two panels against each other and support them with two sticks. Seal off the end that faces the wind, and if you have nothing else to do, make a door using the woven technique. If you are going to be around for a while, make four walls and a roof.

Tips:

- Find a location that is protected from the wind.
- Avoid low spots, riverbanks, open areas, areas near swamps or game trails.
- Trees can provide protection from heavy rains but will continue to drip after the rain passes.
- Don't make your shelter too big, since its goal is to reflect some heat and keep the wind and rain off you.
- Make the best use of naturally occurring shelter and integrate your fire and reflector. Don't forget the fire hazard.

The Snow Cave: Fortress of Solitude

One of the most practical forms of cold weather shelter is the snow cave: a scooped-out hole in a drift. Although all of us would prefer to have nice three-bedroom igloos, they take far too long to construct and are tricky at best.

With the right tools, usually a small snow shovel, you can be inside your new home in less than two hours. This can mean life or death when the temperature drops or a blizzard howls.

It is normal to assume that sitting inside a shelter made of snow is going to be cold. Well, it may be, but it will be less cold that being outside in the wind. Snow is more air than ice (usually between 60 and 90 percent of snow is air), and this air creates insulation.

The first step is to find a large drift, hopefully one that is packed down from wind. Make a hole in the face of the drift and leave enough room so you can stretch out without touching the sides or top. Since cold air flows downward, you want to build a sleeping or sitting platform a good foot above the floor of the cave. Keep in mind that snow will soften from your heat and should be allowed to set, so shape a good-sized platform and stamp it down. Create an insulating layer for your bed from pine boughs, branches, sticks, or whatever is at hand.

If you can remove the snow in chunks or blocks, keep them nice and square to tighten up the entrance hole you made. Use loose snow like mortar to stack and seal the wall. Make sure this wall is tucked up under the edge of the drift so it provides support. You can leave a small crawl space or you can seal it up and poke an airhole in the roof using a long stick.

It is pointless to build a fire or use a stove in a snow cave; a candle is the preferred form of light. The temperature inside will be hovering around freezing: between 32° and 38° depending on how many people are inside and the outside temperature.

Even if you have a tent, a snow cave might be a much more comfortable shelter. It retains less moisture, and can be much roomier.

Snow caves pose a danger from collapse, so don't make the roof too thick. It also takes practice to judge snow textures, shape, and size.

Camp Hygiene and Structure

The final word on shelter is regulating the problems caused by human waste, food preparation, and other activity.

Latrine: If you are in a camp for more than a day, you need to build a latrine. Human waste contains bacteria that contaminate water either directly, through runoff, or from leaching. Dig a hole as deep as you can. Those who are thinking about comfort might want to bend a medium-sized sapling to make a springy seat and build the hole under it. The other method is to dig a hole with a channel leading from a squat area. When you leave, kick in moist leaves and ground debris from around the opening and then bury loosely. The combination of active bacteria and rainfall will break down the waste. It helps to mix everything up to aid the process.

An ideal tip is to choose a place that has privacy and is far enough away so that reversing winds don't perfume your campsite. Your bush loo needs to be at least one hundred yards from water. If you're going to be camping for a long time, it is best to dig a trench and then move down the trench, filling in areas as they accumulate waste.

Water: It may be worth your while to set up water collection areas or even divert a stream, damming it up or building fish traps. Do not bathe in the stream. Instead create an area where soap (if you have any), which is high in phosphates, cannot leach back into the spring.

Cooking/food cache: The location of fuel, visibility for rescue, or a natural reflector such as a rock or upturned tree may dictate where your fireplace will be and hence your campsite. In any case, it is important to have food preparation areas far away from camp and to keep the area clean. Food debris and scraps attract rodents, bears, and scavengers. Burn all scraps and keep your food in a cache, ideally a raised bag suspended by a rope or hung from a tree branch. You can also cool and hide your food by digging a hole, lining it with leaves and sticks, and then covering it with a heavy lid secured by a large rock. Don't forget that grease on clothing or your tent can attract bears.

The PC Thing

After a week or so a campsite has turned from just another piece of wilderness to home. If you've been a good adventurer, you've kept most of the scenery in its place, not burned every bit of available fuel, and not carved your name on every tree.

There are two schools of thought and I'm okay with both of them. The first demands that no blade of grass be bent and no twig be snapped. These are usually activist-type people who work against the devastation wreaked on overused parks and campsites. They're also the same folks who use gravel trails, park their suburbans in the parking lots, use the access roads, and would keep everyone else out of the forest just so they can visit the wilderness when they feel like it.

The "leave no trace" movement makes sense if you are in a completely wild place, but it doesn't work quite as well in used places.

The other group accepts overuse of wild places and pushes for fixed sites where there is a nice flat spot for a tent, a properly constructed fire pit, and even a designated spot for humans and dogs to do their thing. Some of these folks want firewood chopped and waiting so visitors don't tear down the forest every night. This managed approach also makes sense if you think your spot will be used subsequently by someone else. It's up to you to understand both approaches and make the wisest choice.

There is no exception, however, to these things:

- Minimize your impact on the environment.
- Bury all human waste or pack it out.
- Pack out all trash.
- Extinguish, drown, and bury all fires the Smokey Bear way.
- Do not use the scenery for fuel if there is no dead wood. Be conservative in your use of wood and use a portable stove for cooking to preserve wood.
- Even in a survival situation be aware of the dangers of starting a forest fire and control all fires.

· 19 ·

nasty animals

Bambi Strikes Back

E ver since we first slept, cooked, and procreated in caves, we've been scared of animals. We think they're so mean we name our sports teams after them: tigers, sharks, hornets, lions, and other tough-sounding names. But if we took a little reality medicine, shouldn't the meanest, baddest teams be called the Houston Hominids or the Philadelphia People? The Pittsburgh Pedestrians or the Detroit Drivers?

The ever-growing dead alumni list of formerly living species reminds us that the goofy-looking, clumsy, almost hairless *Homo sapiens* can indiscriminately waste mammals, invertebrates, reptiles, or even football-field-sized cetaceans in impressive quantities. And not only can we kill anything that moves, we can defile them by turning them into suitcases and motorcycle jackets, wallets, and edible lingerie. So why is it that we're afraid of animals even while turning Noah's ark into a floating barbecue?

Guilt, pure and simple. It could be that coonskin hat you once had, the bearskin rug you inherited, your grandmother's mink, or even the stupid-looking stuffed alligator you snuck in from Tijuana. Every time we go outdoors, we're just waiting for Hatfield and McCoy payback.

Not very many of us die at the hands of God's creatures. Granted, properly provoked and staged, animal attacks are thrilling stuff, but as a lethal danger, in reality, there's little to fear. Each year, about two hundred people die from animal- and plant-induced injuries in the States. That's eighty fewer than bathtubs kill every year (though *Porcelain Predator* won't be coming to a theater near you anytime soon).

Sure, there are just over a million emergency room visits due to animal bites each year, but it's usually when Junior discovers the family pet doesn't want to go for a ride in the washing machine. There are fewer annual fatalities in the United States from insects than could fill a minivan. A meager dozen people die from snakebites, lizards, and spiders each year. That's not even enough amateur home video to slot in a Fox reality show.

When I was researching this chapter, the one thing people kept telling me to include were "killer bees." "The public has to know about the danger of killer bees!" was the cry. It's as if newly arrived illegal immigrants had formed gangs and were pissed at all the honey they saw on the store shelves. Well, it's true that hornets, wasps, and bees kill forty to sixty people every year, but, still, half as many people do a better job of dying by just falling into holes in the ground.

Others wanted me to write about black mambas, great whites, anacondas, and more. Despite their deep-seated Freudian fears, there wasn't even a statistical blip on the proverbial fatality seismograph. Now, it should be stated that, in the United States, there are under half a million reported cases of emergency room visits due to venomous animals and plants. But we are talking poison ivy here.

Even after digging into my own dark well of experience, I don't have any reason to fear animals. I've been attacked by killer bees twice and have even been tracked by a mountain lion in British Columbia and a leopard in Africa, but after all, I've still eaten a lot more of them than they of me.

I think this is because there is drama in villainizing sharks, crocodiles, snakes, and even amebas in film and television. Sharks make good TV, but hey, consider the ratings if I were to enter a chain-link cage and dangle a Whopper and a six-pack in front of my obese neighbor.

Despite all the nasty PR they get, it seems that animals don't hold it against us. Yes, there are the true stories of Japanese tourists being mauled by a lion because they stood and had their picture taken next to one (they of course sued the tour company), and there are numerous small children cut out of crocodile bellies and smiling surfers showing off their newly reduced and puckered buttocks, but these are still oddities and curiosities. Animals have better things to do than badger humans. Remember, they don't get residuals.

The fact is, the second most dangerous animal in America lives in your house. The most common attack is likely to be when your *Canus domesticus* chomps on your young *Homo sapiens* after they try to put a firecracker in Fido where the sun don't shine. Even in our national parks, pets cause more bites than the wildest, fiercest carnivores.

Animals That Poison You

Things that will poison you usually have to bite you or have you step on them. In both cases you also have to startle them, threaten them, or piss them off in a way that gives them no choice but to strike out.

There may be the odd instant where you are minding your own business and a king cobra comes screaming out of the jungle to protect a nest you never saw. But it's more likely you are at fault.

Top of the poison list are snakes, followed by insects and then marine creatures. We could split hairs and say that the bite of the Komodo dragon is toxic, but if you end up being bitten by a ten-foot lizard, you're probably also going to get eaten long before your bites fester.

Snakes

We have been down on snakes ever since a snake convinced Eve to bite the big one. Snakes are the number one fear of hikers in the South and Southwest, with bears being the bad guys up north. Of the 2,700 species of snakes, only 500 are considered venomous and fewer than 200 can deliver enough venom to be lethal to humans. Around the world about forty thousand to fifty thousand people die from snakebites every year (out of 1 million to 2 million bites reported), and the United States contributes only about a handful to this total. Sri Lanka has the highest number of fatalities from snakebite each year. Myanmar, India, and East (peninsular) Malaysia have the highest number of attacks.

America's pathetic standing in the statistical race for snakebite capital is the result of bites from rattlesnakes and comes from around 45,000 annual snakebite reports (many are plain ole garter snake bites). Approximately 8,000 of the total number of reports in the States are from venomous snakes, and the casualty rate is very low. Just over half of snakebite fatalities are children.

Snakes are not predatory but will attack if stumbled upon by humans. Most bites occur on hands when people reach in and grab bushes, rocks, or logs. People are also bitten when they sit on logs or rocks without looking first. Snakes are active at night and can be found in trees and overhanging branches.

Queeek Queeek, Suck Out dee Poison!

When it comes to treating snakebite, most people have the wrong mental image. If anyone whips out a rusty Buck knife and offers to carve out a canyon of flesh and suck out the poison, run.

This is another area where movies have done us a disservice. Often a bite will not even contain any venom. If it does, you can apply suction to the area in the first five minutes after a bite, which will reduce the harmful effect of the toxin . . . if you keep sucking for half an hour. (You should be on intimate terms with the victim by then.)

The list of what to do when bitten by a snake is more a list of what not to do. Do not cut or open up the bitten area. Gentle suction can be applied in case of a shallow bite immediately after being bitten. Don't rip the poor person's clothes into strips and apply a tourniquet. You run a risk of cutting off blood to a limb in your haste and stressed-out state. Do not give painkillers or a shot of whiskey to ease the pain. Do not soak the affected part in cold water.

Now a few dos. Keep the bitten area below the heart (as opposed to treating a bleeding wound, which would be held above the heart) and calm the victim. Remove any boots, clothing, rings, or jewelry that will cut circulation off from the swelling. These days antivenom is used to counteract the effects of snakebite, so your best use of time and energy is to identify the type of snake and get the person to a medical treatment center.

Dumb tip: Many books tell you to cut off the head of the snake and bring it in for identification. Yeah, sure. Most snakes can outdance a screaming idiot with a machete, possibly creating a second victim.

Rattlesnakes: The pit viper family includes rattlesnakes, water moccasins, and copperheads. Copperheads and water moccasins (cottonmouths) do deliver poisonous venom when they bite, but are substantially less dangerous than rattlesnakes (even if you were hit with every drop of venom they could deliver, you would still be likely to pull through). The rattlesnake's venom is forty-four times as potent. Rattlesnakes are big, can spring (without rattling, by the way), open their mouths wide, and inject their venom in larger amounts than most snakes. They can also strike repeatedly.

The widespread eastern and western diamondbacks are the most dangerous pit vipers in the States. They are large, not retiring when stumbled upon, and have large venom glands.

The bite of a pit viper is painful and swells rapidly. The bite area will turn black-and-blue and can form a blister. Swelling occurs around the bite and may travel toward the heart, causing numbness and swollen lymph glands. Deep bites or large amounts of venom can cause increased rates in pulse and breathing, serious swelling, blurred vision, headaches, sweating, and chills. In nontechnical terms the venom is predigesting you. A bite to a small child is far more dangerous than to an adult.

Coral snakes: Teach yourself this little ditty and you'll do fine: "Red on black, venom lack; red on yeller, kill a feller." Coral snakes with red and yellow bands are venomous, but the lack of a large jaw forces them to make little chewing bites to do any damage. The coral snake is a retiring, shy fellow and more likely to slither away than attack.

Sea snakes: The venom carried by sea snakes found in the oceans can be quite deadly, but they do not deliberately attack humans unless severely provoked. One-third of a drop of their venom can kill a man. They can deliver eight drops in one bite. That bite is from a very tiny mouth, using small sharp teeth, not fangs. Often sea snakes will bite but not release venom.

These warm-water reptiles can be seen floating on the surface, like the yellow-bellied sea snake, or cruising along the bottom. They can dive to depths of over 250 feet and stay under for two hours. They can be found swimming miles from shore and are also found in mating clumps.

Cobras: Cobras kill the most people (mostly in Asia, with about twenty thousand a year killed in India alone) and can claim the most aggressive member of the snake family, the king cobra. This twelve-to-eighteen-foot-long monster is unique because of its intelligence, aggressiveness, and ability to go after animals as large as elephants. In fact, a king cobra has enough venom to kill a full-grown Indian elephant in three hours. The king cobra feasts on other snakes, is the only snake that builds a nest, and is the only snake where both sexes protect their brood of about two dozen with an aggression that makes it the most feared snake in the world.

A king cobra will come slithering out of the woods and repeatedly attack a human and often chase and attack humans who come to the aid of the original victim. It splays its trademark hood, raises up almost to a person's eye level, and then comes after its victim at a high rate of speed. It will lunge, bite, and then chew, injecting its venom. Often it will stay around after the initial attack. Although the venom is not the most poisonous, it kills a human in about twenty to thirty minutes.

Animals That Eat You

Crocodiles/Alligators

Crocs are supposed to be found in salt water and alligators in fresh. Not true. Crocs are also found in freshwater lakes, rivers, and estuaries, and both can be found wandering on land. Alligators are known to snag a small child or dog or two, but are generally not dangerous outside of country and western songs.

Crocodiles are different. They kill about a thousand people a year, mostly in Africa and Australia. "Salties" *(Crocodilus porosus)*, as they are called in Australia, are the Asian version, but the nastiest is the Nile crocodile *(Crocodilus niloticus)*, which is found from Egypt to Madagascar. Asian crocs are big in Australia, Borneo, New Guinea, and other remote areas. Both are very dangerous and both can grow to lengths of twenty-five feet.

Crocodiles look docile but are mean. They sit just slightly submerged at the banks of rivers waiting for game to come and drink. Then blam, out they explode, pulling their prey under the water and doing their characteristic death roll as they try to simultaneously drown and rip the victim. They then stuff the carcass in their underwater dens to eat later. Crocs have very slow digestion, which is one of the reasons you can cut them open and find bits of people long after they've been snacked on.

I was once at an African park where people were watching crocs sun themselves behind a three-inch-high chain-link fence. Never having seen a chain-link fence that small and noting the tourists snapping pictures just a few feet away from the grinning crocs, I asked a waiter who the genius was that built the fence. His answer was not what I expected. "Oh, that fence, sir—well, we had a flood two days ago. Normally the fence is six feet high." I didn't tell the tourists.

If you're ever attacked, bear in mind that the eyes of a crocodile are the only "soft spot," although you can also jam a croc's jaw open with a stick. Don't believe me? Try it.

Sharks

It may be comforting to know that a lot more sharks are eaten by people every day than vice versa. Fishery experts put the number of sharks killed for food or their fins at about 100 million, whereas the twenty-one species of sharks kill fewer than thirty people every year. (That's around the world. The main culprits are the tiger shark, great white, bull shark, sand tiger, and bronze whaler.) This makes it a longer-than-long shot in the statistical category: Odds are one in 100 million that you would be attacked, one in 300 million you would be killed (like playing Russian roulette by remote control from a different state). The fifty to one hundred or so shark attacks that are reported every year make lots of headlines, but less than a third of the victims die from the attack.

Sharks normally feed along the ocean bottom at night and in dim light. Ninety percent of shark attacks occur in less than five feet of water, where visibility is poor. Sharks are attracted by blood, bait, rapid vibrations, and shiny objects. Wearing your Mr. T starter set after you cut yourself shaving is not good here. Peeing in the water at the sight of your first shark is not good either. Ship sinkings attract sharks, as does the dumping of fish entrails and trash.

If you see sharks or feel nervous, swim strongly and rhythmically away or to shore. Scuba divers are best advised to just enjoy the view, but if you're a little nervous, get against the floor or a reef wall. Abandon your catch if you have been spearfishing. If sharks get too inquisitive, you can thump them on the nose, eyes, or gill area and they will swim away. Often victims are cut by a shark's abrasive skin and not by its teeth.

Watch out for sharks in estuaries (where they breed) and off docks where fishermen dump offal.

Overrated but Deadly

There are a number of animals that inspire fear but mostly in the animal, who is more likely to be killed by a human than vice versa.

Bats: Less than 1 percent of bats tested internationally have rabies. In the last two decades there have only been thirty-three human fatalities from bat-related rabies cases. If you are terrified of giant fox bats with three-foot wingspans, relax—they might gum you to death but they prefer munching on fruit. Vampire bats need you to be fast asleep before making a neat painless incision and lapping up the blood. Will you then order your steaks raw and shun daylight? Not likely.

Mountain lions: Also called puma or cougar, the mountain lion is a solitary animal who primarily attacks children. Although the hype is high, the number of actual attacks is low. British Columbia (four deaths, twenty attacks in a year) is the capital of cougar attacks, with California (two deaths, six attacks in a year) close behind. Montana officials report 122 puma/man conflicts in a six-year period. The number of "attacks" or "conflicts" tends to be inflated by reports stemming from the puma's habit of tracking people at a too-close-for-comfort distance (as I have learned firsthand) but not really attacking.

The puma is a highly territorial animal, and being a large cat, it can move quickly and track silently. When cubs are present, there is little if anything you can do to dissuade the mother. Climbing a tree has worked for friends of mine, since the primary goal of the cat is to make you leave (even though they are quite able to climb trees). In their case, numerous flare-gun rounds fired at pointblank range did not deter the cat. Finally, boredom won out and the cat wandered off.

Cougars will track a victim and kill from behind with a bite to sever the spinal cord. Facing the animal and being aggressive is your best bet. Don't play dead or you will be dead. Turning and running is an invitation to an attack. Pepper spray and noisemaking items like whistles or screaming can help.

Tigers/lions/leopards/jaguars: Yes, it is true that large predators will eat humans but only under very extreme circumstances. People-eating tigers typically are sick and old, preying on villagers or their animals. The tiger's domain is limited to India and zoos. Lions will definitely attack a human who is dumb enough to get too close. (Other predators like hyenas and mountain lions will attack but not stay around for supper.) More people are eaten by dogs and crocodiles (as corpses) than by lions and tigers.

Cats typically attack from behind when hunting. For example, tiger deaths in Bengal were about sixty a year before fishermen began wearing masks on the back of their heads, which resulted in a dramatic decrease in tiger attacks. The annual death toll is now around three. So don't break and run if you see any type of cat. Second, cats will always pounce, so look for a twitching, springing action in the loins prior to a jump.

Should you be afraid of large cats? If you are like me and have been stalked by a leopard in Tanzania, mountain lion in B.C., and lions in Kenya, you'll learn quickly that you are the equivalent of a Domino's pizza delivery without the box. The definition of fear is to walk through the chest-high tan grass not knowing exactly how benign or deadly your feline companions will be.

Bison: In fifteen years fifty-six people have been killed by buffalo. That's about the same as cougars. Most attacks are caused by exactly what you would expect, people insisting on treating them like dumb cows and having their pictures taken next to them. Kodak-happy tourists are then treated to a short violent thrill show as they are butted, gored, stomped, and crushed.

Wolves: There has never really been any truth to the image of the lonely trapper being pursued by a pack of red-eyed, slobbering wolves.

Coyotes/foxes: Mainly consumers of chickens, small pets, and rodents, the coyote has an affinity for expensive fluffy dogs who live in pricey new ranchette suburbs. Coyotes often use a bitch in heat to attract Mitsey before the pack descends, ripping it to shreds.

Underrated and Deadly

They are cute, do funny things, sell a lot of stuffed animals, and appear in kids' cartoon shows. They also kill and injure more people than you would guess.

Hippos: You don't have to spend too much time in Africa to learn that hippos are the most dangerous land animals. They kill more locals than crocs, lions, or any other large African game do. Hippos are normally seen floating like giant black turds in water, usually along the banks of muddy rivers. However, at dusk they come to graze on grass—the same nice flat grassy spots that humans camp on. Hippos are harmless once you are safely in your tent (although they do make a god-awful munching and crunching sound when they eat). It's when you wander out for a midnight pee that you should be careful. Once hippos sense there is something between themselves and the water, they rotate their little pig tails, run like hell, and begin thrashing with their long teeth and large jaws.

A hippo is unpredictable in the water and often attacks boats and kayaks. If possible, stay in the boat or head to shore. A hippo can run along the bottom of a river or lake and can hold its breath for five minutes. If you are being charged by a hippo, you will see a curious V-shaped wave as three thousand pounds trundle toward you.

Cape buffalo: Cape buffalo are found in Africa. They are often erroneously called water buffalo, but, unlike their domesticated Asian brothers, the wild African version likes to sit in dense thickets and then explode out at trespassers. Cape buffalo are usually blundered into when you're wandering through thickets or camping too close to water. Listening for the sound of the tick birds is your best and only survival tip.

Elephants: Elephants have become tolerant of humans in game parks, since they are forced to endure thousands of zebra-striped combis dodging in and out of their way in the drivers' tip-fueled efforts to get close snapshots. Elephants outside of the parks are always considered dangerous, and they are very territorial. Male elephants are particularly dangerous in their musth, or mating season. (Look for solitary males and a dark dribbly patch on the side of their head.) All adult elephants get very dangerous toward the end of the dry season when they become hungry and irritable. Despite what you've seen in movies and on TV, elephants do not attack with much bellowing, ear flapping, and stomping. This is a false charge to warn you off. When they do attack, they make no noise, put their head down to get their tusks at eye level, and come at you like a freight train. Typically, an elephant will use its tusks to lift you or your vehicle up and then charge repeatedly. Having been the victim of and around victims of elephant charges in Asia and Africa, I can attest to two things. First, the chargees deserved it for doing something to irritate the animal, whether it was driving too close, ignoring a false charge, or, believe it or not, wearing red socks. Second, we all survived.

Dogs: There are about 2 million cases of attacks or bites from dogs in the United States every year. Worldwide, you can bump into a tame or wild dog just about anywhere. Dog attacks usually occur in an urban environment and around where you live. Many are unprovoked, but often people inadvertently make a dog think it is being attacked. Small children sticking their hands and faces in a dog's mouth is just one nasty example. I recommend not approaching even docile animals.

If you are attacked, the dog will typically go for your arm or leg. If you wrap a jacket or thick protection around your arm, he will go for that and hold on for dear life. A trained guard dog will attack the groin or throat.

If you are bitten by a dog, the first thing that comes to people's minds is rabies. A rabid animal is rare in North America and Europe but can be a real threat in poorer countries. Tetanus is a more likely problem and infection is a definite one. A dog bite must be cleaned out properly and should always be looked at by a doctor. Cleaner than a hound's tooth is a fairy tale, since even kids know that dogs spend most of their time licking their rear end or sniffing others'.

If you do get rabies, it is serious and is considered life-threatening. Rabies is a viral disease and can have a mortal effect on the nervous system. It exists throughout the world with the exception of Sweden, Norway, Malta, Australia, and the British Isles. It is transmitted through saliva (not necessarily through bites).

Rabies vaccines no longer hurt like hell. Back in the old days maybe, but today it is a relatively painless treatment, using intramuscular injections. The days of being tortured with twenty-one daily painful injections of live vaccine into your abdomen are over (in this country at least), so do not risk a very painful lingering death from rabies because you're squeamish about needles.

Worldwide, there are 30,000 deaths each year from rabies, more than 25,000 of them in India, usually from dog bites. Often there are epidemics with raccoons, bats, or other common animals being infected by each other.

Gentle Ben Chows Down

There is about one death by bear every year in the States. Over half (60 percent) are the result of grizzly attacks and the rest due to black bears. This solitary annual occurrence has sparked more fear in hikers than the much more dangerous threat of getting hantavirus from a rodent.

Are there any guidelines? Well, there is something to be learned from one of the very first attacks in Yellowstone. In 1907 a visitor prodded a bear cub with his umbrella to entice it to perform for the camera. He was attacked and killed by its mother for his directorial efforts.

Are there any other grains of knowledge we can glean? Not really. Most grizzly attacks occur at night; black bear attacks occur primarily during the day; and the attacks are more likely to be fatal outside national parks. There are about six hundred black bears and 9 million annual visitors in Great Smoky Mountains National Park, and not one fatality from bears has occurred. The places where we send tourists to be attacked by bears are Glacier and Yellowstone Parks. Not because they harbor a particularly ornery breed of bear, but because they feature a lot of people and a lot of bears. There have been nine bear-related deaths since Glacier became a park. In Yellowstone there have only been six bear-related deaths over the last quarter century, but there have been more attacks (ninety-seven injured) despite the general area being home to only 250 to 350 bears. All in all, more bears are killed by humans than vice versa. Every year, up to thirteen bears are killed by attackees, poachers, and rangers in Yellowstone alone.

Which bear should you fear the most? It is Gentle Ben that should give you the heebie-jeebies and not the Pleistocene-era-looking grizzly. Why? The answer is as obvious as the turds in front of you. Close inspection reveals that the large majority of the grizzly's diet is plants. It is the black bear that hunts down humans as prey.

Making noise in the wild gives a bear advance notice and prevents you from bushwhacking him, but there are conditions where even playing Metallica with a boom box would not rouse a denning ursus. (You thought they were hibernating, didn't you?) Thick brush, loud river rapids, and rustling trees can also mask the noise people make.

Bears have so-so eyesight and average hearing. They also have no predators in the wild and like to cruise through open areas and along trails and
roads. It is because of their laziness, lack of fear, and poor hearing that they
often bump into people on trails and back roads. A startled bear's first instinct is to charge, although if he is far enough away, he'll take off into the
woods. The vast majority of charges are designed to scare you off, not because the bear likes his meat hot and sweaty.

The most nerve-wracking bear meetings occur with bears who are ha-
bituated to campsites, roadsides, garbage dumps, and trash cans, so you not
only get a lengthy rude visit from a bear but you will probably learn his name
from the ranger afterward. These bears won't even pay attention to your
banging, yelling, screaming, and gesticulating as they go about the daily task
of foraging through your nice new tent. Most ranger stations will have a
photo collection of motor homes and camper shells shredded by inquisitive
bears. Your best bet with a bear that doesn't pay attention to you is to leave
and come back when he or she is done.

Anyone who spends a lot of time in the woods finds bears to be a common sight and a good reminder to keep a clean campsite. In areas that have
a lot of "Warning: Bear" signs you have to be extra fastidious in keeping your
site, your clothes, tent, gear, and surroundings free from grease smells, open
toothpaste tubes, and some say even used tampons.

Don't take my cavalier attitude as the reaction to all bear encounters.
Bears do attack and kill people and they do pose a danger in the wild. They
are particularly dangerous when protecting cubs and when surprised or cor-
nered. You may not see the cubs, so it's always wise to back off anytime you
see a bear. Bears also protect kills. If you do come across a bear, in most cases
the bear will inspect you and shuffle off. However, if you meet one ambling
down the trail not paying attention, it might still charge you for reasons
you'll never know. Bears also like to hide in thick brush and can come ex-
ploding out without warning.

The bear facts:

- Bears rarely attack humans who don't bushwhack them.
- It is easy to bushwhack a bear.
- If things appear calm, give the bear an escape route. If things appear
  tense (rapid, aggressive movements from the bear), you are about
  to get mauled. Act accordingly. It's best to back away making
  noise and waving. On the West Coast you can try climbing a tree
  and the worst that can happen is that the bear will sit and wait
  below, occasionally trying to shake the tree to dislodge you. On
  the East Coast black bears may scamper right up after you; grizzlies will flick you out of the tree like a meatball on a satay stick.

- Make your campsite safe by bagging and suspending your food. Secure a rope between two trees (remember that bears climb trees) with your food hanging from the middle at least twelve feet off the ground. If you forget this, you might awaken to see a bear playing piñata with your gorp.
- If a bear casually enters your campsite, try to scare it away. If it's not impressed, let the bear do what it wants. Make sure it has an exit and that you are not blocking it. If you are in a group, gather together to look bigger.
- If you are attacked by a bear, the idea of curling up and playing dead works sometimes (repeat: sometimes) on the West Coast with grizzlies but is not so effective on the East Coast with black bears. Hungry black bears have no problem munching on your supposedly dead but still warm buttocks.
- If the bear falls for your play-dead routine, remember that it may hang around and watch you out of curiosity.
- Pepper spray is the ideal self-defense tool for a bear attack, although the effects only last about ten minutes (one-third to one-quarter of the time a human is incapacitated). Pepper spray should be carried on the belt and sprayed when the bear gets within forty feet (most sprays reach twenty to thirty feet). As the bear runs into the spray, it will stop and run in the opposite direction. If another person is being attacked and you spray both bear and victim, the effects of pepper spray will wear off after about forty minutes (see chapter 9).

Things That Will Sting You

Insects of the order Hymenoptera (thin-waisted insects) include bees, hornets, and fire ants. These insects carry not only a sting but a touch of malicious venom when they strike. They are attracted by heat, motion, and vibration. Often they will swarm and attack en masse, usually in reaction to one of their members being attacked or squashed. The biggest danger here is anaphylaxis, a tough word that describes an allergic reaction that chokes off breathing. Between fifty and one hundred people in the United States die every year from stings, primarily due to the allergic reaction brought on by the venom.

Bees: Bees go about their business of gathering pollen and making nests without any desire to attack or hurt people. Even when bees swarm in large globs, they can be picked up and worn like a hat without fear of stinging. Why? Because they don't have a hive to defend. Bees *will* sting if you squash one or disturb a hive or nest. When confronted with bees, get out of range. It's not worth doing the watusi thinking that you can outgroove thousands of angry flying insects. Running will increase your respiration rate and you may end up ingesting the buggers. Instead—if you can't stand still—being calm and slowly moving away can reduce the threat of being stung. Even if you are stung, resist the urge to freak out. Move away without flailing your arms.

Always carry an injectable epinephrine (ask your doctor for a prescription) in case of serious allergic reaction by you or others. Ten stings are considered dangerous, and a hundred stings can be fatal. In cases where there is mild reaction the victim can be given an oral antihistamine (usually designed for colds and allergy relief). People who have been stung by bees many times (e.g., beekeepers) can be more prone to allergic reactions.

Killer bees: Africanized honeybees are just honeybees with attitude. The kinder, gentler bees (which actually kill more people here than Africanized ones) came from Europe with the settlers in the 1600s. European bees did not do well in tropical areas, so in 1956 researchers brought African honeybees from the Dark Continent to Brazil. They began migrating north and are now found in the Southwest United States. It is expected that they will eventually displace their European cousins as they interbreed and spread. Although there is little physical difference between European and African honeybees, you'll quickly get to know the Africanized variety. They attack more readily, in larger groups, and swarm more often. They also have no problem setting up shop in gopher holes, tires, or places their European brothers would consider the low-rent district.

But let's get to the basics. How do you survive an attack of killer bees? Remember that bees are defending their nest. Often you will not see or be able to prevent an attack by Africanized bees, because they are attracted by vibration, sound, or proximity from up to forty yards away. Within seconds, they will attack in a swarm. Your head is their preferred target. Their goal is to get you away from their nest, so by all means oblige them. Run like hell. Do not flail or swat, since you should be using your hands to protect your head. Don't bother screaming or yelling. Just close your mouth (to avoid breathing in a bee) and move your hands in a crushing, rolling motion around the surface of your head, as if you were brushing them away from behind your ears, eyes, and neck. If a friend is being attacked and you come to his or her rescue, you will also be attacked. Spraying bug killer or DEET is moderately effective, but you should be telling your friend to run like the dickens and have faith that the bees will give up once you reach a safe distance (usually about one hundred yards) from the nest. Once you get far enough away, scrape the throbbing stingers off with a fingernail. Since most of the stings will be around your head, find a volunteer. Also watch for bees trapped in your clothing. Do not grab or try to squeeze the sac or you'll inject yourself with more venom. The normal person can usually stand one bee sting per ten pounds of body weight. If you are allergic to bee stings or are concerned about the number of stings, seek medical help for anaphylactic shock. In severe cases a tracheotomy may be required. It's unlikely you'll ever buy another box of honey-dipped Cheerios again.

I can tell you from personal experience that if a group is attacked by killer bees, your best bet is to stand still and slowly walk away, crushing the insects as they land on you and sting you, keeping your mouth closed and nostrils covered. The swarm will then divert to the frantic screaming and waving victims around you.

Sweat bees: This tropical nuisance should not be confused with killer bees. They are tiny (about 4 mm, or just over a quarter of an inch long) inquisitive insects that mop up the sweat off your exposed skin and clothing. As with all other bees, just being cool and understanding why they sting will prevent you from being stung.

Ants: Africa has given us the killer bee and South America has donated fire ants. Fire ants explode up your leg the second you tread on one of their nests. Up to 25,000 nasty ants will get about crotch-high and then dig in with their mandibles. Not content to just bite you, they then jab their behinds over and over again, redefining the meaning of pain.

The area will blister and itch for about a week afterward. You can experience an allergic reaction from multiple ant bites. The treatment is the same for any severe allergic reaction. Up to thirty people in the United States (mostly in the South) have died from fire ant attacks.

Keeping Them at Bay

There is a whole host of biting insects, but it is rare that people come down with serious infection or disease. Insect bites can be prevented by staying clean, using mosquito nets, and wearing long-sleeved clothing and insect repellent (both on you and in the room you sleep or live in).

This is probably the best spot to talk about DEET. DEET (diethyltoluamide) has been touted as the best, the only, and the "must have" form of insect protection. There is a common misconception that DEET kills insects. It doesn't. It doesn't even repel all insects. And spraying it like a machine gunner on a PT boat is more likely to dissolve your plastic watch, your tent, rain gear, sunglasses, and anything made from vinyl, nylon, rayon, spandex, or other groovy synthetics. DEET is also toxic, causes skin rashes, and has a short life when it's humid or if you're sweating. It can sting like hell when it gets in your eyes or cuts, tastes like shit when it gets on your food or water bottle, and usually spills in your pack or rubs off from your hands, ruining all those nice plastic windows and cases of expensive gizmos like GPS's, compasses, and radios. I have not been hired by the anti-DEET coalition; I just want you to understand the proper use of the stuff before you turn into a babbling psychotic straining through frosted plastic eyeglass lenses.

Apply DEET sparingly on collars, ankles, and wrists. Reapply when necessary. Do not use on children or pregnant women. DEET plus tropics plus slathering it on equals rash. Try a little before you try a lot. Carry it in 100 percent liquid formulation and do not use it as a spray. Double-bag it to protect it in case of spillage. Consider and experiment with other methods of insect deterrent and advise others of the potential problems of DEET. Hey, maybe you'll try a week in the woods without anything.

An alternative—or complement—to DEET these days is permethrin in clothing, which acts as a powerful bug deterrent.

Black flies/horseflies: You see what looks like a large housefly land on your arm. You watch it in amusement and then *Cheeeerisstt!* that hurts. This is a member of the Diptera order, an evil group of biting flies that can drive strong men crazy and convince women to take up tractor pulling instead of hiking. Diptera explode upon the scene when there is water, a short summer, and heat. At that point, clouds of black flies will follow you like Egyptian hawkers at the Pyramids. There is no way to shake them. The only respite you'll have is when the sun goes down and flies stop biting (and of course the mosquitoes begin). Wind, smoke, thick protective clothing, cold temperatures, bug netting (soaked with permethrin), or inviting a fat, sweaty hiking partner along are your only defenses.

Fleas, lice, and bedbugs: If you are going to slum it in third-world countries, you may run into these roommates. Most of these fellows go hand in hand with poor hygiene.

Head lice and genital lice (crabs) are tiny, slow-moving creatures picked up by direct contact, sharing a comb or brush, or sleeping with someone who has lice or crabs. Your best bet is malathion (a strong insect killer) or delousing shampoos.

Bedbugs are exactly what they sound like and wait until you are fast asleep to bite you and drink your blood. Look for small bloodstains on your flophouse mattress. Spray the room with an insect fogger or leave a light on to attract the bugs away from you. Their bite is painful, itchy, and leaves a red spot.

Fleas are found in many places where there are domestic animals and poor hygiene. Fleas do carry plague but it is a very rare occurrence these days. They appear as small dark brown spots and they jump just as you go to grab them. Flea eggs are tiny white orbs that look like round table salt. Young and mature fleas usually hop around the floor or carpets and will bite at your ankles. They can also be in beds and will drill you just like a wildcatter in Oklahoma and leave a series of itchy red bites. Don't scratch them or they can get infected (good advice for any insect bite) and for Christ's sake take a shower, you pig.

Leeches: Leeches are very common in tropical and temperate areas and are picked up as you walk along trails, sleep at night, or swim. They are very thin, slender, and dark when they start, but they can gorge themselves into fat ribbed pigs. Often they nab a vein and look like Liz Taylor after a binge at Dunkin' Donuts.

Leeches enjoy any area where the skin is thin and the blood is close to the surface. The bite is painless and they use an anticoagulant that allows the blood to flow freely.

Insect repellent, salt, tobacco juice, or lit cigarettes will convince leeches to let go. They can also be brushed off but may be stuck to you, encouraging more bleeding. Expect the clean white circular bite to bleed for a couple of hours and itch for a couple of days. If left alone, leech bites leave nice white circles, but if scratched, they can get infected.

Centipedes: Centi- (one hundred legs) and milli- (one thousand legs) pedes always confuse people. Centipedes are the bad guys and have one pair of legs per segment. Millipedes are benign creatures that walk like a wave at a football game. They are found under bark, in leaf litter, and in damp places. Centipedes can give you a painful bite that is not lethal, but will make you pay attention next time you pick up the cute little bugger.

Mites: Mites (or chiggers) are pinhead-sized biting insects that leave a painful, itchy red spot. They usually end up biting where they bump into dead ends or tight clothing. This means your groin, armpits, or waist. Mites can hang on, and the itching, caused by a small hypodermic or straw (called a stylostome) in your skin, can last ten days. Mites crawl up legs when outdoors and can be prevented by socks over pant cuffs and insect repellent.

Ticks: Ticks carry a number of diseases and can lodge under your skin for quite some time. After a day of wood walking check behind your knees, armpits, buttocks, and other soft warm places. Ticks burrow in headfirst and then expand into gray, grape-sized monsters as they suck blood. They must be gently removed or the head will break off and stay in the skin, causing infection.

If you find a tick, brush it off. If it has dug in, gently scrape it off and make sure the head has come with it. A hot match head, a drop of permethrin, or a hot knife will make ticks back up quickly. Spraying or rubbing permethrin will kill ticks; DEET neither deters nor kills ticks.

Ticks are best known as the vectors of Lyme disease (first discovered in Lyme, Connecticut, in the mid-1970s) and Rocky Mountain spotted fever. Look for the bull's-eye rash, and remember that the symptoms of these diseases can take a month to appear (flulike symptoms, headache, nausea, and chills). I once had the pleasure of being swarmed by prenymphal ticks and spent a whole day picking them out of my body. A knife should not be used to cut; you should use a pin or credit card to pick or push them out.

Spiders: All thirty thousand species of spiders can bite, and all have some level of venom. The most venomous in the United States is the female black widow. Between two and four people die each year from black widow bites, but a healthy adult should come through with a good dose of painkillers. If possible, you should have it checked by a doctor as soon as possible.

The black widow female has an orange hourglass on her abdomen and is an inch or less in size. You can stumble on the black widow, found in the U.S. Southwest, but she rarely seeks victims out. The bite delivers a sharp pang followed by a small red bump. Sometimes there is severe muscular cramping in the abdomen and back, burning and numbness in the feet, headache, nausea, vomiting, dizziness, and heavy sweating. Keep the victim calm, and cool the bite area with ice water to prevent spread of venom and reduce the pain.

The fiddleback or recluse spider is found in forests and homes (primarily in the South and Midwest) and has a painless bite. However, in one to five hours a red blister appears and a bull's-eye ring forms a bluish circle around the blister, with a red circle around the outside of the bull's-eye. Any volcanic-style skin ulcers should be looked at by a doctor. The victim may feel weak and develop a rash, chills, or fever. The wound will heal after a week or two, but the bite can be fatal in small children.

Spiders are found just about anywhere. They bite when you squash them in your boots or clothing or reach for firewood or brush.

Rogues' Galleries or Gross-out Winners

In Equatorial Africa there is a fly called the *tumbu (Cordylobia anthropophaga)*. There is nothing extraordinary about this fly other than it likes to lay its eggs in the dirt, which are then transferred to clothes or skin. The maggots then hatch from eggs and burrow into your skin. The baby *tumbus* grows to about 15 mm long, or just over half an inch, and they raise large boils under your skin. If you don't want to replay *Rosemary's Baby,* you can deliver the slimy bugger stillborn by putting mineral oil on the two breathing holes of the invader. This suffocates the insect, and it can then be squeezed or pulled out with tweezers. Make sure you get all the bits or they will cause infection.

I am told that what the thrashing maggot does while it is suffocating is an unusual and not-to-be-missed experience. If you want to be the proud mother or father of a nice fat grub (or just want something you can show off at cocktail parties), wait about two weeks. It will crawl out of the hole in the center of the boil, leaving it to heal.

Not grossed out yet? There is also the much more common chigger *Tunga penetrans* found in dry or sandy conditions (both indoors and outdoors) in Equatorial Africa and South America. These are fleas that bury themselves in your soles or toenails when they are about to give birth. The mother will die, causing an infection and inflammation, and then the whole brood is born into this world in an explosion of pus and blood. You need to dig them out with a needle or razor and then clean the wound area with alcohol or antiseptic.

Still feel like having lunch? Okay, then, there's the human botfly *(Dermatobia hominis),* which actually lays eggs on mosquitoes, which then infect you with their bite. These babies grow to two centimeters after two or three months under your skin and once again don't take kindly to being suffocated. Most folks just whack 'em out with a sharp knife. Some keep 'em as pets.

Finally, there is the much-feared *candiru,* a small fish that lives in the waters of the Amazon. Local guides will tell you that the minuscule and spiny candiru will seek warmth, especially in a stream of warm urine from an unsuspecting eco-trekker. (The fish wiggles into the urethra and lodges itself.) This knee-slapper has made it into just about every adventure book on the Amazon, but, like man-eating piranhas, no actual incidents accompany this hoary old tale.

The World's Most Dangerous Animal

Okay, now for the big quiz. What is the most dangerous animal in the United States? Which fanged behemoth sends more of us to our maker than other species? Bears? Crocs? Cobras? Nope.

Beware the common deer.

Every year startled deer send an average of 150 people to their maker and injure another 9,000 to 16,000. Compare that to the U.S. Park Service report that in one ten-year period only three people were killed by bears in national parks. About 4 percent of the quarter million vehicle crashes involve animals, mostly deer. Some insurance companies report that deer cause, or are involved in, half a million crashes, averaging $2,000 per vehicle damaged. So beware of the 18 million to 28 million deer in this country, since they are growing in number and planning desperate attacks against humans, using roadside suicide volunteers.

· 20 ·

hypothermia

Brain-Dead and Loving It

If your idea of cold weather exploration is picking out dessert in the frozen-food section, you won't have much respect for or interest in hypothermia. This can be a deadly mistake.

Hypothermia means "under" *(hypo)* "temperature" *(thermia)*, but more important, it means "brain-dead and not knowing it." Lowered temperatures can create a sense of well-being and sluggishness before you suddenly realize that you are freezing to death and not able to do anything about it.

The core of your body is the thermostat that controls your brain's decisions to sweat, circulate blood, shiver, and perform other involuntary acts. But the sensors are at skin level. The ideal operating temperature for the skin is about 72° (on your palms and feet) to 78° (your head, groin, and armpits), and the ideal humidity is between 70 and 90 percent. All this temperature control is measured at the thin layer between your skin and the first layer of clothing.

When you are sitting watching the tube, you put out about the same heat as your TV, one hundred watts. If you leave the window open and you start to shiver, your body automatically turns up the heater. Now you're kicking out the equivalent of a five-hundred-watt bulb and you are thinking, "Man it's cold, I better put a sweater on," or something equally intelligent. If you are outside and you stop shivering, your body has begun to focus on other things and you are entering the danger zone.

Cold Stress

During the winter it is easy to travel from car to mall to office without much concern for the raging blizzard outside. As soon as the power dies, however, you can be face-to-face with a survival situation. There are some very simple steps for cruising through these scenarios.

Buy a stand-alone, nonelectrical heating device. Propane-powered space heaters can be fire hazards but will get you through an ice storm or blizzard. Keep a parka, snowpack boots, a sleeping bag, food, water, and spare gas in the trunk of your car. If your car breaks down, you can survive a day or two in comfort. Remember in both cases that operating a heating device or engine generates poisonous gases and you should allow for ventilation.

THE HUMAN BODY LOSES HEAT VIA:	SOLUTION
Respiration	Wear a scarf, enclosed hood.
Evaporation	Wear breathable clothes.
Conduction	Insulate from cold surfaces.
Radiation	Dress in layers, cover parts.
Convection	Find shelter from the wind.

Hypothermia (when the body temperature is lowered to 95°F or less) is easily the biggest danger an adventurer will experience. This life-threatening event usually occurs when people push too far and too hard in inclement weather. It is also a direct result of falling into cold water while boating, crossing rivers, or being in rainstorms at high altitude. Overexertion, windchill, low temperatures, moisture, hunger, and moisture loss can all bring on hypothermia. At greater risk for hypothermia are the newly bred (infants have a larger body surface relative to total mass) and almost-dead (older people have a lower metabolic rate, and 10 percent of over-65s have some temperature-regulating defect; they also consume 25 percent of prescription drugs).

When you're adventuring in cold climates, hypothermia should be the first danger to look for. When a coroner wants to find out when someone died, he jams a meat thermometer into the warm gooey center and measures the temperature. The time it takes for the core temperature to drop determines the number of hours since death. And so it is with hypothermia. It is a slow path to death, but it follows the gradual loss of core heat (usually aggravated by dumber and dumber decisions made by a cold-addled brain).

Keep in mind that people taking certain drugs like antidepressants, sedatives, tranquilizers, and cardiovascular drugs have a higher risk of suffering from hypothermia.

Windchill

Windchill should not be visualized as a hurricane-like force ripping flags and freezing muklukked Eskimos into ice sculptures. Windchill can be as subtle as a light breeze making you shiver or or as harsh as your flesh being frozen within thirty seconds.

The effect of windchill makes a considerable difference to the survivability of someone at risk of hypothermia. Your goal should be to find shelter from the wind either by building a snow cave or windbreak or by wrapping yourself in protective debris or branches. Although much scientific work has been done to determine the effects of windchill, little has been done to research the triple whammy of cold temperatures, wind speed, and the insulation-killing effect of moisture, a common scenario when sweat, rainfall, or immersion occurs in conjunction with low temperatures.

To roughly calculate windchill, add the wind speed to the temperature and then double it. With a 20-mph wind, freezing becomes $-46°$. A more precise table when conditions are dry appears on the next page.

The danger from windchill increases as you gain altitude. Winds tend to be higher (about twice as strong for every two thousand meters ascended) and the temperature drops around $3°C$ every one thousand feet (half if it is overcast). Wind is usually strongest in the afternoon, when it is also warmest, and calmest in the early morning, when it is coldest. The temperature is also warmest on southern-exposed faces and coldest on northern-facing slopes. All these rules of thumb should be considered when traveling in weather extremes.

windchill

TEMPERATURE F°

WIND SPEED	25	20	15	10	5	0	-5	-10	-15	-20	-25	-30	-35	-40	-45
5	22	16	11	6	0	-5	-10	-15	-21	-26	-31	-36	-42	-47	-52
10	10	3	-3	-9	-15	-22	-27	-34	-40	-46	-52	-58	-64	-71	-77
15	2	-5	-11	-18	-25	-31	-38	-45	-51	-58	-65	-72	-78	-85	-92
20	-3	-10	-17	-24	-31	-39	-46	-53	-60	-67	-74	-81	-88	-95	-103
25	-7	-15	-22	-29	-36	-44	-51	-59	-66	-74	-81	-88	-96	-103	-110
30	-10	-18	-25	-33	-41	-49	-56	-64	-71	-79	-86	-93	-101	-109	-116
35	-12	-20	-27	-35	-43	-52	-58	-67	-74	-82	-89	-97	-105	-113	-120
40	-13	-21	-29	-37	-45	-53	-60	-69	-76	-84	-92	-100	-107	-115	-123

EFFECTIVE TEMPERATURE

Bag It

The first step is to prevent hypothermia. First of all dress properly and keep dry. If the weather turns to crap, consider putting up for the night and building a shelter. If you can't, try to create a vapor barrier. This means wrapping your feet in a plastic bag and making an undershirt from a garbage bag with holes cut in it. This low-tech concept keeps heat in and will slow the evapotranspiration that is rapidly cooling your body.

Make sure that all members of your party know what the early signs of hypothermia are and to stop if there is concern.

Mild hypothermia (34°C to 35°C): The first effects of hypothermia begin when the body's core drops to 98°F. That's not a misprint, that's sixtenths (0.6) of a degree from normal. At 98°F the body stops shivering and muscles feel rigid. If you have goose bumps and can't seem to warm up, stop and take steps to rebuild your core temperature. Exercise and rest, have others warm or rub your feet and hands, adjust or change clothing, drink warm fluids, and eat high-energy candies. This is when attention should be paid to all party members to prevent further incidents.

Moderate hypothermia (32°C to 33.9°C): You are hypothermic at a body temperature of 95°F the victim gets stupid, and slurred speech, memory loss, loss of coordination, and convulsions may occur. At this point hypothermia can quickly become a life-threatening emergency. If the victim is wet, strip off his wet or sweat-soaked clothing and get him into a prewarmed sleeping bag. Massage and work his body to slowly build temperature, and help him drink warm fluids to heat the body's core. The areas to heat first are the armpits, groin, chest, and neck. External warming should be moderate, and if the victim does not show signs of improvement after thirty minutes, you should call for a medical evacuation, if available, or proceed to the treatment described in the next level of hypothermia. Many victims will be apathetic and not care what happens to them. Fight this. Keep in mind that hypothermia can continue even if the victim has begun treatment. It is important to watch for the symptoms of increased temperature loss.

Dangerous hypothermia (32°C to 31°C): At 88°F the pulse is faint, and there is shallow breathing, dilated pupils, and a glassy stare. Unconsciousness usually occurs at this point. It is now important to warm the trunk of the body and the head. Do not give food or drink. Do not raise the feet above the heart. Cold blood forced downward can push cold, lactic-acid-rich blood into the core. Wrap in a heat-reflecting blanket and check for frostbite.

Have various members warm the person with their bodies. An IV drip may be necessary to regain core temperature.

Severe hypothermia (below 30°C): When the body hits 82°F, the heart may stop or beat erratically until death occurs. At this point it is debatable whether the person can survive without medical help, heat, IV containing fluids warmed to 43° Celsius, and application of warm fluids. If the heart stops, apply CPR and the above remedies.

The most effective way to warm a victim is to light a fire and heat water bottles, rocks, and clothing worn by other members and then put them on the victim. It is not wise to aggressively warm the victim with hot water or high heat. The most functional areas to apply heat are the areas where large arteries are closest to the surface. This includes the groin/femoral, underarms/brachial, and neck/carotid. Exercise is not a good treatment either, since it can cause cooling of the core as the cold blood recirculates. Have the victim drink warm sugared fluids like tea, fruit drinks, and flavored gelatin to aid in the body's need for energy. Soup and warm water are also fine.

A severely chilled person may appear dead, devoid of pulse or breathing. He may have a heart rate as low as two or three beats a minute. Do a thorough pulse check and warm before attempting CPR, which may cause heart failure.

After sitting in an outdoor restaurant in Uzbekistan ingesting large amounts of alcohol, I found myself admiring the Russian concept of alcohol as antifreeze. Wrong. This is an old babushka tale—drinking too much will rapidly increase loss of core heat. In medical terms drinking to stay warm can cause cutaneous vasodilation (which prevents vasoconstriction), impair the shivering mechanism, and bring on hypothalamic dysfunction. In layman's terms, you will sit there perfectly happy and turn into something out of the frozen-food section. In rural areas over 90 percent of hypothermic deaths are associated with elevated blood alcohol levels.

body temperature effects

F°	C°	
98.6	37	Normal temperature
97	36	*Shivering begins. Metabolic rate increases.*
95	35	*Maximum shivering seen. Impaired judgment.*
91	33	*Severe clouding of consciousness.*
90	32	*Most shivering ceases and pupils dilate. No pulse evident at wrist. Skin may be puffy, lips blue.*
88	31	*Blood pressure may no longer be obtainable. Incoherent and irrational behavior.*
85	29	*Severe slowing of pulse/respiration. Increased muscle rigidity. Loss of consciousness. Ventricular fibrillation.*
84 to 80	28 to 27	*Loss of deep tendon, skin, and capillary reflexes. Patients appear clinically dead. Cardiac standstill.*

The Mark of Jack Frost

Frostbite is your flesh being frozen. It affects the smallest, most exposed areas such as ears, nose, fingers, and toes first. Once the flesh is dead, it can quickly rot or become gangrenous and require removal to prevent infection.

You can feel the onset of frostbite if your skin itches, aches, stings, or feels numb. The skin may look white, waxy, or blotchy. Wiggle your toes and fingers to see if there is sensation. Mind-set here is to protect, exercise, and check.

The key to preventing frostbite is protecting areas from the cold, keeping them dry and movable, and promoting circulation. Tight boots or clothing, contact with metal objects such as a watch, and lack of invigorating movement can create frostbite. Often, gas spills from vehicles or camping stoves will instantly freeze skin. Temperatures below −35F° can freeze skin if exposed. If there is extreme windchill, skin can freeze in less than a minute between −60 and −74.

There are different types of tissue damage by cold. Skin can be killed by windchill and cold, blister, and then appear to be a burn. Windburn at low temperatures can create "frostnip," a condition that creates symptoms that replicate first-degree burns. Third-degree frostbite occurs when the freezing extends below the skin into the muscle tissue.

Prevention of frostbite involves awareness of cold conditions and monitoring of feet, hands, and face for freezing. If you are concerned, try holding warm hands against your face *(do not rub)*, putting hands and feet inside another person's warm clothing, changing into dry socks, and loosening laces.

If frostbite has occurred, rewarm the affected parts in water heated to between 100° and 108°, the temperature of hot tap water. Take the time to make sure the area is completely rewarmed and then keep it dry and warm. Elevate to prevent swelling and place cotton pads between fingers and toes. Be prepared for the pain and itching that occur when parts come back to life. Frostbite hurts like hell when defrosted. Seek medical attention to determine if further treatment is required. Be aware that frostbite damage can also be aggravated when rewarming, as damaged cells release material that constricts and damages other vessels.

If the victim will be exposed to cold weather again, it is wiser to delay rewarming until he is back in a stable warm environment, since the area will be even more susceptible to freezing.

Long-term immersion (a full day) in cold (50° and below) can result in "immersion foot." (Think long-term hiking through springtime conditions in slush and wetlands.) At this point, circulation shuts down and the foot can be sore and numb. Even if rubber boots are worn, perspiration can cool and soak feet, causing the same problem. Treatment consists of drying the foot (do not rub it), elevating it, and letting it warm up.

Finally, the overall effects of long-term exposure to cold and exertion can lead to depression, slow healing of wounds and rashes, and susceptibility to tracheal infections. It is important to maintain hygiene, morale, and proper diet.

Snow Blindness

Snow blindness is the result of overloading UV onto your city-slicker eyeballs, maxing out your iris's capability to close, making you go temporarily blind. You can get this condition in snow, but it also occurs on the ocean and on sand. The symptoms are a loss of vision, bloodshot and running eyes, gritty sensation in the eyes, sensitivity to light, and severe headaches. Your best bet for protection is a pair of good sunglasses. Polarized lenses cut direct reflections off snow and water but may not be dark enough for alpine snow conditions. Alpine and snow goggles have leather side protection and nosepiece and nylon frames to prevent freezing. If you don't have (or lose) sunglasses, reduce light input. This can be done by making slits in bark or leather or pulling your wool hat over your eyes and looking through the mesh. The best method of treatment is to apply a cool compress over the eyes, take painkillers for the headache, and stay out of the bright light.

Getting High Enough to Die: Altitude Sickness

Although altitude sickness is unrelated to weather, it occurs primarily in alpine travel. Most problems occur at altitudes over eight thousand feet, but many adventurous vacationers from low-altitude cities like New York, Miami, Chicago, and L.A. notice the effects of altitude at around five thousand feet in cities like Denver, Nairobi, and Mexico City, where thinner air can combine with pollution, jet lag, temperature changes, and increased exertion to cause sickness.

Altitude sickness is a direct result of less oxygen being taken in. There are three specific problems: acute mountain sickness, high-altitude pulmonary edema, and high-altitude cerebral edema.

Acute mountain sickness (AMS): The trekker's main enemy is acute mountain sickness, which occurs at above eight thousand feet. Headache, fatigue, dizziness, shortness of breath, nausea, and fluid retention are just some of the symptoms. There might also be some blueing around the lips and fingers as well as decreased appetite, stupidness, clumsiness, and strange behavior. Many people ignore or downplay this problem, since it occurs at the beginning of what is probably a very expensive trekking or mountaineering holiday and they don't want to blow it. It is important to review this with members of an expedition and take the time to acclimatize so that it doesn't create more life-threatening problems later on.

Treatment is fairly straightforward. Reduce activity, eat light, high-carbohydrate foods, drink plenty of fluids, and allow two to three days for acclimatization. If things appear more serious, you have two choices: take oxygen (two liters per minute for fifteen minutes) or descend to below three thousand feet.

High-altitude pulmonary edema (HAPE): The climber's nemesis is the more serious HAPE. All the symptoms of AMS are present, plus a dangerous buildup of fluids in the lungs. HAPE is brought on by exertion at high altitudes combined with the effects of oxygen deprivation at altitudes above eight thousand feet. The shortness of breath is now evident at rest and when lying down. The only treatment is to descend and treat with oxygen (four to six liters per minute for fifteen minutes and then decreasing to two liters per minute). Continue oxygen treatment for at least twelve hours. It takes three to four days for a victim to recover. If you have had previous bouts with HAPE, a doctor might prescribe acetazolamide.

High-altitude cerebral edema (HACE): Above twelve thousand feet the brain may swell due to hypoxia, or oxygen starvation. Symptoms are poor coordination and nonstop headache. All the symptoms of AMS will be present. Both HAPE and HACE are very dangerous, and no sympathy or consideration should be given to expedition members who downplay their problems. Their poor mental and physical functioning and the life-threatening nature of this affliction can kill not only the victim but other expedition members who will need to evacuate him.

Someone who has all the symptoms of HACE must be taken to lower altitudes immediately while being administered oxygen (four to six liters per minute for fifteen minutes, then reduced to two liters per minute). Continue oxygen for twelve hours. The victim will usually be stumbling and uncoordinated and will need assistance or even evacuation by helicopter.

The person should not be permitted to reascend even after a successful recovery.

· 21 ·

heat

Think Barry White

Adventure and vacations can take us to places that can be extreme. High mountains, brilliant beaches, scenic deserts, sparkling oceans, thundering rivers. Anyplace that isn't just like where you came from will create environmental stress (heat, altitude, cold, humidity, dryness, etc.). Your basic defense is acclimatization. In the case of extreme heat, for example, plan on spending a few days of nonexertion, followed by up-at-dawn starts, long siestas and lengthy lunches, late dinners, and cool active nights. Just put on some Barry White and you'll get the right pace.

Your Body Is a Badly Built Car

Your body is similar to an automobile. Just as an engine has an operating temperature range, a coolant, and a fuel system, so does your body. You use more if you exert more, and when you're racing, you can run out of gas, water, and air. The problem is that when you overheat, you don't pop a hose, you die.

A human can exist for three weeks without food but only three days without water. If the body temperature rises two degrees, it becomes a fever. An increase of seven degrees puts us near death. If our temperature decreases two degrees, we feel cold, and a seven-degree decrease puts our life in jeopardy.

So it is important to think of your body as an engine running with a massive coolant system (around twelve pints of blood), a huge radiator (lungs, skin), and a fuel system (digestive system), all operating in harmony. The harder you work the system (cold, exertion, heat, stress), the more fuel, cooling, heating, or heat dissipation is required. Human bodies produce heat by the process of breaking down food via metabolism and exercise (muscles are half our body weight and generate 73 percent of our heat during work). The human lungs take in 700,000 cubic feet of air every day, heating or cooling the interior of the body. In extreme cold, shivering provides heat by rapidly exercising cold muscles.

As soon as you affect one of the systems, things happen. Although most people think they will need extra water, clothes, food, and so forth, some have a hard time predicting just how much is required. This is the fundamental reason for emergencies related to heat or cold.

The human body can function in a variety of extremes. There are people functioning by choice in temperatures of 130°+ and in −70° temperatures. It has never occurred to the Dinkas of Sudan to head up to Lapland or the Inuits of Canada to vacation with Tuaregs.

This leads us to the other conceptual idea you need to hold in your head: absolute existence and adaptive existence. Inuits cannot function well in hot areas because of accumulated body fat, diet, body structure, and clothing, just as Tuaregs would quickly freeze if exposed to arctic conditions. But each with a few months of adaption and acclimatization could do just fine.

The Human Machine Doesn't Come with an Air Freshener

A normal human has about 4 million sweat glands, with the forehead, chest, and back having the greatest number. In terms of how much water is pumped, your armpits are the most active.

The source of body odor is the apocrine glands found in (I know this is supposed to be a survival guide, but this stuff is interesting) the armpits, groin, and nipple area. Sweat doesn't smell—it's mostly water—but bacteria on the skin break down the sugars and fats in apocrine sweat after about an hour. Sweat contains sugars, fats, sodium, chloride, and potassium. These are called electrolytes. If you sweat a lot, that's what you will lose. For example, a quart of sweat contains between 500 and 1,400 mg of sodium. Electrolytes allow the nerves and muscles to function in harmony, and if you are out of electrolytes, cramping, spasms, and general fatigue occur.

Perspiration provides 75 percent of the body's cooling capacity. If you are just sitting comfortably in 70° temperatures, you can expect to lose 200 mg of perspiration from your armpits. As the temperature rises to 100°, you can expect to lose three times that much. Perspiration is most noticeable during high humidity, when the moisture does not evaporate as fast as during low humidity. For estimation purposes imagine the body needing two to three liters (four to six pints) of fluid each day just to replace what it has lost. Double this during exertion and triple it in hot areas.

You can drink soda, milk, or juice, but the body craves water and doesn't need the extra sugar or calories getting in the way. Sports drinks that tout electrolytes are fine, but you would need to carry a case for each day you are in the desert or jungle. It is much better to use a powdered electrolyte supplement for long-term use.

"Dry heat" is more bearable than high-humidity heat, but this does not necessarily lead to less fluid loss. My motorcycle ride through Death Valley in the summer is a pleasant proposition at 120 mph, until of course I stop for gas and my black leathers conspire against me. The main difference is that it is easier to overheat in tropical conditions where sweat does not provide the evapotranspiration effect. Evapotranspiration is the cooling effect caused by water evaporating from the skin. This can be used to add extra cooling by wetting your head and face and letting the evaporation cool you.

Heat Stress: Be Cool, Fool

Given a choice (and spending far too much of life growing up with Canadian winters), I choose extreme heat over extreme cold. Extreme heat demands carefully rationing exertion, plenty of water, and being protected from the sun. Push too hard (like I foolishly did scampering up and down the Bandiagara cliffs in Mali in 140° heat) and your body quickly shuts down, forcing you to relax. Or die. My guide, of course, couldn't quite figure out why the big white man couldn't put in a decent day's hiking up and down the three-hundred-foot cliffs.

Heat stress affects the elderly, who perspire less and may take prescription drugs that interfere with perspiration. (Diuretics and medication for high blood pressure, Parkinson's, diabetes, heart problems, and weight loss can alter temperature regulation.)

There are two related but often separate dangers in dealing with high heat: heat exhaustion and heatstroke. The first usually occurs below the canopy of high-humidity jungles, the second in sunbaked deserts. They can also occur in South Chicago or during a day outing at Disneyland.

Heat exhaustion is due to loss of salts and fluids. Breathing will be shallow, muscles may cramp, vomiting and dizziness may occur. The solution here is to hydrate with salt and water (two teaspoons per pint) every fifteen minutes for the first hour and then fluids until the patient cannot drink anymore.

Heatstroke is your body's reaction to excessive sun. The first signs of heatstroke are feebleness, dry throat, unquenchable thirst, and confusion. Your cooling system short-circuits, your skin feels cold, and your pulse will quicken. Flushing of the skin is normal. Get in the shade and try to cool yourself down with water, a cool wet sheet, and fanning.

Close to home, stay cool with fans, cross ventilation, fine mists, and shade trees. Farther afield, heat is easy to deal with: Take it easy. The mental image of a serape-clad Mexican under his giant sombrero is what you're going for. Cover up with lightweight, white, loose clothing, wear a large straw hat (not a baseball or felt hat, which retains heat), find shade, drink fluids, and kick back. Avoid alcohol, which combines with heat to dehydrate you and knock you out, and avoid fatty foods, which require heat-producing energy to digest.

People who live in the desert eat low-calorie food, cover all parts of their body from the sun, and sleep during the hottest part of the day, choosing to spend the evenings and early mornings to work or travel.

· 22 ·

jungles

You in the Jungle, Baybay!

I t is more likely that the reader of this book will get lost in a temperate forest or southwestern desert than in a jungle. Even more likely that you will get lost in a park or along a well-marked trail. Despite this, most survival books go into great detail on jungle survival, a warm, fecund, and remote area where you are less at risk than in a bad neighborhood. Why?

All of these books seem to focus on cutting a vine to drink water (like finding water in the jungle is tough!) and using a big machete (or parang, as it is called in Asia) to slash your way to freedom. Both are myths and both have nothing to do with jungle survival.

Jungle Boogie

Jungles are not to be confused with rain forests. Rain forests can be chilly, coniferous forests in the Pacific Northwest as well as sweltering, fetid jungles in Belize.

There are different kinds of jungles and they all pose some unusual threats. There are primary jungles, which range from lowland mangrove to lowland dipterocarps and then up to montane jungle. These jungles usually have little if any growth on the jungle floor, and there are well-worn animal or human trails. Triple-canopy jungles have huge, 150-to-200-foot hardwood trees that block the sun, and most of the plant and animal life is in the top canopy. Even the animals prefer the upper reaches. Down on the ground you'll meet a lot of leeches, centipedes, snails, scorpions, and other disgusting critters. Montane forests have a lot of moss, an extraordinary amount of rainfall, and very cold nights but contain a lot of wood for fuel. The mangroves are chock-full of good eating (crabs, crustaceans, monkeys, snakes, and fish) but are almost impassable due to the spiky mangrove roots, mosquitoes, and deep mud.

Then there are secondary-growth jungles, found in cleared or logged areas. This type of jungle explodes in a profusion of sharp grasses, small trees, and burned logs and is almost impossible to navigate. Finally, there are what locals call jungles but are really brush or thickets that contain little animal life, few trails, and a lot of razor-sharp thorns and grasses.

The tropics are languorous and the humidity dictates caution in exerting yourself too much. Because of the high temperature and high humidity, there will be severe water loss. The flip side is that there is usually a lot of water around. Don't fall for that crap about cutting a vine and drinking from it. If you can't find water in a jungle, then don't bother looking for sand in a desert. Every time a jungle instructor cuts a vine he kills a rather massive plant that yields very little water.

Dangers of Jungle Travel

There are some specific dangers posed by the jungle. The primary concern is the prevalence of malaria and other insect-carried diseases. This may not be a big factor for the short term, but it can be significant if your malarial prophylaxis runs out or you do not take precautions.

Infections, cuts, and sprains are another major source of debilitating injuries. The jungle floor is muddy and woven densely with roots, vines, creepers, thorns, and rocks. It is easy to become tired in the heat and dim light and trip. My first day in the jungle was made memorable by grabbing at some branches only to find my hand skewered by two-inch-long thorns. Unless cleaned and treated quickly, these types of punctures and cuts can get infected.

If you are lost in the jungle, you are in a bit more trouble than in other terrain. Many of the world's jungles are flat and featureless, and your rescuers above will only see a green monotonous carpet. Depending on who is looking for you and how accurately your last location was communicated, you might want to weigh your options. Lighting a fire in the jungle has probably the least benefit, since swidden farmers regularly burn off hillsides and every little kampong or settlement will have cooking fires going. Your best bet is to forget the compass and machete stuff and look for a navigable river or a trail to guide you to civilization.

Jungle Tips

Sleeping in the jungle is probably one of the most unpleasant parts of tropical travel. Typically, the rains come at night along with insects, rodents, and all manner of large and unnamed species. Although I have slept directly on the ground in times of need, I would not recommend it for health and security reasons. It is possible to drown without some kind of cover. Secondly, the threat of biting or stinging insects is high, and, finally, it is just plain miserable to unglue yourself from the mud.

So, once you find a comfortable spot that has water but is high enough not to be flooded (look for signs of flooding, which include silt, and vegetation brushed in a downstream direction), you should build a simple platform. Make the platform as high as you like, with natural protection from the heavy rains that usually come each night.

(As a minor note in looking for a campsite: Mosquitoes usually don't venture above twelve hundred meters, but it rains more at that altitude and it can get cold.)

If you have a tarp, you can run a single stick underneath it and keep it directly above you. The weight and intensity of the tropical rains are such that your tarp should be as low and as steep as possible to effect runoff and avoid puddling. When you have completed your branch or fern bower, make channels around the higher side of it to direct rain runoff around your bed.

The ideal method of sleeping is to have a jungle hammock that comes with a built-in mosquito net and overhanging tarp. It is advisable to also provide some shelter via thatched palm or branches to break the force of the rain above your hammock.

The basic tools for jungle travel should always include a parang (a machete used not for slashing your way through the bush but for building campsites), a large-capacity water container, a proper pair of jungle boots (cheap canvas with deep lugs and water drains) coupled with a pair of flip-flops for use around camp, disinfectant, malarial prophylaxis, and, of course, a good guide who will carry your gear, regale you with stories, and make your trip enjoyable and not miserable.

Keep your machete in its case in your pack and not hanging from your waist. You don't want to trip and injure yourself.

Everything is wet in a jungle. Clothes, gear, packs, boots, and food soon become moist, moldy, and rotted. There is a window in the morning where the sun shines fiercely and clothes can be washed and dried. If you wear clothes to sleep in, do not wear the same set you wore during the day. This is how bacteria can grow and make your life miserable. Wear clean clothes and the next morning wash your clothes from the day before. It doesn't hurt to boil your clothes or even boots to kill fungus or bugs (or at least use very hot water). Hang sleeping bags or sheets to dry in the sun, and keep on top of any cuts and scratches.

Most local people use the river as both toilet and water supply, but this doesn't mean you should follow in their footsteps. (The sight of somebody brushing their teeth two feet away from somebody defecating upstream is a memorable one.)

When you make camp, you need to create proper latrines, boil and clean utensils, and bury food to prevent the incursion of rats.

Clothing, including socks, underwear, and hats, should not be synthetic, since synthetics breed germs and can cook you. This means you need to wash it, as bacteria quickly make natural fibers foul smelling. Clothing should be loose and absorbent. Long sleeves and long pants are a must. Bathing shorts are ideal for washing in rivers while not offending the locals (who always bathe clothed in shorts or sarong). An umbrella is preferred over rain gear, and a good waterproof poncho is useful when sitting in one place. Once on the trail, rain gear is too hot to keep you dry.

A good terry-cloth hat or sweat rag is ideal to stop the sweat from pouring down your face. A towel wrapped around you or a sweatband around your forehead is good.

When you pack your gear, look for a frameless light pack small enough to be carried by a local porter, stuffed into a canoe, or tossed in a local taxi. The big mountaineering kind won't cut it. Multicompartment packs are ideal, since you don't want to be unpacking your entire bag in the rain. Further compartmentalize your gear by wrapping it in heavy plastic bags and using Tupperware-type containers for delicates, medicines, and personal gear. The pack itself does not have to be waterproof but can be wrapped in a heavy vinyl poncho. Typically, your pack will endure being dropped in the mud, floated in foul bilge water, sweated all over by greasy porters, used as a seat, baked in the tropical sun (cooking everything in it to a foul tropical funk), and generally destroyed.

Water is your best friend, so bring as many bladder-type canteens or containers as you can. Also invest in a good water filtration system, rehydration salts, and purification tablets. A larger-than-normal pot and a small stove are a good investment for boiling water (make sure the pot is not too big for your stove). Salt tablets are a good idea and some form of sucrose to give you a little energy toward the end of the day. Don't take whole salt tablets, but crush them in your food or nibble on the tablets. If you are concerned about infection or stings, get your doctor to prescribe an autoinjector of epinephrine and a strong antibiotic. The most reliable malaria prophylaxis is doxycycline, which as an antibiotic also protects against leptospirosis, typhus, and some forms of diarrhea. There are many resistant strains of malaria in Asia and Africa.

Jungle Tucker

The jungle is one of the most bountiful regions for food. Truckers will often plant bananas and papayas along the side of the road for snacks. Villagers will always have an abundance of rice, fruits, and vegetables, and domesticated fruits like papaya, coconut, taro, breadfruit, durian, mango, and sugarcane grow rampant. In the wild areas of the jungle, however, these fruits will be nonexistent or hard to find. You need to kill a large palm to get a relatively small amount of edible material. Pandanus palms (the thorned, sharp-leaved plant that is used for roofing and thatched material) have edible seeds. The large heart-shape-leaved taro plant provides nutritious roots, but there are similar-looking poisonous species. The roots, seeds, and stems of lilies can also be eaten.

Plants that are edible and in abundance are palms, ferns, and bamboos, where the shoots and hearts are edible. Fiddleheads of ferns can be eaten raw but drain vitamin B after long periods of consumption. A large number of poisonous and stinging plants can kill you or cause allergic reactions. My advice is to spend a few hours with a local who can introduce you to the edible and poisonous plants of the specific area.

Water is stored by many plants, ranging from the convenient pitcher plants and bromeliads to epiphytes that have little pools. Don't worry about pitcher plants being full of poison; just strain the bugs out with your teeth. Pitcher plants are probably the purest and quickest source of water after a rainfall. Streams are usually full of fecal nasties and should be filtered, purified, and/or boiled. Fresh clean water can be collected off of tarps as runoff or caught in leaf containers.

Streams are usually good sources of fish, crabs, and crayfish. There are plenty of reptiles (monitor lizards are big and good eating) and small mammals (rats, bats, and other furry things abound at night). And enough bugs, snails, and insects to keep you grossed out and well fed for years. Any jungle animal, insect, or fish should be well cooked to kill parasites.

Trekking

"Trekking" is a Dutch word used by the Boers to describe a long, arduous journey. It's still true. In the jungles it means hiking from village to village along well-marked trails. Usually, the trails are about twenty feet wide and full of people carrying goods to market or traveling between relatives, although it doesn't take much to wander off to relieve yourself and then find that you forgot which way you came. Also, there are many junctions and forks that can cause confusion. In most cases people hire a local guide, but I have come across many solo travelers who consider jungle trekking fun.

Even if you are in a group, the chances of getting left behind or wandering off the path are high. You can get lost within yards of a trail and not know which direction is back. Your travelmates will probably not notice where you went because after a couple of hours of trekking and tripping, most people just stare at a patch of mud a few feet in front of them. Here is where a whistle comes in handy. Just blast three times and wait to see if anyone responds.

If you are totally lost, you have three choices. Carry on in the direction you think you should go (probably mistaking a pig trail for a hiking trail). Two, try to double back following your tracks; or three, stay put and see if anyone comes looking for you.

The best advice is to backtrack as far as you can reliably track your path and, when it gets dark, hole up for the night. Depending on how far you wandered from your last lost point, you should clearly mark where you were first lost and where you backtracked so that in the morning you can figure out exactly where you got lost.

If you are with a group, often they will not notice you gone until they stop at the predetermined campsite. Even then, few people will head out in the jungle at night to look for you but will wait until the next morning.

The second most common transportation routes in rain forests are logging roads. Often they create a spiderweb of winding dead-end tracks, but they are the quickest land-based way to get out of the jungle. Loggers start in valleys and then work their way up hillsides. If you come across a road, head downward or take the intersection that heads lower. In many cases logging roads may curve up and around for hundreds of miles, but the general direction will be toward a port or river.

Rivers, Rocks, and Falls

In some jungles, like those in Borneo, New Guinea, and Malaysia, there are a number of steep cliffs, thundering rivers, boulders, and/or razor-sharp limestone spires and outcroppings. The slippery conditions (moss, mud, water, vegetation) make serious falls a clear and present danger.

The biggest danger in extended jungle travel is drowning when crossing rivers. Usually, footpaths are connected by makeshift bridges. It is, however, one thing for a 90-pound native to cross and something quite different for a 220-pound heavily laden visitor. Cross native bridges (usually rope bridges with scrap-wood reinforcements that are rebuilt every few years) one person at a time. Send the lightest person across first and then use a safety rope run through a harness fastened by a carabiner. Worst case, the bridge will fail but the rope will secure the luckless crosser. Care must be taken to watch out for flash floods from rainfall upstream.

When there is no bridge, river crossings become complex affairs.

You will need two ropes as long as the river is wide. The first rope will be anchored at each end and the second rope will be used to shuttle gear back and forth, using carabiners as a slide. You will also need to make rope harnesses for the people.

There are essentially two kinds of crossings: shallow and deep. Shallow crossings are more dangerous than deep ones because of the strength of the current and boulders that may trip or trap feet. You can drown if your foot becomes wedged and the water pushes you down.

The best place to cross a river is at a slow bend or calm area. Never cross by yourself.

In a shallow river crossing you should send one person across with a walking stick, no pack, and a lead rope tied to an anchor or tree. At the one end have a floating device and at the other end have at least two or three people upstream and ready to pull in the rope (and the person!) if there is a problem. The rope should be attached to the chest (under the arms and around the back in a figure-eight pattern) and attached in the front with a carabiner.

You can fine-tune the rope by keeping the starting side higher than the destination side, giving you a gravitational boost. Your scout should also bring another "ferry" rope that will be used to pull people and equipment back and forth. Once the scout is on the other side, the rope is fastened to another tree to make a guideline. If your brave scout trips, hold him fast until he can get his balance. Often you can use the water to push your scout to the other side of the river.

Secure the rope on the far side so it can be used by the remainder of the group to steady themselves in the current. In shallow crossings, packs should be carried on the shoulder away from the rope so that they can fall off and not pull you under. In a more secure situation, packs can also be pulled along the security line so that they are not swept downstream.

The last man gets to be towed across. If there is a flotation device (empty jugs, waterproof gear bags, etc.), this is the time to use it.

River Travel

The single most important thing you should know about the jungle is that almost all people live along the shores of rivers. Usually, population increases as the river slows down and meets the ocean. The largest cities are ports where ocean trade meets river trade. This is important because heading overland in tropical regions will not only take you weeks or months of miserable slogging, but just doesn't make sense.

Often canoes and small motorized boats are used. There is not much advice to provide, since you will be at the fate of your boatman. Tie things down to the canoe and make sure that you are unencumbered, in the event of being dumped into the water. If there is anything that looks remotely like a life jacket, wear it.

When your boat capsizes in rapids, stay with it and then swim it to shore when you hit calm water. If you lose track of it, chances are it will be caught in an eddy or backwater downstream.

People are far more likely to become lost in the jungle while trekking than they are on the water.

· 23 ·

deserts

Before You Were Beef Jerky

robably the most inhospitable place to be lost is the desert. A desert is a region that receives less than ten inches of precipitation each year. Most of the world's landmass is covered by desert or arid regions, and that includes Antarctica and the Arctic (a desert is defined by lack of rainfall, not by heat).

For the purposes of this chapter we'll focus on the desert as an arid, hot place. There are a few fallacies that should be dealt with right up front. A desert can be extremely cold, rocky, swampy, lush, and teeming with life.

Deserts are also hot, windy, and completely devoid of life, shelter, or water. Passing the dead cows and camels in the Sahara tells you there isn't a whole lot of room for error.

To the uninitiated, the desert can kill quickly. The sun can cause sunstroke and heatstroke within a few hours. The high heat and low humidity can wring every drop of water out of a human body. Your most precious resource in a desert is water. Often there is water in a desert, but it is buried and a long way between underground sources. Temperature has a direct relationship to how quickly you will lose water. In winter, where desert temperatures may be around 70°, a human can last a week to twelve days without water. If the temperature is around 120°, that window is reduced to three to five days. If any exertion is planned (that includes walking at night), the time that a person can survive is reduced by about 50 to 60 percent. There then becomes a problem with physically carrying enough water to sustain a person without causing more water loss by the weight added (water weighs about sixty pounds a square foot).

Under normal conditions a human will lose one and a half pints of moisture every twenty-four hours. If you are going to be traveling in the desert, your first need is to have at least eight pints of water per day, and that's just for drinking, not cooking, bathing, or washing. The basics of desert travel include lightweight, loose, open-weave cotton clothing. Light colors should be worn. The ideal color is a light tan or khaki to hide the dirt ("khaki" means "dust" in Urdu). Sunglasses and a wide-brimmed hat are indispensable. Boots should be lightweight, thick-soled, and prevent sand from pouring in the top.

Sunscreen and chapstick are a must, and most old hands carry a locally purchased cotton kaffiyeh, shawl, or burnoose to act as a sunscreen, sand mask, and shade provider. Going native is highly recommended for the desert. A wool blanket for nighttime, a turban to cool and insulate the head, and a light cotton robe or shalwar qameez are ideal clothing choices.

The hottest part of the desert is the surface of the sand or rocks, so digging a trench can dramatically reduce temperatures. A trench also makes it easier for the people who find you a month later to bury you.

The methodology for desert travel is simple. Use at least two trucks (cars are not wise) that can carry plenty of water and gas. If your vehicle breaks down, there needs to be another vehicle for help. Often people form convoys for this purpose. You can also use camels (with pack camels for supplies).

If you do have a breakdown, stay with your vehicle; it can provide shade, bedding, and sometimes nonpotable water (from the windshield reservoir or radiator). If you leave your vehicle, however, provide simple and dramatic signage as to where you went. (You might come back, though, to find your car stripped and vandalized and your sign for help still sitting there.)

Having had cars break down many times in the desert when I was all by myself, I can tell you that there is nothing more lonely and forbidding than a Syrian or Jordanian desert, a dead car, and two pieces of gum to survive on. Even a joyride into or across a desert should include enough water to last a week.

Water Where It Ain't

Finding water in a desert is quite simple. Despite what survival guides tell you about munching on cactus guts or boiling your urine, there are a number of wadis, springs, or water storage points in any desert. You just need to know how the hell to get there or have a map or a local along. Most if not all deserts have clearly marked water sources on maps.

It is possible to make a solar still, which transfers the moisture from a cool earth area using solar heat from the sun. Make a hole about three feet across and two feet deep. Put a plastic sheet over it and place a stone in the middle. The runoff collects in a bucket placed under the bottom V of the tarp. Slick versions of this have a plastic pipe coming up from the bucket to drink from. If you were this prepared, however, you would have also brought more water and a radio. Bear in mind that this works best with cold nights and hot days and it takes at least four of these contraptions to provide barely enough water for one person (about one pint of water per still per day under ideal conditions).

You can also stick green vegetation inside plastic bags and put them in the sun. The water will condense, giving a tantalizingly small taste of moisture.

If conditions are right, you can wipe dew off of rocks and plants and enjoy a sweaty and minuscule early morning beverage.

In a high or temperate desert, barrel, pear-shaped, or large tubular cacti store water in their cores. Mash it up and strain or chew the pulp. These areas may also have sources of water that may be marked by palms, willows, or green areas.

Just in case you are completely clueless, the presence of water is indicated by greenery. If there is no greenery, there may be seeps in arroyos or canyons. Surface water or springs are usually found at the base of mountains or where aquifers push up in the sand. If there is water, there will be some form of plant life, insect life, or game activity (footprints or paths). Flies and bees stay close to water. Flies will be within a few hundred yards, and bees will fly in a direct line toward or away from water, usually within three to five miles. Snakes and lizards are not worth following because they get moisture from what they eat. Birds that eat seeds need water to digest their food. When they fly low and straight, they are usually headed for water. (Eagles, hawks, and vultures are not big drinkers.) Hoofed animals need large supplies of water but can walk for miles during the day. Evening and early morning are watering times.

More often than not, you will learn that water in the desert is usually pulled up from very deep wells dug by people a few hundred years ago.

If there is water in a desert, there is more than likely a town or habitation built up around it. This also means there is often a road that heads in that direction.

If you are lucky enough to be in a desert during the monsoon season, there are often violent thunderstorms in the late afternoon. These storms may only last five minutes and the water can quickly disappear into the thirsty sand. Deserts with greenery are a walk in the park compared to rock deserts. Middle Eastern, Asian, or African deserts can be completely devoid of water for hundreds of miles, and if you are in a truly badass desert in South America, China, or Africa, there just won't be any water. Naturally, you as an experienced adventurer don't venture into these places without proper preparation and backup contingencies.

We've talked about heatstroke in chapter 21, but the most dangerous afflictions in the desert are sunburn and dehydration.

Copping a Nuclear Tan

Sunburn is the most common form of affliction in the tropics or a desert region. You can also be severely sunburned at high altitude on the equator, especially when the temperatures are cool but the ultraviolet rays are deadly.

First line of defense is to use clothes and hat to shade against the sun, apply sunblock, and stay out of the sun when possible. I made the mistake of spending a long northern spring day in the sun and couldn't walk for a week afterward. I still have a six-inch patch of skin that fell off.

Sunburn can be mild and cause reddening, itching, and then peeling, or it can be the same as a second-degree burn, with continued blistering, peeling, and permanent skin damage that may lead to skin cancer and growths. If you are badly sunburned, apply liberal amounts of skin cream made with aloe, drink plenty of fluids, and stay cool. As the skin heals, remember that the new layer of skin is even more susceptible to burning.

Long-term effects of high heat include dramatic weight loss, a slowing down of activity, and the potential for skin damage, skin growths, and eye cataracts. Long-term high heat should be combated by proper acclimatization, conducting your strenuous activity during cool hours of the day, and drinking water *before* you are thirsty.

Dehydration, Rehydration

Lack of water leads to a form of dementia where people will try to drink their urine, their blood, or even poisonous fluids from their vehicle. Urine does not provide any beneficial thirst-quenching elements, but it can be distilled by boiling to create drinkable fluids. Even if you drank your best buddy dry, vampire style, the amount of blood in a human would only sustain you for a day. Basically, without water in the desert you're screwed, and it's only a matter of time before your tongue swells up, lips crack, and you literally croak. Sucking a small stone can take your mind off the thirst, but you need to provide enough fluids to replace what you are losing minute by minute. The table below gives you a general idea of the symptoms of water loss. These symptoms are not exact and can occur at different times in different people.

Dehydration victims are in obvious need of water, but they also need electrolytes and salts to regain their functioning. Their body temperature might be too high and they could also be suffering from sunstroke and other maladies. Mix up a small amount of salt and sugar in a water bottle and have them continuously sip the mixture until they feel better.

Before going into a desert area, it is wise to drink as much fluid as possible and then ration your intake while in the desert. By conserving water you extend the amount of time you can exist. Sip a little water frequently, rather

when water goes

1% lost	Thirst, weakness
2% lost	Flushed skin, irritation
5% lost	Nausea, lassitude, no appetite
6% lost	Headache, dizziness
7% lost	Difficulty in breathing, slurred speech
8% lost	Blurred vision, collapse
9% lost	Twitching, darkened vision
10% lost	Delirium, swollen tongue
11% lost	Skin loses sensation, shrinks
12% lost	Death

than gulp it. Always leave some water in case of an emergency and cover yourself from the sun as much as possible.

Avoid drinking alcohol, smoking, and eating dry foods, and expect constipation due to your body stealing water from your digestive system. Avoid laxatives, which can also rob fluid.

Midnight Diner

There is a lot going on in the desert, but it's all happening at night. If you can manage to find a water supply, you are also at the best spot to find a little four-legged food. The most common forms of life in a desert are rodents and birds. Forget trying to capture the birds, but rodents can be lured into traps or right into your hand with bait.

Much of the plant life you find in the desert is edible and of course comes with its own toothpicks. Yucca, prickly pear, mesquite, creosote bush, barrel cactus, and other plants can be peeled, boiled, and eaten.

The desert is one of my favorite places. It has a beauty and serenity unlike any other place on earth. It is also a heartless host which can kill you quicker and more cruelly than just about any other environment.

· 24 ·

getting lost

Why Smart Humans Get Lost and
Dumb Animals Don't

Humans get lost because they don't think they are when they are. Hard on the grammar but a correct statement.

The concept of being lost is not related to navigational misstep but closer to the origin of the Indo-European root word for "to become undone." Your undoing will not be caused by your geographic position but by your mental state.

Lost 'n' Spaced

It's important to understand that there are two main reasons for getting lost:

- Thinking you know where you are
- Trying a different way to where you think you want to go

Getting lost usually begins with underestimating the amount of preparation and attention required to navigate. You can get lost in the woods, in a city, or on a freeway or just snap to attention and wonder where the hell you are.

Let's focus on getting lost in the wilderness, the most dangerous form of lost. A major source of stress is the knowledge that you don't have the equipment to spend a night outdoors and you absolutely need to get back to your car before dark. This overrides common sense and encourages hikers to take shortcuts or head overland.

Unfortunately, as night falls and the stupid hour starts (dusk), many people run out of common sense and race around like rabbits until they collapse tired and hungry. (I take that back. Rabbits don't get lost.) The shift from fun to panic mode can usually guarantee you'll spend a night in the woods. Just north of Los Angeles is a popular place for search-and-rescue workers to pull out bruised and shivering hikers who strayed off a path and spent the night thinking they would be eaten by coyotes.

First Lesson: Don't Get Lost

It may be disheartening to realize that yes, animals do get lost, but very rarely. Turtles can get lost in underwater caves and drown. Birds can get blown off course in storms, and, contrary to what Disney would have you believe, your dog will not follow you all the way from New Jersey to your new home in Santa Barbara. Animals do get lost but people get even more lost.

Human beings don't seem to have a grain of common sense when dumped in the woods and, when blindfolded, will even walk around in circles thinking all the while that they're doing just fine.

That's not to say that animals don't also swim, fly, or walk around in circles in the wild. It's just that they don't have anywhere particular to go.

Try it someday: Go to a parking lot and close your eyes. Use your best efforts to walk a hundred yards in a straight line and then open your eyes. Boy, do you feel stupid. The fact is that the human body is not as bilateral or balanced as we think. One leg is slightly stronger and longer and is probably tweaked to the left or right. This gives us directional windage that we never compensate for. After mentally correcting for your natural left or right drift, see how you do. Not so good, huh? The lesson is that as a navigational machine the human body sucks.

Trail Finding Without a Map:
We're on the Road to Nowhere

What about following trails? Surely once you find a trail, it'll take you straight to somewhere. If you thought that animals and people created trails to get somewhere quickly and efficiently, you're dead wrong. I used to cut the actual boundary between the Yukon and British Columbia. If you stumbled on that twenty-foot-wide clean trail, you'd end up in Alaska or the Northwest Territories about a year later. And you would walk up every mountain and through every swamp on the way there. The North American continent is full of one-way hiking trails, supply roads to defunct gold mines, and a veritable labyrinth of abandoned logging roads. Often these roads weave back and forth not in any directional purpose but to allow total decimation of the forest. Can you get lost when you follow well-marked, well-used trails in the bush? Oh God yes.

You would think that flat, featureless deserts like the Sahara, the Mojave, or the plains of Montana would have arrow-straight paths designed to save time and gas. Sorry. Hundreds of paths weave in lackadaisical ribbons that meander and intertwine across the desert as people and animals pretty much take any line that pleases them. Often trails are designed to inspect fence lines or visit watering spots. Can you get lost in the deserts of Africa with fifty-mile visibility and a local driver? You betcha.

How about getting lost on well-worn jungle paths, packed snow trails, and even paved roads? Why not? Nobody built a road so that you could get unlost. In some countries there are roads that head straight out into the desert with nary a soul for the next thousand miles. There are survey roads neatly bulldozed into the Arctic that serve only to scrape the topsoil off for geological exploration. In places like the Canadian north, trails will neatly circle water and connect valleys but won't take you anywhere scenic or interesting. There are hiking trails that take you hundreds of miles into the wilderness one way and hundreds of miles into the wilderness the other way. After all, who wants to hike in a populated area with food, shelter, and rescue?

It is this very concept of following a trail and not thinking about where you are going that leads to being lost. Even animal trails in the woods are not economical and automatic paths to food or water, much less civilization. Most animals are lazy and take the path of least resistance. Some animals, like goats, like to take the most difficult route. Others, like moose or even elephants, wander pretty much wherever they feel like it. When rutting, they will wander through people's backyards, along roads, through swamps, and into cities.

The other thing that most survival guides forget to mention is that most trail-building animals are about six to eighteen inches off the ground and love running through thickets to slow down predators.

If You Think You Can't Possibly Get Lost, You Probably Are

We've talked about how well-worn trails can lull us into a sense of directional comfort. That's probably why weekend warriors get lost more than arctic explorers. It is completely normal for diligent hikers to jabber away in the woods and walk down the wrong path. When they retrace their steps, they realize that the trail looks totally different and there are dozens of forks they never even noticed on the way in.

The other "biggest" danger is thinking that we can automatically reorient our sense of direction to believe that we are going the right way. It's a sad part of human nature that our cognitive mind can convince our instincts that the sun should be setting in the east because we have been walking north all day when in actual fact we have been walking south. Just have someone spin you around in a darkened room and try to point out north.

If you are fortunate or instinctively attuned enough to find yourself feeling lost, stop immediately and check your bearings. If, like most lost people, you have neither a compass nor a map nor a clue, retrace your steps as far back as you can see them until you feel like you are back on track. Mentally map out where you have been going in relationship to a landmark or the sun and draw a map. Check it with a number of commonsense gauges: Where is the sun? How long have you been walking? When was the last time you passed a known marker? If for some reason you are not carrying a map, mentally create one that retraces your trip and known variables: time, distance, direction, slope, terrain, and landmarks you remember.

It is important to do it sooner rather than later. As you review your "lostness," you begin to doubt the obvious. Soon these initial images will fade and confuse you. Another disease unique to the lost is backtracking a certain distance and then convincing ourselves that we were less lost back where we were. This of course leads to taking shortcuts through dense bush and then usually over a cliff face. Stick to what you know.

The decision now comes as to whether you should stay put, go back, or continue forward. If it is getting dark and you are alone, the best decision is to leave a distinct, easy-to-see mark showing where you came from (I know it sounds silly, but people do camp at night and then start walking in the wrong direction in the morning), do your little map, and prepare to spend the night. In the morning you'll be refreshed, a little sharper, and a little humbler.

Then begin to retrace your tracks or your mental map until you are in sync with your original program.

when lost alone without map or compass

1. **Spend fifteen minutes in one spot.**
Breathe deeply and reconstruct your path from memory.
2. **Draw a map and estimate your walking times to major landmarks.**
3. **Mark your position clearly with a tripod, barrier, or other symbol that could be seen in the dark.**
Write a note with the time you were there and where you went.
4. **Create a highly visible signal for searchers.**

Shame and Fear: Separated from a Group

If you are with a group, it's getting dark, and they just happen to have all your gear and food, they, not you, are in a pickle. They will think you are lying at the bottom of a rocky cliff or hanging from a sapling and will be frantic to find you. Your best bet is to retrace your steps and mark your path with blazes, stones, or bent twigs showing the direction of travel. Depending on the terrain, you may choose to find an elevated or visible point to pull over and wait. If you have no gear, make preparations to stay warm (fire, branches, cover, etc.) and make lots of noise by banging rocks or sticks together, whistling, yelling, or whatever turns you on. The worst thing you can do is hightail it back to where you think you last saw them because you could be rapidly outpacing them as they carefully look for you from behind or you could be heading into uncharted wilderness while they comb the trail all the way back to the bus.

Second Lesson: Don't Get Loster

The amount of lostness is based on time, speed, and direction. If you stay put, you can't get more lost. In fact, you may find you are exactly where you are supposed to be but you just weren't paying attention. If you decide to get unlost, then be prepared for the Las Vegas odds. If you are in a group that gets lost and you don't have a map, compass, or directional guidance, you need to understand that at this point the outing can become a bum weekend or *Lord of the Flies*.

You obviously want to head straight toward where you think you should be. But to do that you have to know where you are. So the first step is, no matter how lost you are, don't leave until you figure out where you are. This might mean overnighting it so you have a full day to extract yourselves. It may mean sending scouts out to map the surrounding terrain.

What if the whole group is lost? Should you roll the dice and charge off back in the direction you came from? Or should you double down and go both ways but cut your distance in half? Should you stay put and hope that someone will eventually find you? All of the above. What you must do is harness the power of the group. Discuss the plan (getting back) and make it fun. Depending on the terrain and what you're looking for, send groups of two (in case of accident) in a well-marked direction to high sight lines or along trails. Give each person a specific pace count, a goal, and a time limit in which to return. Even if you don't know direction (let's say it's foggy or overcast), make up your own direction and method of distance measurement (paces are fine).

Each team of two should sight a far-off object and then send one person toward it. If you need to travel through swamp, brush, or forest to get to the mountaintop, then leapfrog like two survey poles. When you reach the other person, sight past the person to the next point. This method of leapfrogging is dramatically accurate. At the appointed time the teams return and download what they have seen. The team will then choose to pick the most likely path and follow the blazed route.

As you backtrack or search for your last known position on the trail, make sure you always have a known starting point and are expanding your crude mapping. That starting point is where you sat down and wrote down where you were. It doesn't even matter if you have a compass or a map as long as your measurements of direction and distance are constant. You also need to continue to expand your map as you travel, noting down features, elevation (up, down, flat), and time between features.

When traveling in the bush, think of your head as a radar beam sweeping 360° every minute. Your end destination should be the central forward axis, or you can substitute a compass point like north or west. As you move forward, certain items will enter and some will leave. Then, remember how long it took for objects like tall trees, mountaintops, views, soil colors, or foliage to be first and last seen. This will instill a sense of direction, movement, and place, and it will be impossible to get lost. If you make a detour to go swimming or exploring, remember what time it was, how far you had progressed, and what the next object on the horizon was. In other words, pay attention to where you are and where you're going.

distance traveled by lost person

	MAXIMUM DISTANCE	MEDIAN DISTANCE	TYPICAL DISTANCE (50% of cases)
	miles from last known point		
BY DESCRIPTION:			
Hikers	14.91	1.63	.89–2.88
Hunters	12	1.52	.98–2.38
Fishermen	11	.89	.59–2.17
Despondents	3.5	.64	.47–1.12
Walkaways	3	.62	.34–1.19
BY AGE:			
Adults	11.81	1.27	.75–2.24
Youths (13–16)	4.3	1.12	.62–1.78
Children (7–12)	4.97	1.3	.99–1.70
Children (1–6)	1.65	.5	.42– .75

Compiled by Ken Hill, Professor of Psychology, St. Mary's University, Halifax, NS Regional Search and Rescue, based on 252 cases, Nova Scotia.

Recap

- Alone and no one knows where you are: Walk out.
- Separated from a group: Stay where you are or retrace path.
- If you are a group, stay but send out parties to determine position.

Really Totally, Completely Up the Creek Without a Paddle

At this point in the book, with all its smug advice and hardheaded conviction, you probably want to ask, "When should I just give up the ghost?" Are there times when the odds are stacked too high against us? When is survival not worth it?

Never. As long as you adapt your mind to surviving when fear threatens to choke you, your odds are better than when you give in to paralyzing fear or panic. There is no guarantee that applying your survival skills will work, but honing them and linking them to your natural fight-or-flight instincts always sharpens the mind rather than blurs it, often propelling people to superhuman feats of strength and endurance.

· 25 ·

time and direction

Using Nature's Bonus Points

As you read this, do you know which way is north? Where the sun is, where it will set, or even when the moon will rise? Most people have a rough idea of where the sun shines in their apartment or home. Even more can tell you where the cardinal points of the compass are because street grids, highways, and city streets have NSEW designators tacked on.

Humans have a natural center point that instinctively tells us the distance or time or direction from where we are. But put us in a plane, subway, or panel van and we lose all sense of exact distance.

Is anything in nature lost (other than man)? Rarely. Natural disasters may displace animals from their habitat, but most animals know where they are at all times. Seabirds can even travel thousands of miles between island chains with great accuracy. These birds are supposed to have led Polynesian sailors in their colonization of Pacific Ocean islands. But before we get esoteric let's get our head straight on two very simple but confusing measurements: time and distance.

How Long: Time

Time originally meant "to divide." Now it means duration. The concept of time has been regulated to the point that we soon forget that the digits on our watch have nothing to do with the real or solar time. The earth spins, exposing an observer to sun and darkness every twenty-four hours. We have already confused this simplistic concept by using twelve-hour time increments. Adventurers should always think in twenty-four-hour time, giving each hour its own personality.

How Far: Distance

Distance is how far points are apart. The unit to measure it is arbitrary. Whether you use cubits or meters, the distance measured is the same. The problem comes when you try to convert one system to another. Every country in Europe had their own mile. The mile was originally a thousand paces of a Roman legion, or 1,476 meters. There were Irish (2,048 meters), Swiss (8,370 meters), Italian (1,855 meters), Danish (7,538 meters), and even German short, long, imperial, and geographical miles. Long distances have been measured in chains, posting leagues, nautical miles, and of course kilometers (1,000 meters) and our English miles (1,609 meters). The system used in America is based on the English system, where human size and trade customs created feet, yards, rods, chains, acres, leagues, fathoms, miles, quarts, pecks, and many more incomprehensible units. The secret is to train yourself in two methods of measurement: the metric (designed for easy conversion) and the nautical (designed for navigation and celestial conversion).

distance measurements

12 inches	=	1 foot	3 feet	=	1 yard	1,760 yards	=	1 mile
3 miles	=	1 league	5,280 yards	=	15,840 feet	6,076.11549 feet	=	1 nautical mile
5.5 yards	=	1 rod	4 rods	=	1 chain	40 rods	=	1 furlong
8 furlongs	=	1 mile	1,760 yards	=	5,280 feet	320 rods	=	1 mile
7.92 inches	=	1 link	100 links	=	1 chain	80 chains	=	1 mile

A Season and a Reason

Nature works on a schedule. Not the same frenetic schedule that drives FedEx, pizza delivery, and e-mail, but one that if you sped up a film of nature would become evident. If you compressed a month into an hour, you would see the sun drawing perfect but slightly shifting arcs in the sky. You would see the stars blurring around Polaris. The plants and leaves would be following the sun like spectators following the ball at a tennis game. Animals would scurry like rush-hour commuters in well-worn paths to and from dens and water holes. Birds would zip back and forth along paths as straight as arrows. If you were to compress years into minutes, trees and rocks would reveal their more stately but just as predictable life spans and erosion. Fires, landslides, floods, and snowfall would make perfect sense as you notice the lockstep of seasons and their purpose in building a home for wildlife, renewing forests, and creating topsoil and seed generation.

If you can visualize this, then you will have a basic grasp of why you were such a moron in the woods. You were moving like a hyperkinetic ant, your dim, low-rez eyes fixated on a map and compass, without noticing the signs all around you.

Celestial Guidance: Stars

Your best bet for telling direction is the stars. On a clear night the stars give clues as to position and direction. If you are baffled by the millions of twinkling lights, bring a simple star chart. For those who don't want to take the small amount of time to be ace navigators, all you really need to know is where the North Star, or Polaris, is.

Find the Big Dipper handle, go down to the dipper part, then line up the two stars that make up the right-hand side of the dipper and go to the right about four times the distance between these two stars until you hit a bright star. Draw an imaginary line from this star, the North Star, to the horizon and that is north. A shortcut: The North Star is also the tip of the handle on the Little Dipper.

If you cannot find the Big Dipper or it has sunk over the horizon, you are probably in the Southern Hemisphere. Boy, are you lost. Don't freak. Look for the Southern Cross (the stars on the Aussie and Kiwi flags), which is a cross with an extra star under the right arm. Measure the distance between the top and bottom stars and then travel down four and a half times that distance. There is no "southern star," so a line from that dead space to the horizon is south. There are two "pointer" stars that are just below the Southern Cross and provide a cross-reference when a line is drawn at right angles and across the sighting line provided by the Southern Cross.

No matter where you are, if you view from the same position, stars always set and rise in the same position.

A few tips for amateur stargazers who don't have a watch. Planet positions are not fixed and will not twinkle. The brightest "star" in the sky is actually a planet: Venus. It appears three hours after the sun sets and lasts until three hours before the sun rises. Venus, Mars, Jupiter, and Saturn are the brightest planets. Mars has a brownish color.

The Big Dipper rotates around the North Star like an hour hand, with one full revolution every twenty-four hours. The same goes for the long end of the Southern Cross. Obviously, this method can be used with any major constellation as it rotates around the North Star or southern reference point. Stars will always rise and set four minutes earlier each night.

Unless you are cruising around during the equinox (when the days and nights are the same length and the sun carves a perfect overhead path), it is difficult to just look at the sun and know how to calculate direction.

If you want to know which direction is east/west during the day, jam a stick in the ground and mark the end of the shadow. As the shadow moves in the opposite direction of the sun's path, it is marking the direction from west to east.

If you want to know south, remember that the sun is always due south at noon. Noon is actually the "ninth" hour after sunrise. Also know that daylight saving time and the variation caused by time zones can make finding an exact time hard.

If you have a watch with hands on it, you can tell direction (sort of). In the Northern Hemisphere, pointing the hour hand at the sun will give you the direction of south as being between the digit 12 and the hour hand. In the Southern Hemisphere, point the 12 at the sun, and north will be halfway between 12 and the hour hand. This doesn't work, of course, when it's cloudy or dark. And it works only when the watch is set to local time and between the 40° and 60° latitudes.

Another highly unscientific and crude method is to hold your hand straight out in front of you with the palm and fingers flat and the little finger against the horizon. Each rack of four fingers above the horizon to the sun should give you an hour before sunset, and each finger is about fifteen minutes.

Can you make a Flintstones-style, flip-up wrist sundial? Sure. If you remember to stand facing the same direction every time you measure the shadow.

Lunar Lines: The Moon

The moon can give us direction and, more important, time.

It's not strange that we use a lunar calendar. Of all the natural ways of telling time and date, the moon is the most considerate. A line drawn from tip to tip of the crescent moon will give you the north/south direction. A full moon will always directly oppose the sun (that's why it's full). When a full moon is at its height, it's exactly midnight and its setting will herald the sun rising. The moon rises and sets fifty minutes later each day. The moon "waxes" (becomes larger or rounder) and "wanes" (gets smaller or more crescent-shaped) in four distinct phases. The new moon grows into a first-quarter moon in seven days (at its highest point as the sun is setting), into a full moon in fifteen days (its rising is synchronized to the setting of the sun), the last quarter in twenty-two days (which rises at midnight), with the new moon appearing in a thirty-day cycle. The waning crescent moon rises at dawn, just preceding the sunrise.

The moon gives us our month in name but is not directly synchronized to our calendar. To calculate exact time, it is worth having a lunar table or knowing at which time the moon rose on a particular day. Then add those fifty minutes to each day to estimate the time.

The Fluffy Weathermen

Here are some other indicators that will tune you into where you are and what's going on.

Clouds: Clouds can't really help you tell direction, but they can tell where weather is happening and when it will happen. High wispy clouds usually indicate steady fair weather, and low scudding clouds bring drizzle and rain. Clouds a little higher usually bring overcast and light drizzle but not much more. Puffy, well-spaced clouds mean fine weather. Higher, smaller puffy clouds can bring snow or rain within a day.

Basically, clouds look happy or ominous (along with the winds that bring them) and they usually do exactly what you expect.

Winds: Travelers on land can use the prevailing winds to get a general idea of distance and time. The wind typically blows from the west in the temperate zones of both hemispheres. In tropical latitudes the winds blow east. The wind does change with the seasons, but watching the movement of high clouds can give a sense of direction to the traveler.

Desert travelers will note that sand dunes in deserts or sand paths behind rocks align themselves toward the prevailing wind. Snowdrifts in polar regions exhibit the same trait. Once you establish direction, you can maintain it by knowing the prevailing wind.

Get to know the weather patterns peculiar to your home and they will teach you to understand and predict patterns indicated by winds in your new environment.

Trees: The old adage about moss growing on the north side of trees is generally true. Moss grows where the sun shines least. The same is true of snow patches on mountains. The north side is the coolest and gets the least solar energy. Trees, plants, and flowers that grow rapidly will naturally lean toward the south. Trees are also shaped by wind and soil, so be careful. Trees should be a general indicator of direction, not the most exact.

Rivers: Other than the fact that they flow downward, what can we learn from rivers? First of all, rivers follow not the easiest route, but the quickest. If you need a general idea of which way is downhill, rivers never lie, but they may take a long time to tell the truth. Following a river when lost will typically lead you to some form of civilization, but you're going to be old, hungry, tired, and sore when you get there.

Animals: Animals will not stop by your camp and tell you which way the nearest ranger cabin or landfall is, but they come pretty close. Birds are an ideal indication of distance from land if you are cast adrift. The more birds you see, the closer land will be. The colder it gets (or the higher the latitude), the more birds you will see. On land don't assume that a gull means you are by the ocean. About half of the gull species are not ocean birds but shore or land birds. Seagulls, however, never venture more than fifty miles from shore. On the other hand, the large albatross is seen miles from the nearest land. Pelicans are found less than twenty-five miles from land. The Kermadec petrel and puffins fly back to land every evening, but you better know your birds, because some species like the phalarope migrate thousands of miles out to sea.

Testicles: Forget the jokes about the Indian winding his watch and the farmer lifting the bull's scrotum to tell time. This is a directional tip that only benefits half of us, and it's esoteric enough to be useless to all. When the ancient Polynesians sailed between far-flung islands, they followed currents, stars, and seabirds. One means of determining direction was by reading not only the waves but also the reflective waves from islands, which traveled just under the surface of the crests. These delicate waves could indicate the direction of a nearby island by the extent of their force. In order to accurately gauge their direction, the Polynesians employed the most sensitive instrument they possessed. Does it work? Mine always shrink when I jump in the water, so I can't vouch for this method.

· 26 ·

maps

How to Read a Map
(or at Least Look Like You Know How)

ever trust a man who spreads out a map with great flourish, matches his compass to destination, squints off into the distance, and then sets off with stern resolution. This man is usually a complete imbecile who has no idea where he is going. If he did, he wouldn't need a map.

All the great bushmen I have known don't use maps. They measure distance in hours and days, navigate by bends in the river, hills, and outcroppings.

All the world's great land-based explorers never used accurate maps, if they used maps at all. In fact, they had to make their own. Lewis and Clark, Burton and Speke, even Willis and Burke, used the input of local guides who pointed out the way and marveled at the incompetency of these explorers.

If you do any adventuring in remote places and have a choice between a map and an unshaven local guide, choose the guide.

Maps and Why They Suck

Although maps and compasses tend to be lumped together in most survival guides, I should state that compasses are less accurate than a broken watch (which at least is correct twice a day) and maps are extraordinary works of fiction.

A map has character, plot, history, drama, humor, and even a high level of social commentary. Why, one may ask, does northern Europe end up on top of the world and Africa on the bottom? Why don't certain countries appear on maps (like Kurdistan, New Sudan, and a number of breakaway republics)? Why do most maps use Mercator projection, which enlarges the former British colonies at the top and bottom on the globe? The list goes on. Suffice it to say that a map is someone else's view of the world and not remotely close to what you'll find when you actually get there.

Maps have always been partial representations of how to get between point A and point B. For example, someone wants to get from San Francisco to New York. You take a matchbook, make two dots; the one on the left says "San Francisco," the one on the right "NY." A one-inch line connects the two and you write down "80." A map, of course! Accurate? No. But Interstate 80 will take him there in the most efficient manner.

If you were to read most survival guides, you would believe you should provide this same traveler with a set of stereoscopic satellite photos, a compass, topo maps, a preprogrammed GPS, and all the coordinates. Overkill, but you get my point. Maps are just reduced Cliff Notes that record physical features using arbitrary symbols and graphics.

Weah da Fugawi?

The primary purpose of a map is to tell someone how to get somewhere. South Sea Islanders made maps using sticks tied together to represent island groups. Aboriginals and Indians drew maps in the dirt from memory, usually noting only unusual physical features such as lakeshores, hills, or rapids. Often the scale was based on days of travel, with historical events added as landmarks. Sailors used maps that had accurate shoreline representation but empty areas for land. Areas not yet explored were often labeled "Here Be Dragons." Even today, there are maps with large white spaces because satellites have not fully photographed cloud-covered areas. So now that you understand that mapmaking is an inexact art that passes as a science, let's cut to the chase and talk about the map that you as an adventurer will be using: the topo map.

Topo Maps

Topographical survey maps are really the only maps made for hiking, walking, or detailed measurement and contain all you need to know to get around in the bush. You don't even need a compass because you can use the representations of contour, houses, rivers, and roads to get around just fine.

Topo maps evolved from military maps, on which very precise coordinates were needed to locate targets, troops, and distances. And, of course, drop artillery shells on people. A topo map provides a unique point for every place on the planet not only in longitude and latitude but in height. This extra dimension of accuracy allows you to check altitude and to visualize the topography of the terrain.

A good civilian topo map is 1:24,000 scale, where 1 inch equals 2,000 feet. In the United States you want a topo map in the 7.5-minute series because they cover an area that extends across 7.5° of latitude and longitude, or about ten miles across. Two of these give you a day's coverage. Cheapskates or fast walkers might opt for the next size up. The 15-minute series covers about twenty miles, or a good day's hike.

maps

SERIES	SCALE	AREA COVERED (SQ. MILES)	1 MILE =	1 KM =
7.5-minute	1:24,000	49–70	2⅝″ 67 mm	1⅝″ 42 mm
15-minute	1:62,500	140–197	1″ 26 mm	⅝″ 16 mm
1:250,000	1:250,000	4,580–8,669	¼″ 6.5 mm	5⁄32″ 4 mm

Slope

Although old hands can look at a topo map and guess the amount of steepness and effort, it may take a little practice for the novice. On a 7.5-minute map the topo lines show an elevation change of twenty feet and as thicker brown lines every one hundred feet of elevation change. As a rule of thumb, when the brown lines are smashed together in one fat brown mess, you are looking at a nasty cliff. There is no law that says mapmakers must show nineteen-foot trenches, overhangs, or bluffs, so don't assume every place is navigable or accessible.

These contour lines will be used to calculate slope, shape, and degree of difficulty (which affects your distance and therefore time of arrival).

To calculate slope, let's use a 7.5 topo map. A quick glance at the scale tells us that ½ inch equals 1,000 feet. Marking this distance on our compass base allows us to figure out the fall or rise over this constant distance. If we count five brown contour lines, we have a 100-foot rise over 1,000 feet. So 1,000 divided by 100 gives us 10, or a 10° slope. Not so bad. A 45° slope is an equal rise/drop of distance over elevation. Tough going but doable if it's

slope

ANGLE	PERCENTAGE	RATIO	
0°	0	1:0	Flat
5°43′	10	1:10	
10°	17.6	22:125	
11°20′	20	1:5	
16°42′	30	3:10	
30°	57.7	577:1,000	
45°	100	1:1	Steep
56°19′	150	3:2	
60°	173.2	433:250	
63°24′	200	2:1	
90°	Infinite		Vertical

flat. Anything greater becomes really tough and is dangerous. Don't confuse the angle with the grade of a slope.

A couple of shortcuts on figuring out valleys vs. ridges: Ridges will usually appear as U's and valleys as V's. To make a profile map for biking or hiking, simply replot your trail on graph paper using one square up or down for height and an equal distance forward for distance. Smooth it off, put in any navigational points, and you have a good tool to plan breaks, estimate time to viewpoint (for a scenic lunch or camp), determine where you'll find water and even where you'll be tired.

Before we get deeper into maps, though, we should back up and explain what I just explained for the newly oriented. Where do these numbers come from and what the hell do they have to do with rocks and trees? Well, before we discuss the specifics of map and compass reading, let's look more closely at the language of maps.

· 27 ·

navigation

Flatitude and Elongitude

can only remember which is which by using the above phrase. I think of flat sections running left to right and a bungee jumper doing the up and down. But just what is latitude and longitude and why the hell didn't they call it "sideways" and "up and down"? And why do degrees, minutes, and seconds have nothing to do with my watch or temperature? Ah, this is the ancient mystery of navigation, which I will now decipher for you.

Folks have guessed that the world is round since Pythagoras and Aristotle figured that the sun would have no reason to go up and down if the world were flat. Eratosthenes (c. 276–196 B.C.) figured out exactly how big the world was around and, four hundred years later, Claudius Ptolemy was bitching about how maps should all have the same system of measurement and scale. Nobody really paid attention to him and it wasn't until the eighteenth century that sailors figured out that they better stop making excuses for getting lost and stick to some system.

Changes in Latitude

The first idea for global measure is now called "parallels of latitude." Back before maps, sailors noticed that it got warmer the farther south they sailed and then got colder. There were also odd shifts in winds and currents. The length of the day also shifted. They soon figured out they could use this solar-induced climatic information to navigate.

To figure out where they were, they would site the North Star and measure the angle from straight up. If you were at the north pole, you would be looking straight up at 0°, and at the equator the North Star would be just on the horizon at 90°. So by simply measuring the angle that the North Star appeared at (or the calculated south position below the equator), you would know your latitude. Since the latitude also ties directly into the distance, trying to figure out how far north or south you are from your original latitude is a snap: Lines of latitude are exactly sixty-nine miles or sixty nautical miles apart.

The measurements between the north and south poles are called "degrees" (based on degrees originating from the earth's imaginary center and radiating outward). There are 90 degrees from the equator to each pole for a total of 180 "minutes" from north to south pole. "Seconds" are the division of minutes into 60 smaller units. There are 60 minutes in each degree of latitude, with degree having a land distance of 69 miles, 60 nautical miles, or 110 kilometers. Simple math will tell you that there are 180 × 69 miles, which means there are 12,420 miles from North to South Pole, or 6,210 from the equator to each pole (give or take 30 miles).

The fundamental points are the equator (0°), the division between north and south, and the Tropics of Capricorn (23.5° south) and Cancer (23.5° north), the outside limits of the tropics, where there is year-round warm weather. Inside this tropic band is where the sun's rays fall vertically. Above and below this the sun shifts and temperatures change seasonally each year. The Arctic (66.5° north) and Antarctic Circle (66.5° south) are the areas where, depending on the season, the sun never rises or sets. By knowing what latitude you are in, you can measure the position of the sun on the horizon and the time of year to figure out where you are.

So latitude is great if you're packing for a tropical vacation, flying north and south. It doesn't help if you're trundling back and forth to the colonies, however.

Longitude

Longitude was developed in Europe to measure distances from home ports and create a rough grid coordinate. Latitude was dead accurate but longitude required a clock. And as you can imagine back in the olden days clocks were anything but accurate. As a sailor traveled west or east, he would measure the position of the sun at a specific time. That time was in Greenwich, England.

There was never much argument when it came to where the equator should be, but when they had to create a second set of up and down lines, it was "he who has the might has the right." So England, in its glory, chose a place just ten miles south of London to be the center of the world. Greenwich was a place where a lot of figuring and measuring related to stars and navigation went on, so it was a likely place to draw an imaginary line that traveled north/south through both poles. This is where the "prime meridian" can be visited. Keep in mind that a meridian is only half a globe long.

Back then, the idea was to use a clock synchronized to Greenwich mean time (GMT), measure the position of a star above the horizon, and then calculate the difference in position from where the same star would be at GMT. This would tell sailors where they were and how far they had come.

Finding Latitude

After the death of two thousand men in the sinking of four British naval ships due to a navigational error, the British government offered a prize to someone who could invent an accurate clock to prevent further navigational disasters. The method of navigation at the time was called "dead reckoning."

The addition of a highly accurate marine clock, or chronometer, was perfected by John Harrison in 1734. He was a simple man from the north of England who abandoned giant brass sea clocks to concentrate on a watch that would more accurately measure time. This accurate watch, combined with a sextant reading to precisely measure the position of the sun or stars, was pretty much all sailors needed.

There was a minor problem, since the world has a flat spot toward the pole. But since most sea voyages went from landfall to landfall, you could use a compass, a chronometer, and a sextant and get pretty much anywhere in the world. The point of this preamble is to say that even though latitude has perfection of measurement and purpose, longitude is a mess.

The basic tools for measurement of longitude were based on the earth turning one degree every four minutes and the distance between every degree of longitude being 69 miles (60 nautical miles) wide at the equator. But nice perfect squares couldn't be created because the distance between two meridians is always different as you leave the equator. This confusion gives you the dubious privilege of now having to learn about projection.

Scale, Grids, Projection, and Pretty Colors

The world is rather large, wrinkly, and round, and maps are small, square, and flat. Obviously, something has to give in the translation. For instance, if you are flying from New York to Tokyo or from L.A. to London and you check out the map in the in-flight magazine, you think you will be seeing North Carolina or northern California soon. Instead your pilot tells you you are over Greenland and Fairbanks. Huh? You just learned that the quickest route between two global points is a great circle (the shortest constant bearing between two points) and that the world is round and your magazine is flat.

The first world map was created by Belgian Gerardus Mercator in 1538. This was when all compass directions appeared as straight lines for the first time. Because of this, Mercator projection is the traditional way large flat wall maps are made and is ideal for navigation because all north/south/east/west compass lines become straight even if the landmasses and distances are distorted.

The Universal Mercator Grid divides the world into sixty north/south strips. This stretches and distorts the tops and bottoms of the world to make them the same distance as the equator. Keep in mind that it keeps the up and down measurement the same. This means that going north in Alaska looks accurate, but going east/west is dramatically exaggerated.

Robinson projection is like Mercator's view except that the map is squeezed at the top and the bottom to lessen the distortion. Antarctica still covers the entire bottom on the map, but generally things look a little better in the civilized parts of the world. There are also conic, orthographic, Peters, gnomonic, and optimal conformal projections. All with their pluses and minuses. The most common type of projection for topo maps is a conic projection using two parallels of latitude, with a transverse Mercator adaption for large-scale maps.

How Maps Are Made

If you understand how maps are made, you are less likely to get lost. The creation of maps is the process of taking very accurate information and then tossing things out. Knowing what is important on maps makes for clear maps and clearheaded people.

The first step in making modern maps is to take a satellite or aerial photo and then decide how much to shrink (or enlarge). An aerial photo grid of thirty-two ten-inch-by-ten-inch sheets (four up and eight across) covers 100 km north to south and 300 km east to west. The plane usually flies east to west, and each photograph overlaps the next one by about 60 percent. This provides a stereoscopic image that is later plotted onto a computer, which then draws the map with the help of an operator. Newer systems such as GPS can be used to confirm actual position and height of a map point to within one centimeter.

Maps come in different scales, ranging from vague artsy-fartsy globes to precise military maps of 1:25,000, in which one unit of measurement has been shrunk 25,000 times. To estimate actual distance, you simply multiply measurements made with a ruler on the map by the degree of reduction.

To complete the map, topo lines, rivers, and roads are drawn, symbols placed, built-up and forested areas shaded, and names added. The only thing missing is a red arrow and the notation "You are here."

Gridlock

You'll find a number of numbers along the margins of typical 7.5-minute series topo maps. On these maps you'll find latitude degrees written as degrees in the corners, then usually as minutes (') and seconds (") along the left and right margins. On the top and bottom you'll see longitude written as, for example, 118°22'30" (degrees, minutes, seconds). The latitude and longitude measurements are 2.5° apart on 7.5-minute maps and 5 minutes apart on 15-minute maps. Depending on which longitude and latitude you're at, this can give you a wonky grid, since it only provides a grid system along the equator.

You find scale in miles, feet, and kilometers, magnetic declination (to help set your compass to align with true north), and a lot of cover-your-ass verbiage as to date, error, and so forth.

It is hard for most people to think in longitude and latitude and then translate this into the real world. Looking at a map will give you accurate north/south measurements (in degrees of latitude) but ever-changing distance and scale if you use the degrees of longitude that run east/west. Here is a cheat sheet:

latitude

LATITUDE		MILES	FEET	KILOMETERS	METERS
1 degree	=	69	364,800	111	111,000
1 minute	=	1.15	6,080	1.85	1,850
1 second	=	.019	101	.3	30.83
.1 second	=	.002	10	.003	3

To calculate distance per latitudinal degree + 69 × cosine = distance.

UTM (U Talking to Me?)

Travelers like to use a grid with constant distances to figure out where they are and where they are going. On topo maps you'll see another scale along the edges written as large and then small numerals (e.g., **3735000m.N.**). They are put next to blue grid lines along the border: **3735**, with the thousands dropped. These are UTM measurements, or Universal Transverse Mercator. If you don't want to know why the UTM numbers are different than the longitude and latitude, skip this part. All you really need to know is that the distance between two UTM ticks is 1,000 meters, or a kilometer (0.62 mile), giving you a grid of kilometers to measure with.

If you want to know how to accurately measure your route on a map, listen up and take notes.

UTM is a metric grid system designed to be easy. That's why, of course, it takes a whole chapter to explain in most navigation guides. We've learned that Mercator stretched the world at the poles to balance the effect of changing longitudinal measurements. So you know why UTM is not used when mapping the poles above 84° north and below 80° south.

The world is divided into sixty zones. Each UTM zone is 6° of longitude wide (when you add all sixty zones, this equals 360°) and 164° of latitude high. Each zone has a central north/south spine called a zone meridian.

The zones start at 180°, or the international date line (the opposite side of the world to 0° Greenwich).

Measurements only go east. From zone 1 (the date line) from the zone meridian go north from the equator. The zone meridian is always labeled **500000m.E.** The equator is always **10000000m.N.** when measuring below the equator or **0000000m.N.** when measuring above. This may be confusing on a grand scale, but on a local topo map it means you are always increasing when heading north and decreasing when heading south. This is also correct for east/west travel, where traveling east increases the UTM number and traveling west decreases the number. The continental United States only needs ten UTM zones (zones 10 through 19 as we go—c'mon, you can do it—east) and about twenty-five UTM zones to cover us. The effect of the distortion becomes apparent when you realize it takes about twenty-two maps just to cover Alaska but only two for Hawaii.

In the Western Hemisphere this naturally means that UTM numbers go the opposite way that longitude degrees increase. We also know by now that all maps are lies, so it's appropriate to point out that the UTM system has a distortion of 0.04 at its extremes.

UTM is supposedly simple because it provides a constant grid measurement and only two directional attributes: "eastings" and "northings." You read "right 'n' up" using UTM coordinates.

Boiled down, it means that each UTM measurement on a 7.5- or 15-minute topo map is 1,000 meters, 1 kilometer, or just over half a mile. Using these equally spaced E/W and N/S lines, you can calculate diagonal distances with some precision. Remember, a UTM coordinate describes a square area anchored on the bottom right corner and going right 'n' up.

True North and You are Here and How to Use a Map

Like a novel with an unsympathetic character, a map can be an alien device. Where am I in relation to the map? Which way is north? Is this even the right map? What do all those squiggly lines mean?

Let's assume that you are going to spend a weekend hiking, hunting, or adventuring.

- Buy enough maps. Odds are you will want a 1:50,000 topo map that covers the area you think you will be in and enough of the surrounding area "just in case." A lot of people get lost because they wander off the map and don't realize it when they get back on.

- Study the map and chart your course in your mind. Don't draw all over the map because it won't help you when you need it the most. Buy a map case or plastic envelope and carry a couple of grease pencils. This will keep your map dry and you can write and rewrite all over the clear cover.
- Plan out your trip with potential campsites marked. The steeper the elevation, the less distance you'll make. Remember, too, that you will typically get a long way on the first and second days and then gradually slow down. If you are hiking a known trail, look for interesting side trips and note them down. Otherwise, you may completely forget about them once you are on the trail.
- Learn the language. Down at the bottom of the map is the legend. Here you can find the scale, projection, symbols, and notes.
- Get compass declinations (see next chapter). Often the brochure that came with your compass can provide general compass declinations; sometimes they are on the map. Magnetic deposits and even your watch can affect compass readings.

Why the reliance on maps and not compasses? Once again, a map is a collection of lies that is easier to figure out than the truth.

In the Field and in Trouble

- Get used to referring to your map on a regular basis. If you walk off the map or don't maintain a geographical relevance to your map, you're asking for trouble. Note when you cross streams or roads and pass certain geographic features by writing down the time. This habit alone will ensure you will never be lost. If you space out and get confused, you will only be as lost as your last entry or reference point.
- Lay the map out with the place you want to go in front of you. This way the topographic features will be recognizable and you can make a note where north is based.
- Look for hilltops, roads, rivers (usually evidenced by larger, greener growth along the banks) that provide clear reference points. If you are picky about finding your position, simply point your compass at two widely spaced reference points and note the intersection. That's where you are.
- If you are traveling with a group, point out on the map where you are, where you are going, and any major intersections or navigational aids along the way. Set another resting point to regroup.

- Plenty of features will not be on the map: new trails, washout bridges, flooded rivers, barbed-wire fences, overgrown thickets. Check the date the map was made and updated. On topo maps purple areas designate new information about the area.
- Don't forget your road or general area map that will get you to your entrance and exit points from civilization (river, road, town, etc.).
- Only the leader gets to carry the map; that way you appear like you know where you're going and those that really need it will be lost without it. This gives rise to Pelton's rule that the person least likely to get lost is most likely to be hogging the map. Make photocopies with your route marked in fluorescent marker pen.

measurements

1 millimeter	.039 inch	.1 cm	.001 meters
1 centimeter	.394 inch	10 mm	.01 meters
1 inch	25.4 mm	2.54 cm	.039 meter
1 foot	304.8 mm	12 inches	.305 meter
1 yard	3 feet	36 inches	.914 meter
1 meter	39.37 inches	3.28 feet	.001 km
1 fathom	6 feet	18.28 cm	1.83 meters
1 kilometer	3,937 feet	.62 mile	1,000 meters
1 mile	1,760 yards	5,280 feet	1.609 km
1 nautical mile	2,026 yards	6,080 feet	1,852 meters

Angular

1 mil	1/6,400 circle	0.5625 degree	0.0625 grad
1 grad	1/400 circle	16 mils	0.9 degree
1 degree	1/360 circle	17.8 mils	1.1 grad
A circle	360 degrees	6,400 mils	400 grads

· 28 ·

compasses

Using a Compass
(or at Least Look Good While You're Trying To)

A compass does one thing well, and that is remind you of how easy it is to become disoriented. What you thought to be north turns out to be south and so on. Without a compass, you just have this nagging feeling you are going in the wrong direction; at least with a compass you'll know.

By now, you should be more than comfortable with maps. Compasses are far more daunting. After all, they have all sorts of numbers in circles and straight lines, magnifying glasses, a mirror, and even some little adjustment thingy-majiggy.

The Scent of the Rose

When you look at a compass rose (the directional pointers that show direction), you can't help wondering why a compass always points north. The only problem with getting too enamored with the magic of a compass is that, in fact, a compass *doesn't* always point north, and, of course, there are three different norths. More about this later.

In the past, compasses were viewed as mystical devices with no actual function. The Chinese, who first used the compass, were convinced it pointed south. When sailors in the thirteenth century discovered that this simple device was unerring in its devotion to pointing northward, however, the compass came into widespread use.

Despite the time we have had to get used to compasses, most people still view them as a bizarre and unexplainable phenomenon. They point but they don't direct, they are precise but confusing, they are part of every survival kit but don't tell you where you are. Just what the hell are you supposed to do with a compass?

Finding Your Direction

When most of us think about compasses, we assume that compasses are for when we are lost. Sorry, compasses can only work when you know where you are.

Think of a compass as the white lines on a road. After you've begun traveling in a certain direction, you need to know if you are still on track. For example, you don't need a compass to climb to the top of a mountain or even to find the mountain. But if you are traveling across open desert and need to find a water hole, you could definitely use a compass.

You can buy a cute little bubble compass for your key chain, but if you are going to do some serious navigation, you should know that compasses are only truly useful if they have a sighting device and a sense of directional measurement.

Now you have to stop and think about something. If a compass points to the poles and the poles are the only places where all 360 longitudes meet, why is a compass divided into 360°? The answer is it isn't. The other question you should be asking yourself is wouldn't a compass be pointing straight down (up?) when you are standing on the south pole? It would if it weren't weighted.

Compasses can be divided into four methods of measurement:

- Magnetic north/south: A simple magnetized object like a needle on a thread or floating on a cork will align along a magnetic north/south axis.
- Compass rose: This is the traditional form of direction measurement in which the four "cardinal" points (north, south, east, west) are

subdivided by their proximity between the four points. For example, the west to north quadrant is divided by nine descriptions (west, west by north, west-northwest, northwest by west, northwest, etc., clockwise around the face).

· Bearing scale: This divides the compass into four quadrants of 90, with the north or south direction preceding the easterly or westerly. So northwest would be N45°W.

· Azimuth: Probably the only precise measurement scale worth using (along with the compass rose descriptions for rough work), the azimuth divides the outer circle into 360 equal divisions. Why 360, you ask? Well, the ancient Greeks thought that it would mesh nicely into measurements used for the earth's rotation, and 360 divided by 24 (hours in the day) gives you 15, the number of degrees the earth rotates every hour. (Every 60 seconds the earth rotates 0.25 of a degree, which gives you 15 angular minutes.)

Slice the world along the equator, pretend it's a watch face, and then realize it takes twenty-four hours for the world to return to the same spot, and it starts to make sense.

How the hell does a revolving world neatly divided into 360° match up with a compass divided into 360°? It doesn't. The best you can do is imagine yourself standing where the prime meridian intersects with the equator and measuring north, south, west, and east. Latitude and longitude use the center of the earth and its poles as a reference; the compass uses the magnetic poles and your position as a reference. Now keep in mind that the units of measurement are based on the same thinking but are completely different measurement systems.

There are only two measurements you need to understand with a compass. The first is magnetic north.

Who's Got the Magnet?

A compass will direct its attention to whatever provides the most magnetism. That means when you are desperately lost, your compass is cruelly pointing at your magnetized belt buckle instead of magnetic north. You must remember to use your compass away from metallic or electrified ferrous objects (like your car, computer, or even manhole covers).

In an open area free from ferrous deposits, power lines, electric disturbances, and operator interference, a compass will point to magnetic north. It doesn't hurt to take a couple of readings and to experiment how your vehicle and simple objects like your watch affect readings.

distance from interference

High-tension lines	50 yards
Large trucks, ships, containers	20 yards
Cars, transformers, pylons	10 yards
Electric fences, telephone lines	8 yards
Large hand tools, poles	3 yards
Small metal objects	1 yard

The True North: Strong and Confusing

We're looking pretty good since we are getting clean strong readings from our Boy Scout compass. But remember that true north is where all those up and down lines meet at the top and bottom of your globe. That's okay, you say, just tell me where magnetic north is and I'll figure out where true north is. Well, I guess I should bring up another problem. Nobody quite knows where magnetic north (or south) is at any one time.

The magnetic poles are 1,284 kilometers from their respective geographic poles (the axis that the world spins around) on a spot that wanders about one degree every ten years.

You can't physically visit the poles. The north magnetic pole can be found about twenty miles north of Bathurst Island and the south magnetic pole is buried under 3,700 feet of ice in the Russian-controlled slice of Antarctica and is supposed to be the coldest spot on earth (−88° centigrade on August 24, 1960). You can measure it and stand on the ice and have your picture taken, but it is really just an odd phenomenon of mass and movement that has even been known to reverse in ages gone by.

As for the question of using a compass in a journey around the world, the needle does have to be counterbalanced as you head southward. Compass needles are counterweighted to prevent them from standing on their head in extreme southern and northern regions.

This errant wandering won't bother most of us unless we set off on a two-decade hegira but it can cause confusion when you use old maps. Most topo maps will provide the appropriate declination from true north. Here are the various choices in north:

- **Magnetic north:** This is the direction your compass points before you adjust the declination. This is really a misnomer because there are many things that can throw your compass off. Following a magnetic heading can lead you around in circles in areas with large ore deposits, power lines, or strong magnetic objects.
- **True north:** After you've adjusted your compass for declination it will point to the geographic north pole, which is the top axis around which the world rotates. Stateside you can be off as much as 22° from true north if you don't adjust for the declination.
- **Grid north:** These are the up and down lines on a map that are adjusted for the projection, magnetic declination at the time of map manufacture. In the continental United States this can be as much as 2 percent off from straight, and much higher as you go north to Canada.
- **Your north:** You are going to have to balance the age of your map (which will have an older declination bearing), where you are on the map (declinations are from the center of the map), your compass accuracy, and extenuating circumstances to decide how you'll set your map.

It's a Deviant Thing: Declination

We're all a little deviant sometimes, but the magnetic poles (let's forget the magnetic pole's propensity for wandering) are perverse mothers.

Every area of Planet Earth has a slightly different deviation (it is officially called declination, but that would give you the erroneous image of a standard deviation) from true north due to the earth's molten core, magnetic flux, mineral deposits, or global position. In the Canadian tundra it's so bad the magnetic declination lines look like a topo map. You might as well throw your compass away.

The changing magnetic influences (primarily due to the earth's molten core changing our magnetic flux) means that the declination is 22° east in Banff, Alberta, but only 15° east of true north in Los Angeles, even though they are on the same general longitude.

Imagine a swinging pendulum with the center point running from Thunder Bay, Ontario, to Havana that is 0° declination. This is the *agonic* line (no angle) where both magnetic and true north are found in the same direction. The isogonic lines (lines *with* angles) then curve up to 20° east in Washington State (120° long.) and 20° west in Maine (66° long.). These declinations also change at different rates, with the isogonic lines changing 5°

west. (It will take twelve years for the declination to change 1° degree in California, 10° west in the prairies, and around 5° easterly in Maine.)

Greenwich, England, the central measuring point of longitude, has changed from 8° east to about 4° west over the last four hundred years. There are plenty of local tweaks when it comes to declination, but this is a good rule of thumb for setting your compass.

Setting your compass, you say, what compass?

Your First and Last Compass

Buy a good compass. For a measly forty or fifty dollars you can have the Rolls-Royce level in compasses.

Your compass should have a folding cover with a mirror inside for sighting your direction, precise markings on the base to measure distances and slope on your topo map, a rotating bezel for setting and locking course, a tiny screw adjustment that allows you to dial in local declination, and luminous markings to allow night usage. (You will also need to buy a good topo map of where you are going, a plastic cover sheet or plastic map case, and a grease pencil.)

Looking Good and
Knowing Your Way Around

The first rule in not getting lost is knowing where you are and where you are going. This does not require a compass or a whole lot of bush smarts. Look at your map and translate the topos into hills and valleys. Look for interesting points on the map and then figure out where you'd like to go.

In the field, the first thing you'll notice is how much taller the hills are than you imagined and how many more features there are. Once you are in the woods, you will also wonder what use the map is if there is not a trailhead park or a start in a spot that has an identifiable curve, hill, stream, or location. Spend some time matching your map to your environment.

Before you leave the trailhead, create a mental or written overlay on your map of where you are, rough distances, your path, and end destination. Find a distant object (not the sun, you fool) like a hilltop, shore point, lone tree, telephone pole, or other recognizable object. Find where you think it is on the map and mark it. If you don't know where, and even if you think you do know, you need to triangulate your position.

- Line up your map to the same view as you are facing.
- If there are no visual navigational points, adjust your compass so that the north needle is over the north pointer and then line up the up and down grid lines on the map to your compass.
- Find your first bearing and then rotate the compass, but not the map, to that bearing and set the bezel to line up the north indicator with the north needle.
- Find a visual aid that lines up behind your sighting mirror and walk toward it. Do this as many times as you need to.

If you lose your position:

- Your map needs to be "set." Find two objects and take a reading from each. The V created is pointing right at your spot.
- Find an object that is due north to check your deviation. You may want to tweak your compass for the deviation difference.

Pick Up the Pace

It's one thing to know where you are going. It's another to figure out how long it takes to get there. The original function of a compass was not as for direction but as a measuring device.

So now comes the most important and difficult part of compass navigation: your pace. In most cases you don't need a compass to walk to a recognizable object over flat ground with a clear view. You just wander over. In the real world people follow winding trails in forests or canyons, at night or in fog.

Your job now is to figure out not where you are but where you are going. You must pick up the farthest visible marker, set a compass bearing toward it, and then count the number of paces to each way point. Why? Because if you sighted a tall mountain but there are a number of little mountains in the way, you will be wandering in an S, weaving back and forth along a river or trail.

So if you are heading north but you end up walking 100 paces northwest along a path, then you know you need to walk 100 paces northeast to correct your course. Once again this is an ideal situation, since you will be wandering like a drunk on payday hoping against hope that it was 560 paces, not 660 you counted. (If you are humping it without taking scenic beauty rests, you could use time instead of paces on land.)

To estimate arrival time, length of trip, and speed, you need to measure your own and your group's pace. A "pace" is whatever the average of your stride is during your typical type of walking, but you need to set a pace that allows the group to stay together. As a general rule it is better to walk slower over a longer period of time than faster with breaks. Adjust your pace so your perspiration, breathing, and heart rate are within your aerobic range.

Knowing your average speed over certain terrains will be invaluable in predicting where and when to make camp and help in finding lost persons.

The most capable person should be the "sweeper," or the person who makes sure no one gets left behind. The sweeper should also have the first-aid kit and ideally a two-way radio and a GPS to report position.

If you need to take a break, take it. Use that time to adjust boot laces and pack straps and to note where you are. A watch with a regular timer will remind you to make a note of where you are in case of being disoriented.

If you are a first-run dufus, you will spend so much time checking your compass and position you will forget to have a good time. It is important to plan for a one-hour goof-off if you find a stream, cave, or interesting spot.

Altitude is a major factor in estimated distance, as is terrain. There is no way to predict the terrain, but you can use the chart on the next page as a general rule of thumb for height.

Continually measure and calculate your speed and mark it on your map as the day progresses. Simply writing the time, the GPS point, and any landmarks every thirty minutes will give you good reference should anything go wrong.

If you feel comfortable with the spatial relationship between a map, a

estimating speed and time

ACTIVITY	SPEED	TIME FOR COVERING 1 MILE
Sprinting	5	12 minutes
Jogging	4.5	14 minutes
On paved roads/no load	3.6	17 minutes
On pavement/normal load	3	20 minutes
Gravel roads/load	3	20 minutes
Smooth trail, no hills	2.5	24 minutes
No path, flat/using compass	1.4	43 minutes
No path, hills/using compass	1	60 minutes

compass, and distance measurement, try to do tougher little jaunts or even look into orienteering, an army training exercise that has turned into a sport, where contestants run a premeasured course with a compass and map, looking for markers.

The bottom line is that some people have spatial skills and others couldn't find their way up in an elevator shaft. Practice relaxes the latter and cockiness kills the former.

the going rate

ASCENT	4 by 400 rule	Estimate 1 hour for every 4 km (2.5 miles) of flat travel and 1 hour of travel for every 400 meters (1,312 feet) of ascent.
FLAT	4 by 8/2	Estimate 1 hour for every 4 km (2.5 miles) in an 8-hour day of hiking, with 2 hours of stops in a typical 10-hour day.
DESCENT	6 by 600	Estimate 1 hour for 600 m (1,968 feet) of vertical distance plus 1 hour for every 6 km (3.7 miles) down.

I'm Not Lost— I Just Don't Know Where I Am Yet

Being comfortable with the concept of location, time, map, and compass is the cornerstone of surviving in the wilderness or the city. "Being lost" causes panic and poor judgment. Knowing how to read your gut feeling, and honing your instrument-driven, pathfinding and analytical positional skills will get you out of more problems than anything else. Slavish addiction to map, compass, or other tools can lead to major direction mistakes that can only be corrected once your innate sense of "I think we took the wrong turn back there" kicks in.

Since we are on the subject of balancing tools with logic, let's look into other directional tools.

God's Gift to Yuppies:
The Global Positioning System (GPS)

GPS could be called the greatest innovation since the creation of longitude and maybe even the invention of the compass, certainly since the arrival of the BMW and Sharper Image catalogs. But like any other breakthrough, the hype is usually about the benefits and little about the drawbacks.

The global positioning system is a network of twenty-four satellites (and spares) that rotate around the world twelve thousand miles high. Each satellite makes a pass around the world every twelve hours. It started in 1960 as a think-tank military concept to assist Uncle Sam in outnuking the Soviet Union and to aid military and naval navigation. Called NAVSTAR (Navigation Satellite Timing and Ranging), the first satellite went up in 1978, and the final one went up in 1993. Since our government was smart enough to figure that this bunker-door-accurate guidance system could also be used against us, they built in a high-security software program to control the downlink signals and introduced an ever-changing margin of error that turns the one-meter-square accuracy available to the U.S. military (and, one would expect, our allies) into a football-sized slop factor for us taxpayers. Russia has its own GPS system without the error factor but with some serious atmospheric-introduced problems. Let's explore what GPS is and isn't.

Weah da Fugawi: Part Duh

Having man-made celestial signposts sounds like you can toss your compasses, maps, and common sense. But you must know that there are some serious flaws.

The GPS satellites send out a constant radio signal. This signal when interpreted by your GPS ultimately provides atomic clock time, latitude, longitude, and altitude. The signal can be picked up by a tiny handheld receiver which can be manufactured for under $100 (and less as their popularity spreads).

The signals travel twelve thousand miles from the satellite at the speed of light. If there was just one GPS satellite, you would get the time (shifted by the transmission lag) and that's about it. This would give you distance from the satellite to you and what side of the world you are on. Not a very helpful bit of information unless you are Charlton Heston and you just crashed on the Planet of the Apes in the wrong century.

A second satellite adds the dimension of a more general sense of location, but things start to hum when a third satellite locks on. This is called 2D mode. Now you have the magic of triangulation. Now you can determine exactly where you are anywhere in the world. Sort of. It is only when the fourth satellite knocks on the door that timing errors from the other satellites are corrected. This is 3D mode.

Now accurate position and elevation (over the averaged calculation of sea level) are yours. Sort of.

Your GPS receiver will display this in longitude and latitude and height in meters or feet . . . subject to the introduced error provided courtesy of Uncle Sam.

You Can't Get There from Here

Despite looking like it should be a compass and even having compass dials and measurements, a GPS is not a compass. Remember, a GPS is very good at figuring out where it is sitting but has no idea where it is going.

Once you start moving, things change dramatically. Since you are now picking up position readings every fifteen seconds, the little math monkeys inside your GPS receiver can start calculating speed, direction, and way points. (Way points are specific readings that you enter or that the receiver remembers in evenly timed intervals.)

Now you have a compass, a speedometer, an altimeter, a watch, a timer, and—in the newer models—a map, time of sunrise/sunset, and even your home street . . . sort of. The only accurate element of a GPS is the time. The other calculations are precise, but—except for the mathematical calculations—they are not accurate, since the original data are sloppy. Many systems have a fudge factor that reads the introduced errors in the satellite signals and then compensates. A measurement to within thirty feet is pretty good for a civilian GPS. Specifically, the introduced error (one of the few areas where our government actually admits to lying and sending out disinformation) can be over one hundred meters 20 percent of the time and three hundred meters 1/1,000 of the time.

You'll notice this error the most when you are walking and, magically, your speed varies widely, or your home way point is off by a different amount every time. The most egregious error is the altitude measurement, which can be off 50 percent more than the positional reading error. In other words, your GPS receiver can be off by five hundred feet when it comes to altitude.

Hey, what more could you want for free?

Finding Your Way Back Home

The real strength of GPS is in its ability to remember specific points, creating navigation way points where no visual clues exist. Sailors and desert and arctic travelers simply can't do without a GPS these days. Yes, they can rely on sextants, knot meters, chronometers, compasses, radio signals, and dead reckoning, but the GPS automates and simplifies direction finding.

Jungle, forest, alpine, and urban explorers are subject to the fickle signals that are blocked by canopy, buildings, canyons, and other obstructions. Even a car-mounted unit will need an expensive auxiliary antenna to work well. Cavers and divers can use a GPS to find a cave opening or dive spot, but it is useless once they are underground or below water.

The correct use of a GPS is to mark your starting point by entering a way point and labeling it as "home." As you travel, you can enter more electronic markers to coincide with trail junctions, depth sounds, or whatever your heart desires. You can also read off coordinates from maps and enter them into the GPS receiver manually. There is always the chance of a mistake, but a little common sense can set you right.

Hitting the "go to" button and your next way point then provides an estimate of direction, arrival time, a handy pointer arrow, and measurements. At its simplest, you could find the place you want to get to, enter its longitude and latitude, and then just follow the arrow until you get there.

GPS receivers are made for aviation, nautical, fishing, and automotive uses. Car units can calculate the quickest directions with vector map software, and a GPS unit is offered with detailed maps for your car, boats, and aircraft, allowing you to store and view hotel information, marina dock plans, airport layouts, and so on.

This means that you can travel the globe without a map, altimeter, compass, phone book, or even an alarm that tells you when you have arrived at a predetermined spot. Or can you? Well, the concept is great, but it is so easy to get hooked on a GPS that you may forget to actually remember where you are. The first time your batteries conk out or you leave your GPS back at camp, you'll learn to love GPS only when you use it as an enhancement to your normal navigation skills. The other drawback to GPS is that it doesn't work where your receiver can't get a lock on the relatively weak satellite signals, places like forests, buildings, underwater, caves, canyons, or other places where people get lost a lot.

How Deep Are You Lost? Using an Altimeter

The least used and least accurate tool for determining location is the altimeter. I've belabored the faults of the map, compass, and GPS, but even the altimeter manufacturers will boldly tell you that an altimeter, despite its name, doesn't measure altitude. Like depth meters used by divers, they simply measure pressure. Water pressure is very stable, but air pressure is subject to temperature where cold air is denser and hot air lighter. This can be a significant problem when traveling from north to south faces at the same altitude. They may have large temperature differences of about 22 percent for each degree of Fahrenheit at the same altitude. For every 5 percent change in temperature, an altimeter will be 1.1 percent off, reading higher when it's hotter than the first reading and lower in altitude when it's cold.

An altimeter is ideal for alpinists on rugged terrain, where you will be traveling up and down more than back and forth. You need to set your altimeter from a set point: a topo map (ideal), the seaside (don't forget tide), or a highway or city marker sign that shows elevation (sloppy but better than nothing). Do not use your GPS to set altitude or you will be going from bad to worse.

You can also measure time and distance when ridge traveling. Just match up the altitude with a topo line. You can then figure out rate of travel and distance to the next elevation by calculating your rate of speed and measuring off the map. Good altimeters are expensive, and if your budget forces you to choose between a GPS or good altimeter, go for the GPS.

When You Lose All Those Cool Gizmos

We've spent a lot of time talking about bushlore. The best way to develop those skills is to practice direction finding by using moss on trees, the flow of rivers, the sun and the stars and using your gizmos as backup. That way, when you screw up, you're comfortable with these cruder but more fallible methods of not getting lost.

Just remember what you read in the beginning about using some of the classic guides like the sun or the stars. Polaris, or the North Star, is the only star that appears fixed in space. This is because the earth rotates and this star happens to be perfectly lined up to the axis of our rotation. Back when the Pyramids were built, a star called Thuban was aligned to the earth's axis, but changes in the earth's rotation have caused things to shift.

This means the Pyramids and Stonehenge don't quite line up as neatly as those TV documentaries tell you, but you calendar and astrology nuts will be happy to learn that your star sign is one sign ahead of the ancient definitions and birth dates.

· 29 ·

pack lists

What Did You Forget?

The major source of pre-trip anxiety always centers around what you forgot to pack. The lists below are just bare-minimum lists and should be expanded upon as you feel necessary. Also, if you're traveling in a group, you can bring more (or less), but each person should have the basic emergency and subsistence kit to get by if separated.

How to Pack

Pack light. According to military and expedition standards, the maximum load for hikers is 30 percent of body weight. Hikers should not exceed 25 percent of body weight as a maximum load. That means a 150-pound person should be able to slog forty pounds, and a lummox like myself should be able to carry seventy pounds. Males are able to carry between fifty and one hundred pounds, but it is extremely debilitating and can lead to all types of injuries, slips, twists, falls, and exhaustion. Even half that amount (twenty to forty pounds) will wear you down. I like to travel with about twenty to twenty-five pounds on my back and then another ten pounds in camera gear, water, books, and junk.

Your pack should not be stressed when full, so choose an appropriately sized pack. I suggest a frameless model unless you are really humping some serious gear. Keep in mind that on expeditions, or even on some treks, you can hire porters to carry some of your gear. They don't like to carry more than thirty pounds each.

Keep your heavy stuff aligned along a vertical and horizontal axis that puts the weight in line with your pelvis and toward the top. Imagine a cross across the shoulders and along the spine and then load heavy stuff across the top of the cross center. Keep your survival kit on your belt and your first-aid kit in a separate, easily accessible pocket on your pack.

General Purpose

clothing

Underwear/bra (two)

Shirts (two loose-weave bush-style cotton, one dark wool)

Pants (one bush pair, one khaki for city)/one skirt for women

Velcro in money pocket or ankle holster

Thin wool socks (three)

Heavy wool socks (two)

Money belt

Boots

Canvas sneakers or sandals

Fleece sleeveless black turtleneck (long-sleeved for cold climates)

Windproof/waterproof shell

Wool hat/balaclava

Absorbent hat (for sun)

Large bandanna

first-aid/medical kit/ personal kit

Scissors

Tweezers

Single-edged razor blades/scalpel

Needles

Safety pins

Sunscreen

Lip balm

Small first-aid manual

Toilet paper

Alcohol swabs

Painkillers

Antihistamine

Anti-motion-sickness pills

Insect repellent

Rehydration packets

Disinfectant fluid

Antibiotic creme

Autoinject epinephrine (optional)

Prescription medicine

Tape

Moleskin or blister bandages

Sterile gauze

Absorbent pads

Water purification tablets

Sanitary napkins (can be used as absorbent bandages)

Condoms (can be used to waterproof gear, carry water)

gear

	Backpack (frameless, dark color)
	Heavy vinyl liner for pack
	Canteen or water bladder
	Large garbage bags and small freezer bags
	Caribiners
	Head flashlight/waterproof spare batteries
	Towel
	Spare shoelaces
	Extra rope
	Extra compass
	Sunglasses
	Water filter/extra purification tablets
	Extra ground sheet
	Compact multifuel stove with small gas canister
	Cooking pots and frying pan
	Emergency food bars/jerky/sweets

survival kit

Small survival booklet

Knife (multipurpose)

Disposable lighters (two or more)

Compass with sighting mirror

Signaling mirror (use compass mirror in a pinch)

Magnifying glass (primarily for splinters but useful to light fires)

GPS unit

Pens/notebook

Flashlight/spare batteries/spare bulb

Wire saw

Snare wire

Whistle

Foil survival blanket (Store in folding mess tin and then in separate belt pouch)

Nylon line/hook

Sewing kit/needle selection

Altimeter

papers

	Passport/driver's license/visas/tickets/copy of all
	Money/traveler's checks/credit cards/ATM cards
	Eyeglass/medical prescriptions
	Plastic container for above
	Map (spray with plastic coating to waterproof)
	Plastic overlay or envelope for maps
	Guidebooks/phrase book/plant and animal ID guides

bush/camping kit

Tent (optional)

Dried food/spices/energy bars

Straps for sleeping bag, jacket

Insulating half-body mat

Sleeping bag

Cooking equipment/pots/larger gas bottle

Cooking grate/large knife

Compact two-way radio/spare batteries

Ground sheet/poncho/tarp

Metal cup (with folding handle)

Lighter

Get a wider belt to carry canteen and survival kit

Special Purpose

tropics

Jungle hammock
Malaria prophylaxis
Mosquito coils
Foot powder with fungicide
Sarong (can be used by men and women)
Swim trunks
Flip-flops
Swap boots for jungle boots or canvas lugged sneakers
Head and shoulder mosquito net
Goggles (for diving)
Extra bug repellent
Umbrella

desert

Extra water containers

Plastic bags

Larger spare hat

Extra sunglasses (prescription if needed)

Replace boots with desert boots

Extra sunblock/lip balm

Extra water purification tablets

Substitute short cargo pants

Kaffiyeh/turban or light cotton wrap

winter

	Gloves	
	Ski pole	
	Large toque	
	Parka	
	Snow pants	
	Snowpack boots/spare liner	
	Extra wool socks	
	Ice axe	
	Zinc cream	

alpine

Long sleeping mat
Hand warmer
Snow goggles
Climbing helmet
Climbing gear
Glacier cream

Before you go traveling in dicey countries, black out any logos, check and waterproof seams and tape with colored ID tape to minimize sticking out. Use Sharpie to mark all gear with name and initials, as well as a local contact so when your gear does get stolen, they know who to sell it back to.

· 30 ·

and in the end

Surviving for Fun

By now I hope you're locked into the survival groove. The Look, The Walk, The Style, and hopefully The Message all make perfect sense. You know who survives, who doesn't, what is dangerous, where not to go, why stuff happens, why things go wrong, and how to avoid bad things.

This book is just a well-meaning attempt to communicate some simple concepts in a memorable fashion. A manual can't really show you the hard look of a kidnapper, the sound of thin ice, or the stink of a bad water hole. These are things you need to get out there to experience.

Actively practicing the techniques of self-sufficiency, bush skills, cultural sensitivity, weapons, first aid, hygiene, and cuisine should be fun and something you incorporate into your daily life. You need to approach it with a sense of humor, a dash of cynicism, and a lot of energy.

Integrate the concept of experimenting with every outing, and in your choices of books and entertainment. Attend a couple of different classes and build a library of reference books to review. But by no means accept any tip as gospel until you've had a chance to try it out for yourself.

If you were to nail a list over the outhouse to keep you in survival mode, start with this one:

ryp's 10 ws

1	**worst**	*Plan for the worst-case scenario. Ponder and plan the various positive and negative permutations of your trip or outing. Do a mental walk-through before you go, which will give you a plan and a healthy expectation for a worst-case scenario. Check out the weather and altitude effects and plan accordingly.*
2	**word**	*Tell people where you're going. Where you might be wandering off the trail. How long you'll be gone and when you'll be coming back. Read up on where you're going, talk to locals. Use the Internet, telephone, books, and other sources of information. Tell the members of your group about the potential dangers, discuss emergency plans, and establish responsibilities before you hit the trail.*
3	**where**	*Know where you are at all times. Bring and understand navigational aids. Practice tracking, trail finding, and dead reckoning before they become necessities. Knowing where you are eliminates the major reason for search and rescue.*
4	**warmth**	*Make sure that you can remain warm under any conditions. If you pack even simple items like thermal reflectors and a plastic tarp, you have just eliminated the number two reason for rescue (after getting lost). The right clothing, boots, spare socks ensure that everyone's comfortable. When you buy new clothing or footwear, wear it for at least three weekends before you go.*
5	**water**	*You can never drink or have too much water. Having enough eliminates the number three reason for problems.*

6	will	*You need to want to overcome any situation. Without this, tools and nature's resourses are useless.*
7	wits	*Be creative, and life in dangerous places and the woods becomes much easier and more fun.*
8	wound	*Are you prepared to handle a backwoods accident, an evacuation, or a painful injury? If not, get training.*
9	wisdom	*If you bring one thing, bring this.*
10	wander	*Make sure you have a good time and enjoy our planet.*

index

about the author

Robert Young Pelton, forty-four, leads an adventurous life. His interest in adventure began at age ten when he became the youngest student ever to attend St. John's Cathedral Boy's, called "the toughest Boy's School in North America" by *The Globe and Mail*. Pelton went on to become a lumberjack, boundary cutter, tunneler, driller, and blaster's assistant, in addition to his more creative occupations as an award-winning designer, photographer, producer, strategic planner, and marketing consultant. On his time off, his quest for knowledge and understanding have taken him through the remote and exotic areas of more than seventy-five countries.

Some of Pelton's trips include demining in Afghanistan, surviving a bomb attack in East Africa, visiting Algeria without a military bodyguard, thundering down forbidden rivers in leaky native canoes, plowing through East African swamps with the U.S. Camel Trophy team, hitchhiking through war-torn Central America, setting up the world's first television interview of the Taliban leaders, the first circumnavigation of the island of Borneo by land, and raising identical twin girls. He dismisses his numerous adventures, misfortunes, expeditions, expulsions, and incarcerations in the world's most dangerous places as just the price he pays for knowledge and enlightenment.

Stories about Pelton or his trips have been featured in publications as diverse as *Outside, Shift, Soldier of Fortune, Star, The New York Times, Los Angeles Times, Playboy, The Globe and Mail, Blue, Class, El Pais, The Sunday London Times, Der Stern, Die Welt, Washington Post, Outpost,* and hundreds of other newspapers around the world. He has also been featured and interviewed on a variety of networks, including the BBC, CNN, NBC, CBS, ABC, ATV, Fox, RTL, CTV, CBC, and other networks. He is currently producing and starring in *Robert Young Pelton's The World's Most Dangerous Places* for the Discovery Channel and international syndication.

Pelton is a Fellow of the Royal Geographical Society in London. He is also the author of *Borneo, Hot Spots, Travel in Harm's Way,* and *The World's Most Dangerous Places.* He lives in Los Angeles, California.